Location-Based Information Systems

Developing Real-Time Tracking Applications

T0100478

CHAPMAN & HALL/CRC
COMPUTER and INFORMATION SCIENCE SERIES

Series Editor: Sartaj Sahni

PUBLISHED TITLES

ADVERSARIAL REASONING: COMPUTATIONAL
APPROACHES TO READING THE OPPONENT'S MIND
Alexander Kott and William M. McEneaney

DISTRIBUTED SENSOR NETWORKS
S. Sitharama Iyengar and Richard R. Brooks

DISTRIBUTED SYSTEMS: AN ALGORITHMIC APPROACH
Sukumar Ghosh

ENERGY EFFICIENT HARDWARE-SOFTWARE
CO-SYNTHESIS USING RECONFIGURABLE HARDWARE
Jingzhao Ou and Viktor K. Prasanna

FUNDEMENTALS OF NATURAL COMPUTING: BASIC
CONCEPTS, ALGORITHMS, AND APPLICATIONS
Leandro Nunes de Castro

HANDBOOK OF ALGORITHMS FOR WIRELESS
NETWORKING AND MOBILE COMPUTING
Azzedine Boukerche

HANDBOOK OF APPROXIMATION ALGORITHMS
AND METAHEURISTICS
Teofilo F. Gonzalez

HANDBOOK OF BIOINSPIRED ALGORITHMS
AND APPLICATIONS
Stephan Olariu and Albert Y. Zomaya

HANDBOOK OF COMPUTATIONAL MOLECULAR BIOLOGY
Srinivas Aluru

HANDBOOK OF DATA STRUCTURES AND APPLICATIONS
Dinesh P. Mehta and Sartaj Sahni

HANDBOOK OF DYNAMIC SYSTEM MODELING
Paul A. Fishwick

HANDBOOK OF PARALLEL COMPUTING: MODELS,
ALGORITHMS AND APPLICATIONS
Sanguthevar Rajasekaran and John Reif

HANDBOOK OF REAL-TIME AND EMBEDDED SYSTEMS
Insup Lee, Joseph Y-T. Leung, and Sang H. Son

HANDBOOK OF SCHEDULING: ALGORITHMS, MODELS,
AND PERFORMANCE ANALYSIS
Joseph Y.-T. Leung

HIGH PERFORMANCE COMPUTING IN REMOTE SENSING
Antonio J. Plaza and Chein-I Chang

INTRODUCTION TO NETWORK SECURITY
Douglas Jacobson

LOCATION-BASED INFORMATION SYSTEMS:
DEVELOPING REAL-TIME TRACKING APPLICATIONS
Miguel A. Labrador, Alfredo J. Pérez, and
Pedro M. Wightman

METHODS IN ALGORITHMIC ANALYSIS
Vladimir A. Dobrushkin

PERFORMANCE ANALYSIS OF QUEUING AND COMPUTER
NETWORKS
G. R. Dattatreya

THE PRACTICAL HANDBOOK OF INTERNET COMPUTING
Munindar P. Singh

SCALABLE AND SECURE INTERNET SERVICES AND
ARCHITECTURE
Cheng-Zhong Xu

SPECULATIVE EXECUTION IN HIGH PERFORMANCE
COMPUTER ARCHITECTURES
David Kaeli and Pen-Chung Yew

VEHICULAR NETWORKS: FROM THEORY TO PRACTICE
Stephan Olariu and Michele C. Weigle

Location-Based Information Systems

Developing Real-Time Tracking Applications

Miguel A. Labrador

Alfredo J. Pérez

Pedro M. Wightman

CRC Press
Taylor & Francis Group
Boca Raton London New York

CRC Press is an imprint of the
Taylor & Francis Group, an **informa** business
A CHAPMAN & HALL BOOK

CRC Press
Taylor & Francis Group
6000 Broken Sound Parkway NW, Suite 300
Boca Raton, FL 33487-2742

First issued in paperback 2019

© 2011 by Taylor & Francis Group, LLC
CRC Press is an imprint of Taylor & Francis Group, an Informa business

No claim to original U.S. Government works

ISBN-13: 978-1-4398-4854-8 (hbk)
ISBN-13: 978-0-367-38348-0 (pbk)

Visit the Taylor & Francis Web site at
http://www.taylorandfrancis.com

and the CRC Press Web site at
http://www.crcpress.com

Preface

Location-based services (LBS) are finally coming out of research labs and getting into the hands of final users. It is fairly common to see cellular carriers and private companies offering LBS to locate your children, friends, and sites of interest, track assets, enhance the security of key personnel, help people with disabilities use public transportation, guide tourists, and many others. Location-based advertisement is becoming a very big business. Very soon users will be receiving customized advertisements in their cellular phones according to their current location. Military-related LBS systems have also been implemented to provide real-time situational awareness. Soldiers are receiving alert messages with additional information according to their current location. The interesting aspect is that LBS applications are just starting to emerge and the potential for growth the next several year is tremendous.

One common aspect of all these LBS applications is that they are built on top of an infrastructure that includes not only the cellular phone and the application that runs in it but also a communication network, a back end application that runs in a server somewhere, and a series of supporting servers and databases that together provide useful information back to the user. This entire infrastructure on top of which many LBS applications can be efficiently supported and run is what we call Location-Based Information Systems (LBIS). LBIS are being developed to target problems in many, if not all, sectors of the economy. In this regard, the timing of this book could not be better.

Looking into the future, current research is bringing new refinements and improvements and is pushing the technology even further. We can see LBIS systems transforming into what is being called "Participatory Sensing" and "Human-Centric Sensing" systems. In addition to having the location of the user in real-time, the cellular phone could integrate and provide information coming from other sensors or devices. For example, the user could be wearing Bluetooth-based sensors to continuously measure his or her temperature, heart rate, and other vital signals. Accelerometers are already integrated in several cellular phones. They are very useful in determining the type of activity that the user is doing, which along with their vital signals could be used in many health care-related applications. Cellular phones could also integrate measurements from other types of sensors and be used to address large-scale societal problems. For example, if all cellulars phone were equipped with air-quality sensors, and all users participated in the application, we could have information about the pollution level in an entire city very easily. Similarly, we should be able to easily determine the congestion level, travel times, etc., in most of our major roads. As you can see, the future of location-based information systems is very promising.

Book Origin and Overview

This book is the result of more than six years of research and development in location-based information systems. This research involved the investigation of new architectures, middleware, algorithms, protocols, mechanisms, etc., to address particular problems related to the implementation of a variety of location-based applications, mostly for the transportation industry and the military. It is also the result of our active participation in the definition of the Java ME Location API 2.0 as part of the JSR 293 working group. After all these years, we thought it was time to include this topic into the mainstream of courses in our university, so we prepared a junior-/senior-level course and wrote this book to support it.

The book contains information and examples to implement a general real-time location-based information system. In fact, all chapters of the book target the implementation of a general real-time tracking system example. It is general in the sense that the system should be easily adapted to target any application domain. Further, the incorporation of other sensors's data to make the system "participatory" or "human-centric" should be a straight-forward extension.

The book consists of twelve chapters and one appendix. Chapter 1 introduces the definition and classification of location-based services and the types of LBS applications. It also describes the three most important location provider architectures. This chapter describes an entire real-time tracking system that will be used throughout the book as an example. Each subsequent chapter of the book shows how to implement a piece of the tracking system example. The chapter concludes with a description of the software architecture we used to implement the tracking system and a look into the future, including concepts such as participatory sensing and human-centric sensing. Chapter 2 describes the hardware and software architectures of a typical cellular phone. Chapter 3 describes the Java Platform Micro Edition, or Java ME, the Java platform for resource-constrained devices. The chapter includes the description of the entire software stack: the Connected Limited Device Configuration 1.1, the Mobile Information Device Profile 2.0, and the optional packages. Chapter 4 shows how to create MIDlets, those Java-based programs that comply with the Java ME platform. Some of the most important APIs used in the development of MIDlets are also described there. The chapter also touches on security and privacy issues and mechanisms. Chapter 5 is devoted to other important programming aspects such as memory management, concurrency, dynamic linking, and energy management, all especially important for resource-constrained devices. Chapter 6 is about obtaining the user's position, the different technologies, systems, and players. At the end, the Java Location API 2.0 is also described in detail. Chapter 7 is about relational and geographical databases, how to define them, and how to store and retrieve information from a cellular phone. Similarly, Chapter 8 covers the topic of communications, or how to exchange data between the cellular phone and the main application server. Chapter 9 explains how to create and use Web services from cellular phones. Chapter 10 introduces the reader to the Google Web Toolkit and how to use it to create system administration functions, such as creating and deleting users, modifying the user information, and the like. Chapter 11 shows how to display the location of the users in Google Maps or Google Earth in real-time using the browser of any computer connected to the Internet. Finally, Chapter 12 includes some examples of additional processing functions at the cellular phone and the server meant to improve the system's performance and provide enhanced services. The Appendix A tells the reader where to download all the software needed to implement the entire location-based information system and guides the reader through the installation procedure.

Intended Audience

The book is intended for undergraduate students in their junior or senior years, professors, researchers, and industry professionals interested in the design and implementation of location-based information systems. The book can also be used as a reference book in a graduate class on the same topic.

Resources

A companion Website has been set up to provide additional information and supporting material. The Website contains all software packages and applications utilized in the book as well as the PowerPoint slides and laboratory examples utilized to teach the course CIS 4930 Location-Based Information Systems at the University of South Florida (USF). All this material and more can be found at `http://www.csee.usf.edu/~labrador/LBIS`.

Acknowledgments

We would like to acknowledge the financial support that we have received from the federal Department of Transportation and the Florida Department of Transportation through the National Center for Transit Research (NCTR), AT&T, the National Science Foundation, and more recently, TeamTaclan. Special thanks to Sprint, which has given us access to their development environment and A-GPS server, as well as considerable support in terms of cellular phones and data plans for our research. They have supported our research and development efforts on location-based information system over the past six years. We would also like to acknowledge the help and support of our research team mates Sean Barbeau, Phil Winters, Nevine Georggi, and

Rafael Pérez, as well as the large number of past and current graduate and undergraduate students who have worked in all our projects. We would also like to thank the staff of Taylor and Francis, and Randi Cohen in particular, for their support during all the phases of the book. Finally, we want to acknowledge our own families for their patience, support, and understanding during all these months of continuous, hard work.

About the Authors

Miguel A. Labrador received the M.S. in Telecommunications and the Ph.D. degree in Information Science with concentration in Telecommunications from the University of Pittsburgh, in 1994 and 2000, respectively. Since 2001, he has been with the University of South Florida, Tampa, where he is currently an Associate Professor in the Department of Computer Science and Engineering. Before joining USF, he worked at Telcordia Technologies, Inc., New Jersey, in the Broadband Networking Group of the Professional Services Business Unit. He has more than fifteen years of industry experience in the telecommunications area. His research interests are in design and performance evaluation of computer networks and communication protocols for wired, wireless, and optical networks, energy-efficient mechanisms for wireless sensor networks, bandwidth estimation techniques, and location-based services. He has published more than 50 technical and educational papers in journals and conferences devoted to these topics. Dr. Labrador has served as Technical Program Committee member of many IEEE conferences and is currently member of the Editorial Board of Computer Communications and the Journal of Network and Computer Applications, Elsevier Science. He is the lead author of the book *Topology Control in Wireless Sensor Networks*, Springer 2009 and served as guest editor of the special issue of Computer Communications on "Advanced Location-Based Services." Dr. Labrador is a senior member of the IEEE Communications Society, and member of the ACM SIGCOMM and SIGCSE, ASEE, and Beta Phi Mu honor society.

Alfredo J. Pérez received his B.S. in Systems Engineering from the Universidad del Norte, in Barranquilla, Colombia, in 2006, and his M.S. is in Computer Science from the University of South Florida in 2009, where he is a Ph.D. candidate in the Department of Computer Science and Engineering. His research interests are in the areas of mobile sensor networks, location-based systems, evolutionary algorithms, and multi-objective optimization. Alfredo is a member of the IEEE Computational Intelligence Society and member of the Location Aware Information Systems Laboratory at USF.

Pedro M. Wightman received his B.Sc. in Systems Engineering from the Universidad del Norte, in Barranquilla, Colombia, in 2004. He received his M.S. and Ph.D. degrees in Computer Science and Engineering from the University of South Florida in 2007 and 2010, respectively. Dr. Wightman worked as an adjunct instructor at the Universidad del Norte during 2004 and 2005 and since 2010, he has been with the Universidad del Norte, Barranquilla, where he is currently a Professor in the Department of Systems Engineering. In 2005 he was selected to participate in the National Program of Young Researchers in Colombia, sponsored by the Colombian Institute of Science and Technology, Colciencias. In 2005, he was selected by the Universidad del Norte to participate in the Teaching Formation Program, which gave him the opportunity to start his doctorate. His research interests are in the development of energy-efficient topology construction and topology maintenance protocols for wireless sensor networks. Dr. Wightman is co-author of the book *Topology Control in Wireless Sensor Networks*, Springer 2009. He is a member of the IEEE Communication Society, and co-founder of CommNet, the Communication Networks Group at USF.

Tampa

May 2010

Miguel A. Labrador

Alfredo J. Pérez

Pedro M. Wightman

Dedication

Dedicado a mi esposa Mariela, y a mis hijos Miguel Andrés y Daniel Ignacio.
Miguel A. Labrador

Dedicado a mis Padres, mis hermanas y a Rossana. Ad Maiorem Dei Gloriam.
Alfredo J. Pérez

Dedico este trabajo a mi familia por todo el apoyo que me han bridado desde
que tengo memoria, en especial a los Arango y a los Chiriboga.
Pedro M. Wightman

List of Figures

List of Tables

Contents

Acronyms

A-GPS:	Assisted GPS
AJAX:	Asynchronous JavaScript and XML
AMS:	Application Management Software
AOT:	Ahead of Time Compilation
API:	Application Programming Interface
ARM:	Advanced RISC Machines
ASP:	Active Server Pages
BSC:	Base Station Controller
BTS:	Base Transceiver Station
CA:	Certificate Authority
CDC:	Connected Device Configuration
CDMA:	Code Division Multiple Access
CLDC:	Connected Limited Device Configuration
CPA:	Critical Point Algorithm
CUT:	Coordinated Universal Time
CSS:	Cascade Style Sheet
DAC:	Dynamic Adaptive Compilation
DBMS:	Database Management System
DDL:	Data Definition Language
DML:	Data Manipulation Language
DOP:	Dilution of Precision
DRAM:	Dynamic RAM
DSP:	Digital Signal Processor
E-OTD:	Enhanced Observed Time Difference
GCF:	Generic Connection Framework
GGSN:	Gateway GPRS Support Node
GIS:	Geographic Information System

MMAPI:	Mobile Media API
MMS:	Multimedia Messaging Service
MMU:	Memory Management Unit
MS:	Mobile Station
MSC:	Mobile Services Switching Center
MSISDN:	Mobile Subscriber ISDN Number
NSS:	Network and Switching Subsystem
OGC:	Open Geospatial Consortium
PDA:	Personal Digital Assistant
PHP:	Hypertext Preprocessor
RAM:	Random Access Memory
RFC:	Request for Comments
RISC:	Reduced Instruction Set Computer
RMI:	Remote Method Invocation
RMS:	Record Management System
ROM:	Read-Only Memory
RPC:	Remote Procedure Call
SDK:	Software Development Kit
RSS:	Radio Subsystem
SDE:	Software Development Environment
SEQUEL:	Structured English Query Language
SGSN:	Serving GPRS Support Node
SIM:	Subscriber Identity Module
SMS:	Short Message Service
SOAP:	Simple Object Access Protocol
SPI:	Service Provider Interface
SQL:	Structured Query Language
SRAM:	Static RAM
SSL:	Secure Socket Layer
SWWT:	Sprint Wireless Web Toolkit
TCP:	Transport Control Protocol
TLM:	Telemetry Word
TLS:	Transport Layer Security
TTFF:	Time to First Fix

TTP:	Trusted Third Party
UDDI:	Universal Description, Discovery, and Integration
UDP:	User Datagram Protocol
URI:	Uniform Resource Identifier
URL:	Uniform Resource Locator
U-TDoA:	Uplink-Time Difference of Arrival
VLR:	Visitor Location Register
WKT:	Well-Known Text
WLAN:	Wireless Local Area Network
WMA:	Wireless Messaging API
WPS:	Skyhook's Wi-Fi Positioning System
WSA:	J2ME Web Services API
WSDL:	Web Services Definition Language
WSN:	Wireless Sensor Network
XML:	eXtensible Markup Language
XPS:	Skyhook's Hybrid Positioning System

Chapter 1

Introduction

The availability and pervasiveness of powerful mobile phones along with advances in software development platforms, databases, positioning technology, Geographic Information Systems (GIS), and communication networks have led to the creation of Location-Based Information Systems (LBIS), which promise to change the way we live. LBIS, consisting of GPS-enabled cellular phones capable of interacting with other systems and databases, combine all these technological advances to create a new breed of applications known as Location-Based Services (LBS).

Global demand for location-based services continues to skyrocket because of the availability of cellular phones, the new level of service these applications provide, and the important role LBS will play in future software systems. Once large, awkward devices owned only by the wealthy, mobile phones are now becoming accessible to the majority of the world. In 2007, there were 3.25 billion mobile phone users, which is more than half the world's population [53]. Market research also confirms that the world's number of LBS subscribers using Global Positioning System (GPS)-enabled cellular phones will grow from 12 million in 2006 to a projected 315 million in 2011 with North American growth reaching 20 million users up from 500,000 users in 2006 [14, 15].

Creating LBS is very challenging, as there are many players involved and many issues still unsolved. LBS have to deal with erroneous and variable information, as the accuracy of GPS fixes depends on the positioning system, user location, weather conditions, interferences, and others. Cellular communication networks also introduce challenges due to the nature of the wireless transmission where signals fade, transmissions disconnect, and errors in the data occur. Cellular phones themselves introduce several challenges as well, as they are very resource-constrained in terms of processing power, availability of memory, and energy. LBIS need to be conscious about the limited resources available in mobile devices. LBS, as part of a LBIS, interact with other systems and databases to retrieve context information and therefore, be able to provide better information/responses to the user. Finally, cellular phone applications need to have a standard way to access position information and interact with the rest of the system, regardless of the cellular phone manufacturer and cellular system.

This book is about location-based information systems. It describes the technical components needed to create location-based services with emphasis on non-proprietary, available (free) solutions that work across different technologies and platforms.

The rest of this chapter includes a formal definition and classification of location-based services, a description of the major architectures for location providers, an example of a software architecture for LBIS, and the description of a LBIS tracking system example with visualization capabilities that will be used throughout the book to explain, with precise examples, how to implement each of the individual pieces of a LBIS.

1.1   Definition and Classification of LBS

A location-based service is an application that provides users with information based on the geographical position of the mobile device. This is one of the main differentiating features of LBS systems with regard to other systems, such as well-known enterprise systems, i.e., the system knows the physical location of the mobile device (user). This minimal piece of additional information opens up a whole new spectrum of possible applications in many domains. Further, the location of the user is the major differentiator between first-generation LBS applications and current ones, which provide more advanced and useful information. A typical first-generation LBS application example is the subscription-based service that provided traffic congestion notifications to mobile users. In those applications, users had to choose the roads they wanted to receive congestion notifications about using the service provider's Web page; however, since the user location was not available, a particular user could receive a notification of congestion in I-75 in Tampa while being in a business trip in California. On the other hand, current LBS applications will never send this unwanted and irrelevant notification message.

The next section describes current types of LBS applications, which can be categorized as reactive or proactive according to whether the response is triggered by the user or automatically generated by the system.

1.1.1   Types of LBS Applications

A *reactive LBS application* is triggered by the user who, based on his current location, queries the system in search of information. These applications are of the request/response type in which the user queries the system, including the current location, and the system responds with the specific information after searching in other systems and databases. There are many examples of reactive LBS applications:

- Finding a nearby restaurant, friend, or service such as taxis, ATMs, and the like.

- Obtaining directions to a place from the current location.

- Locating people nearby and display their locations on a map.

- Obtaining local weather information.

- Sending emergency notifications to police, insurance companies, roadside assistance companies.

In *proactive LBS applications*, on the other hand, queries or actions are automatically generated by the LBIS once a predefined set of conditions are met. Since the user does not initiate the request of information, these types of applications require the LBIS to continuously know the location of the user. Conditions are included in the LBIS by the user according to his needs or application needs. For example, a proactive LBS application will send you a congestion notification about I-75 in Tampa only when you are close to it or whenever the system knows that I-75 is in your route toward your final destination. A similar proactive application will send you an alert message anytime your children go beyond a pre-defined boundary. In addition to traffic notifications and geofencing, there are many other examples of proactive LBS applications:

- Fleet management.

- Real-time tracking of people and/or assets.

- Location-based advertising.

- Turn-by-turn navigation.

- Real-time friends location.

- Proximity-based actuation.

- Travel assistance device for riding public transportation and museum-guided visits.

1.2   Location Provider Architectures

As said before, the location of the user is a fundamental piece of information in the provision of location-based services. Therefore, it is important to know the different players and techniques involved in the provision of location information and their advantages and disadvantages in the development of location-based services. According to who provides the location information, the location provider architectures can be categorized as network-based, mobile-based, and location provider-based.

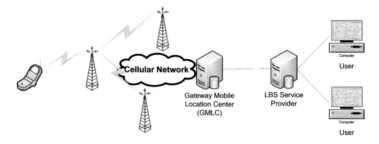

FIGURE 1.1: Network-based location provider architecture.

A *network-based location provider* is usually the same cellular network carrier, which locates the users and stores their locations in a server located within its own network. Figure 1.1 shows a diagram of the network-based location provider architecture. Using this type of location provider, a location-based services provider needs to obtain permission (and possibly pay) for getting access to user location information. The LBS application needs to include mechanisms to query the location server and obtain the location information. This type of location provider is the natural and preferred type of cellular carriers, as they maintain ownership and control of the location information. Further, it may be an additional source of income, as they may charge LBS providers to get access to their location server, usually known as the Gateway Mobile Location Center (GMLC).

Network-based location architectures have not contributed to accelerate the development of LBS. First, this architecture forces cellular network providers to install advanced (and costly) positioning technologies to provide accurate user location information. In the United States, given the FCC mandate to improve the accuracy of location information for 911 emergency services, most cellular network providers have improved their positioning systems over the coarse cell ID technique. However, this is not the case of many cellular providers across the world. The second problem with this architecture is that cellular carriers may limit the number of location fixes and/or the frequency at which they can be queried and impose very expensive charges to query the location server, limiting the development of certain applications. Further, applications need to be aware of which users belong to which network-service providers to query the appropriate server or servers.

In order to overcome the limitations explained above, a *mobile-based location provider* architecture is also available. In this architecture, the LBS provider also develops the application running in the client device, and the client device has the capability of obtaining its location. This capability may be through the use of an embedded Global Positioning System (GPS) chip, in collaboration with the cellular network provider, or both at the same time. Once the client obtains its location information, it uses either the data connectivity through the cellular network via packet services like GPRS or any net-

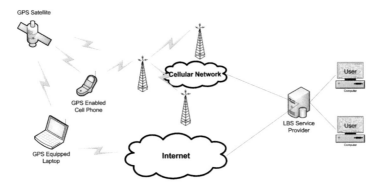

FIGURE 1.2: Mobile-based location provider architecture.

working interface to send the location information to the LBS service provider server for storage and further processing according to the particular application. The location server receives location updates and queries from the clients and, after some filtering and additional processing, sends information back to the client. It is worth mentioning that under this architecture, as shown in Figure 1.2, clients are not limited to cellular phones. Any GPS-enabled client with network connectivity can be part of the LBIS.

The main disadvantage of the mobile-based location provider architecture is that it has the potential to flood the network with unnecessary information, as different LBS providers implement their own applications and do not share the location information. For example, a user of two LBS providers runs two different applications in its client device, which may be obtaining the location of the device at the same time and sending the same information to two different servers. Although the first problem might be solved, including some sort of location manager on behalf of all applications in the client device, the second problem is harder to solve, as the same location information is needed at two different locations. On the plus side, this architecture favors the rapid development of LBS applications, as it imposes no major financial nor technical barriers.

The third location provider architecture is the *location provider-based* architecture, which is shown in Figure 1.3. This architecture is meant to solve the flooding problem of the mobile-based architecture. Under the location provider-based architecture, an independent entity collects users' locations using different methods and makes the information available in a server to all LBS application providers. The independent entity's business is to provide location information to LBS providers, information that can be obtained querying the location server of the cellular network, as in the network-based architecture, or using the model of the mobile-based architecture. This architecture is scalable and perhaps the best architecture for the wide development

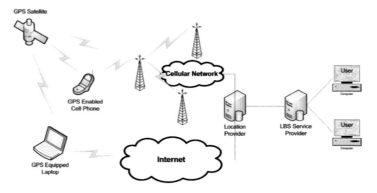

FIGURE 1.3: Location provider-based location provider architecture.

of LBS. However, provisions need to be in place to guarantee fair prices and competition.

In this book, the focus will be on developing proactive LBS applications using the mobile-based location provider architecture.

1.3 A Complete LBIS Real-Time Tracking System Example

This section describes a Location-Based Information System (LBIS) that will be used as an example throughout the book. It describes the different components of the system and explains how each of these components work and interact with each other.

The LBIS system example is a tracking application that can be used in many application domains. The system follows (tracks) devices (people, cars, machines, etc.) in real time to provide services such as tracking your children and company executives as part of a security service, or similar, providing you with timely and appropriate road congestion notifications, and many other services like the ones outlined in Section 1.1.1. As said before, the application is proactive and uses the mobile-based location provider architecture.

The LBIS tracking system example consists of the following five major components, as shown in Figure 1.4:

- The positioning system.

- The client device.

- The transport network.

- The main control station.

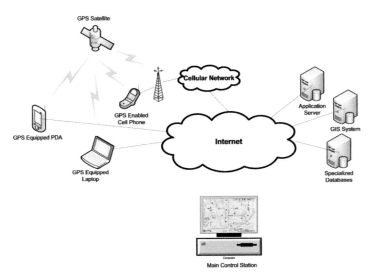

FIGURE 1.4: A complete LBIS real-time tracking system example.

- The servers.

The positioning system provides the location of the client device as requested by the application. In the specific case of our tracking application, the main positioning systems utilized are the GPS and the Assisted-GPS (A-GPS) systems (more on positioning systems in Chapter 6). The client device can be any device capable of 1) obtaining the location of the device, 2) running the LBS application, and 3) communicating with the other components of the LBIS. A typical example of a client device is a GPS-enabled cellular phone, or a laptop with a GPS or embedded positioning system. The transport network is the network that the LBIS system will use to exchange information among the client devices, the servers, and the main control station. Normally, this transport network corresponds to the data packet cellular network (GPRS service), or any other IP-based networking technology available to the clients, servers, and main control station, such as regular Ethernet (wired or wireless) access networks connected to the Internet. The main control station can be any desktop or laptop computer connected to the Internet. Its main functionality is to control (administer) the system and provide a visual representation of the whereabouts of the LBIS clients in real time. For example, the main control station might be used for system administration tasks such as including new users in the LBIS system, deleting users, modifying their information, etc. It might also be used for control tasks such as establishing the virtual boundary of a geofencing application. The control station will also serve as the main monitoring station where to visualize the positions of the users in real time. In addition, the main control station might serve as a device to exchange bi-directional real-time information with the LBIS users, such as sending a text message to any of your children who trespassed the virtual fence. Finally, the servers are machines where most of the intensive processing operations take place. Among the most important servers in our LBIS tracking system example are the database server, where all the locations sent by the clients are stored, the Geographic Information System (GIS), where these locations are translated into known places and vice versa (geocoding and reverse geocoding), and the application server, where specialized applications are run to enhance the service and provide better performance.

From the software point of view, our LBIS tracking system example utilizes available and free software tools as well as standard protocols. The client and server-based applications are programmed using the Java platform in its three different versions, i.e., the Java Platform Micro Edition (Java ME) for resource-constrained devices, the Java Standard Edition (Java SE) for powerful clients, and the Java Enterprise Edition (Java EE) for client-server enterprise applications. NetBeans is the main software development environment utilized. Sun Microsystems' GlassFish is used as the main application server and Google's Web Toolkit the main tool to develop dynamic Web-based applications. Google Maps or Google Earth are the main applications in the main control station used to visualize and track the devices in real time. Postgres and PostGIS are the databases utilized in the LBIS under consideration. Postgres is an object-relational database management system. PostGIS is an add-on to Postgres that supports geographic objects. Finally, the tracking application utilizes standardized communication protocols to transfer information. As such, HTTP, TCP, UDP are the application and transport layer protocols of choice. In terms of networking, the tracking application is IP-based, so it should work without problems over any IP-based network, such as the Internet, regardless of the underlying physical layer communications technology. Appendix A contains a complete list of the software utilized in the LBIS tracking system example as well as specific information about all these components, where to download them from, how to install them, etc. All the software can be found in the book's Website at `http://www.csee.usf.edu/~labrador/LBIS`.

1.4   Software Architecture

A software architecture includes all those software components that together make up the entire system. The architecture not only describes these components and what they do, but also how they are related or connected with each other. The LBIS tracking system example just described includes two key components in terms of the system architecture: the mobile device, or client-side, and the server-side where the application and databases reside to receive, process, analyze, and store the data. These two components have their own software architecture to support the system as a whole, including

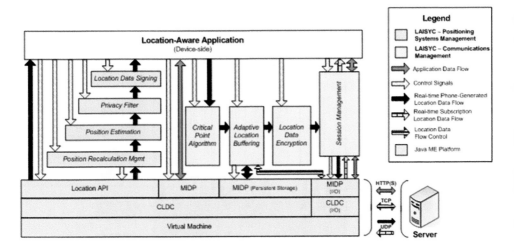

FIGURE 1.5: Client-side software architecture [19] ©2010 IEEE, Inc. Included here by permission.

the relationship between them. These architectures, the client-side and the server-side software architectures, are described next.

1.4.1 Client-Side Software Architecture

The client-side software architecture includes those software components that reside in the mobile device, i.e., the cellular phone. Figure 1.5 shows an example architecture that can be used to support all the functions required to implement the client-side of our LBIS tracking system example. The architecture sits on top of the mobile device's operating system, which is not shown in the figure. Since our application is developed using the Java programming language, the Java virtual machine sits on top of the device's operating system and the Java programming platform sits on top of the virtual machine. In our case, this platform corresponds to the Java Platform Micro Edition or Java ME platform for resource-constrained devices. All these components are common to all Java-based applications and are explained in detail in Chapters 2 and 3.

The architecture shown in Figure 1.5 has the Java platform at the bottom and the location-based application at the top, which is the application that runs in the mobile device and possibly interacts with the user. Between these two layers, the architecture presents several modules, each in charge of performing specific functions. For example, it can be seen how the positioning data is obtained using the Location API included in the Java platform and how these GPS fixes are passed up to the application, either directly or through some other modules in charge of recalculating and estimating the po-

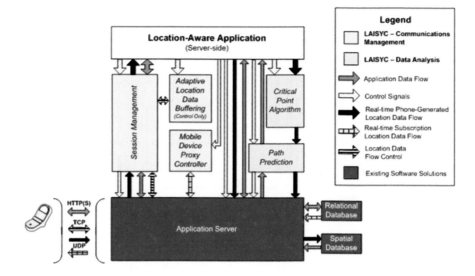

FIGURE 1.6: Server-side software architecture [19] ©2010 IEEE, Inc. Included here by permission.

sition and making the position private. The GPS fixes can be sent from the application to the server directly using the UDP transport layer protocol, or they can be passed through some other modules in charge of saving energy not transmitting unnecessary fixes (Critical Point Algorithm — explained in Chapter 12), storing fixes temporarily not to lose them if the network momentarily fails (Adaptive Location Buffering), and encrypting the GPS fixes and data, if necessary. Finally, the architecture also shows a Session Management module, which is in charge of getting the log-in information from the user and establishing a new session with the server to store all the data from this particular device and user. This information is sent to the system's database using the TCP transport layer protocol for reliability purposes.

1.4.2   Server-Side Software Architecture

The server-side software architecture shown in Figure 1.6 is similar to the client-side architecture in the sense that the application server and the location-aware application are located at the bottom and top of the architecture performing similar functions as their client-side counterparts. Similarly, some modules between these two layers are included to perform specific functions such as the session manager, which receives the session information from the mobile devices and stores that information in the relational database, and the path prediction module, which predicts the user travel direction based on past travel data. The sever has associated a relational database to store all information about users, devices, and sessions, and a spatial database to support the storage of spatial information, such as the GPS fixes from all the mobile devices. The location-based application here also responds to queries sent from the "control station," or main monitoring station, to obtain the GPS fixes of a particular user or group of users and display their positions in a graphical user interface in real time.

Additional literature on software architectures and middleware for location-based services can be found in [38, 20, 18] and the references therein.

1.5 A Brief Look into the Future

The LBIS system described and implemented in this book is just the tip of the iceberg. In addition to GPS fixes, the same system could be used to send other type of data such as environmental data and/or personal health-related data. This take us to the new topics of "Participatory Sensing" and "Human-Centric Sensing."

Participatory sensing is an application that, with the collaboration (participation) of many users, could obtain large amounts of data capable of determining or solving some large-scale societal problems. For example, imagine that your cellular phone, in addition to a GPS chip, comes equipped with a CO_2 sensor that measures the level of pollution around you. If all the cellular phones in the system sent their positions *and* the pollution level to the system's database, we could obtain enough information to determine the pollution index of a particular city or country. Not only that, it should be fairly straightforward to determine which sectors of the city are more polluted than others. The government could use this information to implement environmental policies, you could use these data to decide where to live, and where to go to, and also at what time of the day, as the pollution index would change according to the time of the day. Many more applications based on this concept of participatory sensing can be developed. For example, instant traffic congestion in major roads could be determined if all cars would be sending their locations in real time. Popular sites, restaurants, and events to visit could be easily found in real time. Other sensors could be integrated into a cellular phone to collect data and solve other problems. More information on participatory sensing can be found in [48, 54, 51, 44, 50] and the references therein.

Human-centric sensing is more related to obtaining additional information from a human being to solve a particular problem or improve somehow his or her quality of life. This additional information is obtained in the same manner, integrating specific sensors in the person's cellular phone. For example, if in addition to the user's location, the cellular phone sends data coming from a 3D accelerometer, the system should be able to determine what type of activity the person is doing, for how long, etc., useful information to determine whether

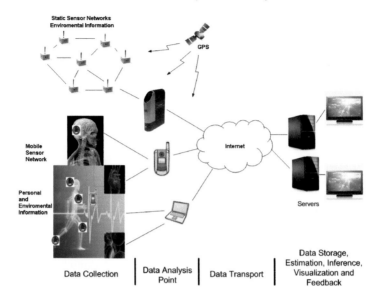

FIGURE 1.7: A high-level architecture for future location-based sensing information systems [46] ©2010 IEEE, Inc. Included here by permission.

the person is concerned about the amount of calories he or she is burning. If in addition to accelerometer data, the cellular phone also transmits the person's temperature, pulse, and breathing depth the system could eventually warn the user about a possible health problem while jogging. The same system could be used by the caregiver of an old person to continuously monitor his/her whereabouts and health condition. A system like this could potentially be used to determine possible effects or the effectiveness of some medications. Literature on human-centric sensing can be found in [41, 43, 24] and the references therein.

As it can be seen, the possibilities are many. Whether it is participatory sensing, human-centric sensing, or both combined, the integration of sensors (mobile with your cellular phone or fixed through the use of wireless sensor networks) into a location-based information system offers many ways to help society and individuals. Figure 1.7 shows a high-level architecture of this integrated system. Reference [46] describes and explains the software architecture of this integrated system, which can be used in location-based services, participatory sensing, and human-centric applications.

1.6 Organization of the Book

The book is organized in a sequential manner so the reader obtains the necessary knowledge to build the LBIS tracking system as needed. Chapter 2 starts describing the mobile phone in terms of hardware and software. This information is important because the application developer needs to understand the resources and capabilities of these devices to develop good applications. The following chapter is Chapter 3, which introduces the reader to the Java Platform Micro Edition, or Java ME, and a summary of its most important optional packages. Chapter 4 briefly describes the most important Application Programming Interfaces (APIs) available to develop MIDlets, or applications, for the Java ME platform. Chapter 5 presents additional programming concepts with emphasis on resource-constrained devices. Chapter 6 includes information about positioning systems, the different systems and techniques available to obtain the location of the client device. The chapter ends with a detailed explanation of the Java ME Location API. Chapter 7 introduces the reader to databases and explains how to set up a database and how to interact with it, i.e., how to store and retrieve information. Chapter 8 is about communications, or how to send and receive information through the network using standard protocols. The reader is introduced to Web services for mobile devices in Chapter 9. Web services is an important technology that has been extended to mobile devices. Chapter 10 explains how to use the Google Web Toolkit to implement system administration functions. How to visualize the data in real time using Google Maps and Google Earth is explained in Chapter 11. Chapter 12 describes client- and server-based applications meant to enhance the service and improve the performance of the system. Finally, Appendix A lists the software needed to develop the entire LBIS system as well as download information and installation procedures.

Chapter 2

The Mobile Phone

2.1 Introduction

Over the past several years, we have witnessed an impressive change in the size and capabilities of cellular phones and their individual components. First-generation cellular phones for analog cellular networks were very big and for voice processing only. Today, on the other hand, with the advent of digital networks and standard IP-based networking technologies, and the technological advances and breakthroughs that we have witnessed in memory, displays, cameras, batteries, microprocessors, digital signal processor, etc., cellular phones are integrated mobile multimedia devices capable of playing and recording video, pictures, TV channels, and MP3 audio; interacting with IP-based servers around the world using the packet radio and other wireless networking interfaces and, of course, continue processing voice calls.

Nonetheless, cellular phones continue to be different from other multimedia devices, such as laptops or personal computers. Cellular phones continue to be resource constrained in terms of memory, energy, and processing power, which requires extra care and knowledge from the application developer. This chapter is meant to provide this extra knowledge about the mobile phone, describing its hardware and software architectures.

2.2 The Hardware Architecture

Figure 2.1 shows a general hardware architecture of a cellular phone. It consists of a microprocessor, digital signal processor, memory, battery and power control module, radio frequency (RF) interfaces, and peripherals, such as keyboard, speakers, microphone, and display. A description of the most important components of the architecture is included in the following sections.

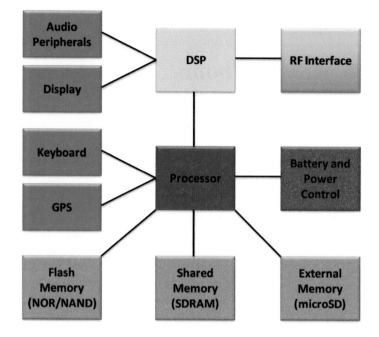

FIGURE 2.1: General architecture of a cellular phone.

2.2.1 The Microprocessor

The mobile phone market is dominated by Advanced RISC Machines (ARM), a 32-bit architecture developed by ARM Limited [2]. It has become very popular in mobile devices given its low power consumption. ARM processors are manufactured by ARM directly or by any company that licenses the architecture. The most recent ARM family of microprocessors manufactured by ARM Limited include the ARM9, ARM11, and Cortex.

The ARM9 family is very common today. They are based on the ARMv4T, ARMv5TE, and ARMv5TEJ architectures. It is a general purpose 32-bit RISC architecture with 5-stage pipeline, 16-KB cache for instructions, 16-KB cache for data, and a memory management unit (MMU). It provides a typical computing power of 200 MIPS at 180 MHz and also includes some enhanced DSP extensions and instructions to better support digital signal processing functions and multimedia applications. The ARM9E also supports Jazelle, a technology that allows Java bytecode to be executed directly in the ARM architecture. Jazelle provides significantly higher performance than a software-only based Java Virtual Machine (JVM); it not only accelerates Java execution by 8x but also reduces the power consumption by 80%. Popular devices using the ARM9 family include the Nintendo DS, the SUN SPOT wireless sensor network device, and several Sony-Ericsson cellular phones. Qualcomm, Texas Instruments, Freescale, and Samsung are among many of the ARM9 licensees.

The ARM11 family of processors is based on the ARMv6, ARMv6T2, ARMv6K, and ARMv6KZ architectures. They include a 8-stage pipeline, variable cache for instructions and data, and a MMU. These processors provide 740 MIPS at 532-665 MHz of computing power. The ARM11 family also supports Jazelle and includes the Thumb-2 technology for the first time. Thumb-2 technology expands the instruction set of the 16-bit set of Thumb with additional 32-bit instructions to handle bit-field manipulation, table branches, and conditional execution. In addition, the ARM11 family includes Vector Floating Point (VFP) technology that provides single- and double-precision floating point computations, which are very useful in graphics and image processing applications such as scaling, 2D and 3D transforms, font generation, and digital filters. Popular devices using the ARM11 family of processors include Apple's iPhone and iPod Touch and Motorola's RAZR. Texas Instruments, Nokia, and Qualcomm are among the most important licensees.

The Cortex family of processors utilizes the ARMv7 architecture, which comes in three flavors. The ARMv7-A architecture is designed to support sophisticated, virtual memory-based OS and user applications. The ARMv7-R architecture is designed for real-time systems. Finally, the ARMv7-M is optimized for microcontroller and low-cost applications. All ARMv7 architectures implement the Thumb-2 technology. The ARMv7-A architecture includes NEON technology extensions, which are designed to address the demands of high-performance, media intense applications such as video encode/decode, 3D graphics, speech processing, compressed audio decoding, image processing, telephony, and sound synthesis. ARMv7 A and R architectures also include VFP technology and dynamic compiler support. The dynamic compiler supports Just-In-Time (JIT) compilation, Dynamic Adaptive Compilation (DAC), and Ahead Of Time (AOT) compilation. The new iPhone 3GS uses the Cortex A8 CPU, which runs at 833 MHz.

2.2.2 Digital Signal Processors (DSPs)

Digital Signal Processors are included in cellular phones to improve their performance. DSPs are optimized processors to handle computationally intensive and repetitive mathematical operations quickly such as Fast Fourier Transforms, compression, and coding/decoding algorithms. Further, they are programmable, so different algorithms can be implemented in the same chip. Although general-purpose processors and DSP algorithms can be successfully implemented in software, these solutions are not suitable for cellular phones because of power supply and space limitations. A specialized DSP provides a lower-cost solution with better performance and lower latency.

Texas Instruments is the world leader in the DSP market, although other companies such as Lucent, Motorola, Analog Devices, NXP Semiconductors, and Freescale have also been very active in this sector. TI offers several DSP platforms, such as the DaVinci digital media processors, the series C5000 of low-power DSPs, and the series C6000, the most recent family of high-performance DSPs. The TI series C6000 supports floating point computations and implements separate instruction and data caches as well as an 8-MB 2nd-level cache. These models are capable of as many as 8000 MIPS, use very long instruction word (VLIW) encoding, and perform eight operations per clock cycle.

2.2.3   The GPS Receiver

The GPS receiver is a key hardware component for any LBIS utilizing the mobile-based location provider architecture, like the real-time tracking system example described in this book. The GPS receiver is important not only because no position will be available to the application without it but also because of its features and performance. There is always the trade-off between cost and quality, and the GPS chip is not the exception. Accuracy and energy consumption are usually traded off for lower prices, so the chips can be integrated in as many devices as possible. It is the application service provider's responsibility to test their applications in the supported devices and assess whether the accuracy and performance provided by the GPS receiver meet the application's requirements or not. Bear in mind that some applications need very precise GPS fixes while others may have more relaxed requirements and cellular phones may provide very different levels of accuracy. Power consumption is another important issue that application service providers should look into. Having the GPS receiver always on and transmitting GPS fixes very frequently will tend to drain the cellular phone's battery very fast. Therefore, some ways to make the application more energy efficient while meeting the tracking requirements of the application need to be devised. (More on this in Chapters 5 and 12.)

Nonetheless, this is one area where more technology advances are expected very soon. For example, better receivers with parallel, hardware correlator architectures can provide faster acquisition of satellite signals, more accurate fixes, and lower power consumption. Further, they can also improve the receiver's sensitivity, meaning that weaker satellite signals could be detected and used to obtain GPS positions in places where we are not able now. One example in this direction is the Broadcom BCM4715 single-chip GPS receiver, which integrates all chip components in less than 30 mm^2 and also supports additional satellite constellations [23].

2.2.4   Memory

Cellular phones, as any other computer, utilize Read Only Memory (ROM) and Random Access Memory (RAM). Information stored in ROM chips cannot be modified once it is written and does not disappear if power is removed. As such, ROM is utilized to store programs that need to be permanently stored in the device. Most of the time, these programs are read from the ROM memory and stored in RAM for execution. In cellular phones, the amount of ROM is usually in the order of 64 MB or more.

RAM, on the other hand, is memory that can be utilized to read and write. However, information in RAM is volatile, meaning that it is lost after the power is switched off or not refreshed periodically. RAM is usually used to store the programs to be executed and the variables related to them. Mobile phones are usually equipped with 128 MB or more RAM memory. For example, the very new Nexus One phone comes equipped with 512 MB of RAM. There are two types of RAM: Static RAM, or SRAM, and Dynamic RAM, or DRAM. Information in Static RAM is stored in flip-flops and as such it does not need to be refreshed. On the positive side, SRAM is faster, more power efficient, and easier to control than DRAM. However, it is more expensive. As a result, SRAM has been used to improve the system's performance utilizing it in intermediate storage, such as cache, which consists of a small amount of memory with fast access times for frequently used data. Dynamic RAM, on the other hand, is less expensive, slower, and more hungry in terms of power since it needs to be refreshed periodically. As such, it is mainly used as main memory in computers.

Another type of non-volatile memory widely used in mobile devices is flash memory. Flash memory comes in two flavors, NOR and NAND flash memory, and depending on the type, it can be used for different purposes, i.e., as a substitute for ROM or RAM, or as a hard drive. NOR-based flash memory provides long erase and write times but full address and data buses, allowing random access to any memory location. Compared with RAM, it provides excellent read times. This makes it as a suitable replacement of ROM to store more permanent programs and run them from there, or even RAM. NOR flash memories present an endurance between 10,000 to 1,000,000 erase cycles.

NAND-based flash memory, on the other hand, presents faster erase and write times and up to ten times better endurance than NOR flash memory, but higher random access times. The main difference is that NAND flash memory does not have an address bus capable of addressing memory locations individually, and rather, data must be read in blocks. This design decision makes NAND flash memory suitable as a secondary storage device such as hard drives to store data and programs on a more permanent basis. Micro SD cards are examples of NAND-based flash memories. As an example, the new Nexus One cellular phones comes equipped with a 4 GB Micro SD card expandable up to 32 GB.

Table 2.1 summarizes the types of memory available, their main use, and characteristics.

2.2.5 Future Trends and Challenges

As explained before, cellular phones are becoming an integrated mobile multimedia device capable of handling voice calls, media streams, and data over multiple types of networking wireless interfaces. These and other new

Memory Type	Main use	Characteristics
ROM	Main memory for permanent programs	Read only
DRAM	Main memory for program execution and variables	Slow and cheap
SRAM	Cache for quick and repetitive access	Fast and expensive
Flash NOR	ROM or DRAM replacement	Long write times; excellent read times; fully addressable
Flash NAND	As a mass storage device	Fast write times; block addressable

TABLE 2.1: Summary of memory types, usage, and characteristics.

capabilities have placed very strong demands for more computing power. At the same time, there are similar demands in terms of making the device more energy efficient, smaller, and cheaper. In the past, these challenges were addressed by making smaller and more energy efficient transistors, which satisfied the required increment of computing power. However, the integration of more and more transistors into the same chip increased the energy consumption.

In order to address these, sometimes contradicting, challenges of providing more computing power while reducing the energy consumption, chip designers have recently come up with several solutions, which are all derived from Equation 2.1. This equation says that the power consumed by a processor is proportional to the product of the square of the voltage V, the frequency of operation f, and C, the capacitance being switched per clock cycle, which is proportional to the number of transistors whose inputs change.

$$Power \sim CV^2f \qquad (2.1)$$

According to Equation 2.1, one option to reduce energy consumption is to make the chip slower by using a lower frequency; however, this alternative reduces the chip's speed, which goes against the trend of more computing power. Similarly, the equation says that lowering the voltage of operation reduces the energy consumption in a quadratic manner. This trend has been pursued by chip manufacturers aggressively. Lower voltages of operation and different modes of operation, e.g., sleep modes, are currently available in most chips inside battery-powered devices, such as laptops and cellular phones.

However, new solutions are needed because as integration of more and more transistors per area of chip continues, the power consumption and energy dissipation become the dominant issues. One option is parallelism. Let us go back to Equation 2.1 and assume that at voltage V_1, the frequency of operation is f_1. If the voltage is divided by half ($V_2 = V_1/2$), the frequency is also reduced by half ($f_2 = f_1/2$), but the power P_1 is now reduced to one-eighth of the original ($P_2 = C(V_2)^2f_2 = C(V_1/2^{(2)})f_1/2 = CV_1f_1/8$). Of course, this comes at the expense of having a chip that is twice slower. If another unit is now added to the chip, it would increase its capacitance C_2 (by an amount that is less than $2C_1$) but would make the whole chip as fast as it was before; however, the voltage needed to run the two units is reduced by half, and the power is decreased by a factor of four! Therefore, important power savings can be achieved by multiple or parallel processors while keeping the computational power constant. Of course, this also brings new challenges, such as finding more efficient ways to perform operations in parallel.

Other important trends in processors, digital signal processors, and memory are the following:

- Multi-core, multi-threading designs.

- Deeper pipelines to achieve more per cycle.

- More multimedia support not only for audio but also video, imaging, graphics.

- Multimedia centric DSPs.

- More and better caches.

- Faster memories.

- Others.

2.3 The Software Architecture

Cellular phones, as any other computer, contain the following three layers of software [42]:

- Application-level software.

- Middleware software.

- Low-level software.

Application-level software consists of all those programs running in the device that are meaningful to the user. One example of an application-level software is the tracking application described in Chapter 1, which is meant to be developed using the Java programming platform for resource-constrained devices.

Middleware software provides the application developer with easy to use interfaces that automate commonly used tasks. It hides the developer from the details of providing the specific service, much in the same way drivers do, but at a higher level. Middleware has the double effect of shortening the application development time and reducing programming errors by offering well-designed and proved service interfaces.

Finally, low-level software consists of the device's operating system, the drivers, and virtual machines. The operating system is in charge of coordinating the activities and assigning the resources of the computer in a controlled fashion to all running applications. As such, the operating system is directly attached to the hardware of the computer. Drivers are hardware-dependent-specific programs utilized by the operating system to communicate with a particular hardware device, such as a printer or a network interface card. Virtual machines are an additional software layer on top of the operating system that also executes computer programs. The importance of virtual machines is that they make the applications operating system independent allowing real portability of applications among computers. Virtual machines offer applications the same services and interfaces and hide the particularities of each operating system. Of course, there must be a specific virtual machine for each operating system. Since applications developed using the Java programming language run on Java virtual machines, the following section describes the Java virtual machine for resource-constrained devices, which is the most relevant one to this book.

2.3.1   The Java ME Virtual Machine

The Java Virtual Machine (JVM) is in charge of the execution of compiled programs that generate *Java bytecode*, which are a low-level, architecture-independent representation of the program. Although there are many JVMs available, they all support the same bytecode. This means that a Java application potentially can run on any machine without modifications. Sun Microsystems has developed the Kilo Virtual Machine (KVM) and the Connected Device Configuration (CDC) Hotspot VM for resource-constrained devices. Other manufacturers have also implemented their own JVMs, which run on specific hardware.

Figure 2.2 shows the entire Java programming flow of execution. At the top, it is the application written in the Java programming language. These `.java` files are passed through the Java compiler, which produces Java bytecode or `.jar` files. The bytecode is executed in the virtual machine, which is on top of the real operating system running on the device. It is worth mentioning that Java is not the only programming language that can be run in the JVM. Any programming language that can be compiled into bytecode can be run as well.

The Java ME virtual machine consists of the *execution engine*, the *heap*, the *stack*, the *garbage collector*, the *loader*, the *verifier*, and the *thread manager*. The description of these modules is based on Sun Microsystems's Kilo Virtual Machine (KVM), one of the most popular virtual machines built by Sun for resource-constrained devices.

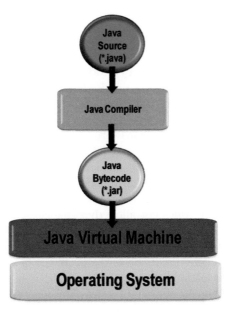

FIGURE 2.2: A Java program flow of execution.

2.3.1.1 The Execution Engine

The execution engine is the module that executes the Java bytecodes. Each Java method consists of a series of bytecodes that are executed in the execution engine. Similar to low-level machine languages, each bytecode consists of the operational code and the operands. The Java virtual machine has 200 standard bytecodes that perform standard tasks such as load and store, arithmetic functions, type conversions, push and pop stack operations, branching, method invocation and return, and exception management, among the most important ones.

The execution engine can be implemented as an interpreter, a compiler, or a Java processor. As an interpreter, the Java execution engine reads each bytecode at a time, translates it into machine code, and finally executes it in the machine's hardware. The main disadvantage of interpreters is speed, as it usually takes longer to run an interpreted program than a compiled one. Interpreters are slower because they have to analyze each statement in the program each time it is executed and then perform the desired action. Interpreters continue to be the execution engine of choice for resource-constrained devices.

The good thing about the Java programming language is that a high-level language compilation, from Java code to bytecode, always takes place before the code is run by the execution engine, regardless of how the execution engine is implemented. This first compilation makes the Java interpreter more efficient, as the interpretation of bytecodes can be done in a more efficient manner than the direct interpretation of the high-level Java language.

The execution engine can also be implemented as a compiler. In this case, the bytecode is compiled by a bytecode compiler that translates the entire code into machine's language, which is then run in the hardware directly and at once. Java compilers are faster because they avoid the translation process on a bytecode by bytecode manner. Java bytecode is compiled into native machine code and run in the hardware as any other compiled program.

The compilation of Java bytecode can be done before the program is run, a process called *static compilation*, or at runtime, *dynamic compilation*. Static compilation is the usual procedure in which the program is compiled entirely offline and then the compiled program is run. Static compilation produces high quality code but does not allow dynamic class loading and only runs on a specific machine.

Dynamic compilation compiles Java code into native machine code at runtime, on the fly. Therefore, it solves the problems of static compilation allowing dynamic class loading and not being specific to a particular machine. The performance of dynamic compilation heavily depends on the amount of methods that are repeatedly run, as each method is only compiled once. Keep in mind that interpreting and executing is faster than compiling and executing. Dynamic compilation is also known as *Just-In-Time compilation (JIT)*.

Another option to improve Java's performance is to use Java processors. Instead of emulating the CPU in software, the Java virtual machine is implemented entirely in hardware. In other words, the bytecodes that make up the instruction set of the abstract machine become the instruction set of a specific machine. Java processors have the advantage that many of the functions in the virtual machine are optimized to run more efficiently in hardware.

2.3.1.2   The Heap

The heap is the memory area used by the Java virtual machine to store data and code during runtime, i.e., perform dynamic memory allocations. The heap is usually partitioned in two areas, one where the methods to be executed are loaded, and one with the JVM stacks. The methods area is also called the permanent area because it is outside of the garbage collector's domain of execution. The stacks, on the other hand, are within the garbage collected area.

The Java virtual machine is a stack-based machine, as it carries out all operations through a stack. The JVM creates a stack for each thread, and each stack consists of frames where local variables and operands to execute a method are stored. One frame can only be active at any given time. The JVM has three pointers to handle the operation of the stacks. The *stack pointer* points to the beginning of the active stack. The *local pointer* has the address of the local variables. Finally, the *frame pointer* points to the beginning of the frame. Once a method is executed, the garbage collector claims the frame space and makes it available for new methods.

2.3.1.3 The Garbage Collector

The garbage collector module is in charge of claiming the memory space occupied by objects that are no longer referenced by the program. One of the advantages of having a garbage collector is that it liberates the programmer from the burden of knowing which objects have or have not been referenced. On the down side, a garbage collector may introduce a performance penalty, which may vary depending on the algorithm utilized.

The garbage collector included in the KVM is a simple, non-moving, single-space mark-and-sweep garbage collector [58]. This means that the garbage collector marks referenced objects and sweeps unreferenced or unused ones.

2.3.1.4 The Loader

The loader is the module in charge of loading the main classes of the Java ME platform, optional APIs, and the application's class files (MIDlet Java Archive JAR files). It may be called at the beginning of the execution or dynamically during the execution of the application. A conforming virtual machine for resource-constrained devices does not support user-defined class loaders; instead, for security reasons, it has to use a built-in "bootstrap" class loader that cannot be overridden, replaced, or reconfigured [59]. Further, MIDlets can load the classes included in their own JAR file only, ensuring that applications running in the same device do not interfere with one another. This means that the Java ME platform supports dynamic linking of classes that are included in the application's JAR file only; however, dynamically linking classes from different JAR files is not allowed.

2.3.1.5 The Verifier

The verifier is the module that checks whether the loaded bytecode can be safely run in the virtual machine. The verifier checks for bytecodes wrongly typed, stack overflows and underflows, and correct branching of subroutines. The conventional class verifier included in the Java SE virtual machine occupies a minimum of 50 KB of binary code space and between 30 and 100 KB of RAM at runtime [59]. These numbers, in addition to the CPU power required to run these algorithms in real time, result very burdensome for resource-constrained devices. As a result, an off-device preverification and runtime verification approach were designed for the KVM.

The verification process takes place in two steps. In the first step, the class file is run through a *preverifier* tool that is run in the developer's workstation. This part of the verification process includes in the class an additional attribute in a `StackMap` that, in the second step, the *runtime verifier* in the resource-constrained device uses to perform the verification efficiently.

2.3.1.6 The Thread Manager

Given that Java supports multithreading, a thread manager is needed to coordinate the execution of all the threads created by the application. The Java KVM also supports multithreading but does not support thread groups or daemon threads.

2.4 The Mobile Phone and the LBIS Tracking System Example

According to the description of the LBIS tracking system example presented in Chapter 1 and looking at Figure 1.4, it is very easy to know where this chapter fits into the LBIS system: the mobile phone is the device that the LBIS system will track. The device runs a client application that obtains the device's position using the GPS chip and transmits those fixes in real time to the LBIS system servers for storage, processing, and visualization. This chapter describes the most important hardware and software components that make up a cellular phone, so software developers can develop robust and adequate applications for the specific device.

Chapter 3

The Java Platform Micro Edition (Java ME)

3.1 Introduction

The Java programming language consists of a family of Java platforms, each targeting different types of devices and applications. Currently, there are three platforms, the Java Enterprise Edition (Java EE) for server and enterprise applications, the Java Standard Edition (Java SE) for desktops and laptops, and the new Java Platform Micro Edition (Java ME) for resource-constrained devices, as shown in Figure 3.1. The size of the stacks in the figure represents the size of the libraries and, therefore, the footprint of the platforms. The Java editions sit on top of a Java Virtual Machine (JVM) that is also relative in size with the Java edition that it supports.

This chapter introduces the Java Platform Micro Edition (Java ME), formerly known as Java 2 Micro Edition (J2ME), the newest Java-based platform for resource-constrained devices. The chapter describes the Java ME architecture and its relevant configurations and profiles along with a brief description of the optional packages and APIs available for mobile devices.

It is worth mentioning that the Java ME platform inherits the advantages of the other Java-based platforms. First and foremost, it avoids the significant problems that software developers face when porting applications from one mobile phone to another. While still not a perfect "write-once-run-anywhere" solution, Java ME applications run over a Java virtual machine that is operating system independent. Therefore, Java ME applications should run on any Java-enabled mobile device without substantial changes to the code or structure of the program. Secondly, this newer Java platform is based on the well-known and popular Java programming language, which eliminates the steep learning curve of mastering a new language. Finally, there is a vast number of cellular phones that support Java virtual machines and therefore can run Java ME applications. These advantages have made Java ME an excellent candidate for mobile application development.

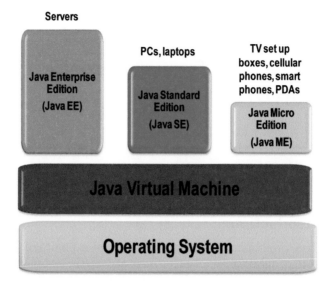

FIGURE 3.1: The family of Java platforms.

3.2   The Java ME Platform

The Java ME platform was designed for mobile devices and embedded systems, such as mobile phones, PDAs, and set-top boxes, those devices that are constrained in terms of computational power, memory, and energy compared with other computing devices such as laptops, desktops, servers, and workstations. For this reason, the Java ME platform has the smallest footprint and runs over the thinest virtual machine of the Java family.

The architecture of the Java ME platform is shown in Figure 3.2. As it can be seen, the architecture differentiates between different types of resource-constrained devices. The left side of the architecture contains the layers for those devices with a relative larger amount of resources, such as set-top boxes, automobile navigation systems, and the like. The right side of the figure shows the stack for more constrained devices, such as cellular phones, PDAs, and pagers. The rest of this chapter is devoted to the right side of the architecture, as it relates to our LBIS system tracking example using cellular phones.

Regardless of the size and the type of device, the architecture consists of four layers. At the bottom, there is the Java Virtual Machine that sits on top of the operating system running in the device. The JVM is in charge of the execution of the Java compiled programs. Next is the *configuration layer*, which includes those Java classes specific to a particular class of devices. On top of the configuration layer is the *profile layer*, which consists of the APIs

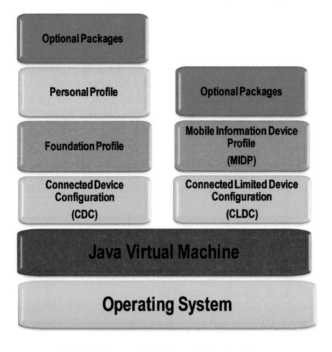

FIGURE 3.2: The Java ME platform.

implementing the services supported by the specific configuration. These three layers are required in all implementations. The last layer represents those optional packages that implement specific APIs and classes needed by some applications only; these optional packages are loaded in the device as needed. A more detailed description of the configuration and profile layers follows along with a brief description of the most important optional packages. The Java virtual machine was already described in Chapter 2.

3.3 The Connected Limited Device Configuration (CLDC) Layer 1.1

A Java ME configuration contains the Java libraries needed to support a particular class of devices. As such, configurations specify the features of the Java programming language, the features of the virtual machine, and the Java APIs that are supported. The Java ME platform has two configurations, the Connected Device Configuration (CDC) and the Connected Limited Device Configuration (CLDC), which is the one supporting cellular phones and more resource-constrained devices.

The Connected Limited Device Configuration layer, currently Java Specification Request (JSR) 139 version 1.1, implements the minimum components required to support small connected devices. It targets devices with 192 KB of total memory, 16-bit or 32-bit processors, low power consumption, and intermittent connectivity and limited bandwidth such as cellular phones, pagers, PDAs, home appliances, and the like. The CDLC 1.1 specification contains the components to support the Java programming language and virtual machine features, core Java libraries (`java.lang.*`, `java.util.*`), and APIs for input/output, security, and networking.

3.3.1 Java Programming Language and Virtual Machine Features

The CLDC 1.1 specification supersedes specification 1.0 introducing several important new features and fixes. Among the most important new features are the inclusion of floating point support with the classes `Float` and `Double` and the redesign of the classes `Calendar`, `Date`, and `Timezone`, and the `Thread` object to be more Java SE-compliant.

A Java virtual machine conforming to the CLDC 1.1 specification is compliant with the Java virtual machine of the Java SE except for the following:

- **No finalization of class instances:** The method `Object.finalize()` to finalize class instances is not included in the CLDC 1.1 libraries.

- **Exception and error handling limitations:** In CLDC 1.1 asynchronous exceptions are not supported and error handling capabilities are limited.

- **User-defined class loaders:** The CLDC 1.1 virtual machine does not support user-defined class loaders; it only supports the "bootstraping" class loader for security reasons.

- **Thread groups and daemon threads:** The CLDC 1.1 only supports operations with individual thread objects.

- **Class file verification:** As explained in Section 2.3.1.5, the CLDC 1.1 specification supports off-line preverification and runtime verification with stack maps.

3.3.2 Libraries and APIs

The CLDC 1.1 specification includes libraries that are a subset of the standard Java SE and EE platforms, for upward compatibility, and a subset of libraries that are specific to CLDC 1.1.

The classes derived from the Java SE platform are the following [59]:

- **System classes:** These are classes that are essential to the Java programming language, and they are included in the `java.lang` package. The system classes included in the CLDC specification are the following:

  - `java.lang.Object`
  - `java.lang.Class`
  - `java.lang.Runtime`
  - `java.lang.System`
  - `java.lang.Thread`
  - `java.lang.Runnable`
  - `java.lang.String`
  - `java.lang.StringBuffer`
  - `java.lang.Throwable`

- **Data type classes:** The following data type classes are supported:

  - `java.lang.Boolean`
  - `java.lang.Byte`
  - `java.lang.Short`
  - `java.lang.Integer`
  - `java.lang.Long`
  - `java.lang.Float`
  - `java.lang.Double`
  - `java.lang.Character`

- **Collection classes:** The package `java.util` supports the collection classes `java.util.Vector`, `java.util.Stack`, `java.util.Hashtable`, `java.util.Enumeration`, and two additional utility classes, the `java.util.Random` class to generate random numbers and the `java.util.Math` class that provides `min`, `max`, `abs`, `ceil`, and `floor` functions.

- **Input/output classes:** The package `java.io` supports the following classes:

  - `java.io.InputStream` and `java.io.OutputStream`
  - `java.io.ByteArrayInputStream`
  - `java.io.ByteArrayOutputStream`
  - `java.io.DataInput` and `java.io.DataOutput`
  - `java.io.DataInputStream` and `java.io.DataOutputStream`

- java.io.Reader and java.io.Writer
- java.io.InputStreamReader and java.io.OutputStreamWriter
- java.io.PrintStream

- **Calendar and Time classes:** The CLDC 1.1 specification only supports the java.util.Calendar, the java.util.TimeZone, and the java.util.Date classes. To preserve more space, it only supports one time zone, which is the GMT by default.

- **Exception and Error classes:** The list of exception classes is very comprehensive to preserve upward compatibility with the Java SE and EE platforms. The specification supports the following exception classes:
  - java.util.Exception
  - java.util.ArithmeticException
  - java.util.ArrayIndexOutOfBouondsException
  - java.util.ArrayStoreException
  - java.util.ClassCastException
  - java.util.ClassNotFoundException
  - java.util.IllegalAccessException
  - java.util.IllegalArgumentException
  - java.util.IllegalMonitorStateException
  - java.util.IllegalThreadStateException
  - java.util.IndexOutOfBoundsException
  - java.util.InstantiationException
  - java.util.InterruptedException
  - java.util.NegativeArraySizeException
  - java.util.NullPointerException
  - java.util.NumberFormatException
  - java.util.RuntimeException
  - java.util.SecurityException
  - java.util.StringIndexOutOfBoundsException
  - java.util.EmptyStackException
  - java.util.NoSuchElementException
  - java.io.EOFException
  - java.io.InterruptedIOException
  - java.oi.IOException
  - java.io.UnsupportedEncodingException

– `java.oi.UTFDataFormatException`

Error handling on the other hand is very limited. The CLDC 1.1 specification only supports the `java.lang.NoClassDefFoundError`, `java.lang.OutOfMemoryError`, `java.lang.VirtualMachineError`, and `java.lang.Error` classes.

The CLDC 1.1 specification also includes some CLDC specific classes described within the *Generic Connection Framework (GCF)*, meant to support input/output and networking capabilities in a generalized and extensible manner. The idea is to provide the minimum I/O and networking support needed by all devices while opening the door for extending these capabilities and implementing new ones as needed by specific devices and implementations. In that manner, the very large footprint of code included in the Java SE platform is reduced to fit in a small device. More details on the Generic Connection Framework are included in Chapter 8, which is devoted to communications.

3.4 The Mobile Information Device Profile (MIDP) Layer 2.0

If the CLDC is a contract between the device and the Java programming language, the Mobile Information Device Profile is a contract between the Java programming language and the application developer. The MIDP, currently JSR 118 version 2.0, is the profile designed for the CLDC. Other profiles, such as the Foundation Profile, the Personal Basis Profile, and the Personal profile have been designed to work on top of the CDC configuration. These later profiles will not be discussed here.

The MIDP 2.0 specification includes the minimum set of APIs required to develop graphical and networked applications for resource-constrained mobile devices. These applications, called *MIDlets*, are the mobile equivalent of the *applets* developed under the Java SE platform. As applets, MIDlets can also be downloaded from a Web server and installed and run in the mobile device. MIDlets, by definition, are those applications that use only the APIs defined in the MIDP and CLDC specifications.

The following list contains those APIs that are part of the MIDP 2.0 specification. They are part of the list of minimum requirements to develop applications for resource-constrained devices. In other words, it is expected that most applications will have a graphical user interface, communicate with other applications or databases over a network, store data either locally or remotely, secure the data transmissions, etc. The APIs included in the specification are grouped according to the type of function they perform. Each API consists of one or more packages as follows:

- **User Interface API:** These APIs provide the functionality needed to implement graphical user interfaces for the MIDlet application. They are included in the `javax.microedition.lcdui` package.

- **Game API:** These APIs include a series of classes to develop games for wireless devices. The classes are included in the `javax.microedition.lcdui.game` package.

- **Application Management API:** These are the APIs used to install, update, and remove MIDlets. The classes are included in the `javax.microedition.midlet` package.

- **Networking API:** Networking support as specified in the *Generic Connection Framework* is provided by the networking APIs. The networking-related classes are included in the `javax.microedition.io` package. The networking APIs will be described in more detail in Chapter 8.

- **Security API:** These are the APIs used to protect the mobile device and secure the communications. They are included in the `javax.microedition.pki` package.

- **Sound API:** Packages `javax.microedition.media` and `javax.microedition.media.control` provide the APIs related to media and `control` types used with a `player`.

- **Storage API:** MIDP includes APIs to store and retrieve data in the mobile device. The classes are included in the `javax.microedition.rms` package.

These APIs will be further described in the following chapter or in those chapters related to the topic of the API.

3.5   Optional Packages

The Java ME platform is very rich in terms of additional packages. These packages, which are not part of the MIDP 2.0 specification, provide the functionality needed to perform those tasks that are specific to some applications. The optional packages, as seen in Figure 3.2, sit on top of the MIDP layer and are loaded into the stack on demand as dictated by the applications. The following list briefly describes some of the most important optional APIs.

- **Mobile Media API (JSR 135):** This API includes the functionality to access and control multimedia resources and files. The sound API part of the MIDP specification is a subset of this API.

- **Security and Trust Services API (JSR 177):** This API provides security services to make *trusted* mobile devices.

- **Session Initiation Protocol API (JSR 180):** The Session Initiation Protocol is a signaling protocol to establish and manage multimedia communications over IP networks. This API provides this functionality to mobile devices.

- **Mobile 3D Graphics API (JSR 184):** This API is designed to develop 3D graphic applications such as games, animated messages, product visualization, etc. It is flexible enough to be used in resource-constrained devices as well as higher-end devices with better color displays, DSP, floating point unit, etc.

- **Event Tracking API (JSR 190):** This API was designed to standardize the tracking of application events in the mobile device and transmit those events to a server maybe for billing purposes, update notification, usage tracking, etc.

- **Wireless Messaging API (JSR 120):** The Wireless Messaging API includes the interfaces to send and receive Short Message Service (SMS) and Cell Broadcast Service (CBS). This API is described in more detail in Chapter 8.

- **Location API (JSR 293):** This API defines methods to obtain the mobile device's position. This API is described in more detail in Chapter 6.

- **Java ME Web Services API (JSR 172):** This API enables mobile devices to use Web services. This API is described in more detail in Chapter 9.

Except for those APIs that will be used in subsequent chapters in the development of our LBIS tracking system example, these APIs will not be described here any further. More information about these APIs can be found in the Website of the Java Community Process at `http://jcp.org`.

3.6 The Java ME Platform and the LBIS Tracking System Example

This chapter provides basic information about the Java ME platform. It lists the components, features, classes, and APIs that are available to develop the client application that will run in the cellular phones of the clients of our LBIS tracking system example. This chapter is a brief guide to the programmer. The following chapters introduce the reader on how to use those components and APIs to actually build MIDlets.

Chapter 4

MIDlet Development

4.1 Introduction

This chapter is devoted to MIDlets and those APIs that are commonly used in the development of MIDlets. The chapter begins with general information about MIDlets and the typical "Hello World" example. Then, the chapter includes example code to describe how to use the user interface, sound, security, and storage APIs.

4.2 MIDlets

A MIDlet is a Java program compiled using the APIs included in the CLDC and MIDP specifications. The compilation can be made using the command line invoking the Java SE compiler *javac* with the appropriate `classpath` option indicating the location of the CLDC and MIDP APIs, i.e., `javac -classpath path\CLDC-MIDP-API applicationName.java`, or selecting the appropriate compilation options in NetBeans or Eclipse.

Once the compilation of the MIDlet is successfully completed, there are several additional steps before loading the application in a real device for testing. First, the application should be debugged and tested in local emulators, like the Mobility Pack that can be integrated into NetBeans, to debug and test the graphical user interface and event handling functionalities. Second, the application needs to be passed through the off-line preverifier, so it can be later verified by the device when loaded. Third, the MIDlet's source code needs to be packaged. The *packaging* process creates two files, a Java Archive file (JAR) that contains all the class files and resource files such as audio, video, pictures, and data files, and a Java Application Descriptor (JAD) file. The JAR file also contains the *manifest* file, which is generated by the JAR tool and provides specific information about the MIDlet, such as the MIDlet name, vendor, version, and configuration and profile utilized. The JAD file contains additional information about the MIDlet, such as the URL and the size of the MIDlet, useful information for the mobile device to decide whether to download the MIDlet or not. The preverification of the MIDlet as well as the creation of the JAR, JAD, and *manifest* files is performed automatically by NetBeans when the MIDlet is compiled and built. The preverifier is usually part of the software development kit platform used to develop applications for a specific vendor device or carrier, which includes all or most cellular phone models of that particular carrier or device manufacturer. One example is the Sprint Wireless Web Toolkit (SWWT), which can be integrated into NetBeans as the device platform to be used by the compiler. The installation process of the SWWT is described in the Appendix, Section A.5.1.1. Listings 4.1 and 4.2 show examples of a *manifest* and JAD files, respectively.

```
 1  Manifest−Version:  1.0
 2  Ant−Version:  Apache  Ant  1.7.0
 3  Created−By:  1.6.0_03−b05  (Sun  Microsystems  Inc.)
 4  MIDlet −2:  CalculatorWebService ,  ,  edu.cse.usf.book.ws.
        CalculatorWebService
 5  MIDlet −1:  TCPTest ,  ,  edu.cse.usf.book.TCPTest
 6  MIDlet−Vendor:  Vendor
 7  MIDlet−Name:  TCPTest
 8  MIDlet−Version:  1.0
 9  MicroEdition−Configuration:  CLDC −1.0
10  MicroEdition−Profile:  MIDP −2.0
```

Listing 4.1: Content of a *manifest* file.

```
 1  MIDlet −1:  TCPTest ,  ,  edu.cse.usf.book.TCPTest
 2  MIDlet −2:  CalculatorWebService ,  ,  edu.cse.usf.book.ws.
        CalculatorWebService
 3  MIDlet−Jar−Size:  12747
 4  MIDlet−Jar−URL:  TCPTest.jar
 5  MIDlet−Name:  TCPTest
 6  MIDlet−Vendor:  Vendor
 7  MIDlet−Version:  1.0
 8  MicroEdition−Configuration:  CLDC −1.0
 9  MicroEdition−Profile:  MIDP −2.0
```

Listing 4.2: Content of a JAD file.

All MIDlets have the same life cycle shown in Figure 4.1. When the application is loaded, the constructor of the MIDlet is called and an instance of the application is created. At that time the MIDlet is in the *Paused* state. Calling the `startApp()` and `pauseApp()` methods cause the MIDlet to change its state from *Paused* to *Active* and vice versa. During the lifetime of the MIDlet, its state can change back and forth between these two states as many times as necessary. When the MIDlet is no longer needed, the `destroyApp()` method terminates the instance of the application.

The MIDP layer contains a piece of software called the *Java Application Manager (JAM)* or *Application Management Software (AMS)* that manages the MIDlets in the device, i.e., installs, updates, starts, removes, and pauses the MIDlets.

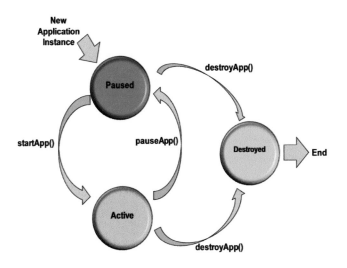

FIGURE 4.1: The life cycle of a MIDlet.

4.3 A Hello World MIDlet

A MIDlet is an extension of the `javax.microedition.midlet.MIDlet` class, which implements the methods that define the behavior of the MIDlet such as `startApp()`, `pauseApp()`, and `destroyApp()` methods. The Hello World MIDlet implementation shown in Listing 4.3 shows how to implement this small application.

```
1  import javax.microedition.midlet.*;
2  import javax.microedition.lcdui.*;
3
4  public class HelloWorld extends MIDlet implements CommandListener{
5    private Command exitCommand;
6    private TextBox tbox;
7
8  // MIDlet constructor
9  public HelloWorld() {
10
11 // Create "Exit" Command
12 exitCommand = new Command("Exit", Command.Exit, 1);
13
14 // Create TextBox to display the output
15 tbox = new TextBox ("Hello World MIDlet", "Hello, World!", 15, 0);
16
17 // Include the Exit Command in the interface and set its Listener
18 tbox.addCommand(exitCommand);
19 tbox.setCommandListener(this);
20
21 // Set the TextBox as the current screen
22 Display.getDisplay(this).setCurrent(tbox);
23 }
24
```

```
25 // The system calls this function to start the MIDlet
26 protected void startApp() {}
27
28 // The application is switched to the paused state
29 protected void pauseApp() {}
30
31 // The application is destroyed
32 protected void destroyApp() {boolean force}
33
34 // MIDlet destroys itself if user gives the Exit Command
35 public void commandAction (Command c, Displayable d) {
36    if (c==exitCommand) {
37       destroyApp(false);
38       notifyDestroyed{};
39       }
40    }
41 }
```

Listing 4.3: A Hello World MIDlet.

Let us digest this simple MIDlet. First of all, the application imports the packages related to MIDlets and the user interface API. As a MIDlet, the HelloWorld MIDlet extends the class `javax.microedition.midlet.MIDlet` and implements the command listener to listen for commands. Then, the constructor is called by the Java Application Manager (JAM) to instantiate the MIDlet. The application creates the Exit command as well as a text box and screen to display the application's text and command. The application then implements the methods to start, pause, and destroy the MIDlet. As it can be seen, this MIDlet does not take any action when the start and pause commands are given by the user. However, it does reacts to the Exit command, which utilizes the destroy method. Notice that the `destroyApp()` method has the boolean `false` parameter. This means that the destroy request is not unconditional. In this case, the MIDlet may throw an exception and stay in the current state of execution. If the parameter is `true` the request is unconditional, the MIDlet will free its resources, and the application will terminate. Figure 4.2 shows the Hello World MIDlet as run in the cellular phone emulator included in NetBeans.

4.4   The User Interface API

The package `javax.microedition.lcdui` contains most of the classes and methods utilized in the design of graphical user interfaces. This section presents the hierarchy of the classes included in the package as well as a brief description of each of them.

The classes included in the user interface package follow the hierarchy shown in Figure 4.3. At the highest level of the hierarchy, there is the `Display` class. This class manages the display and input devices of the system. There is only one instance of `Display` per MIDlet. A reference of that instance can

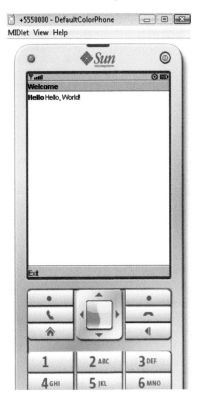

FIGURE 4.2: The Hello World MIDlet in NetBeans' cellular phone emulator.

be obtained by calling the `getDisplay()` method. The class also contains methods to retrieve the properties of the device and to request the display of objects.

The `Displayable` object contains the user interface objects that are shown in the display. The `Display` class `setCurrent()` and `getCurrent()` methods are utilized to set and retrieve the current `Displayable`. Normally, the application changes the current `Displayable` based on user action. If the current `Displayable` is visible, the application is in the *foreground*; otherwise, it is said to be in the *background*.

A `Displayable` object may have listener and command objects associated with it through which the user interacts with the user interface of the application. When the user selects a particular command, the application is automatically notified. The application may react to user command notifications changing the current `Displayable` by another one. In other words, the transition from one `Displayable` to another is controlled by the command associated with the current `Displayable`. All `Displayable` objects have the following properties:

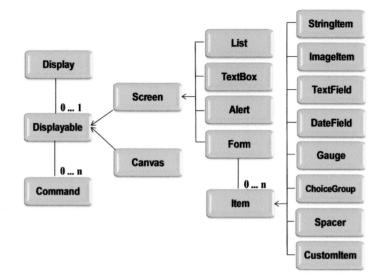

FIGURE 4.3: Hierarchy of the most important classes in the user interface package.

- Zero or more commands associated with it.

- A `CommandListener` that is notified when the user issues a command.

- A title string to identify or name the object.

- A ticker object that shows scrolling text.

`Command`s provide users with a way to navigate through the `Displayable`s of an application. If a `Displayable` object has no command associated with it, the user has no way to change the current `Displayable`. `Command`s are added and removed using the `addCommand()` and `removeCommand()` methods.

All `Command`s have a string label, priority, and command type. The string label can be short or long and represents the description that identifies the command. The priority is a number that defines the importance of the `Command`s of the same type on the same `Displayable`. The lower the number the higher the importance. More important `Command`s are displayed before less important ones. There are six specific command types and two generic command types, as follows:

- **Specific command types:**

  - BACK: Goes back to the previous screen.
  - OK: User accepts question or data in current screen.
  - CANCEL: User rejects question or data in current screen.

- HELP: Activates online help.
- EXIT: Used to exit the application.
- STOP: Used to stop a process running on the current screen.

- **Generic command types:** Used to describe the intent of a Command not described by the specific commands.

    - ITEM: Relates to specific items of a Screen or the elements of a Choice, e.g., "Delete" item in a List.
    - SCREEN: Typically relates to all items of a Screen or elements of a List.

Listing 4.4 shows an example that implements three Commands, two generic commands, save and delete, and one specific command, the exit command. The application responds to commands because the listener of the command is called. Listeners are registered using the setCommandListener() method. An object must implement the commandAction() method of the CommandListener interface to define itself as a listener.

```
1  class ExampleCommand extends Screen implements CommandListener {
2    Command save = new Command ("Save", Command.SCREEN, 2};
3    Command delete = new Command ("Delete", Command.SCREEN, 3};
4    Command exit = new Command ("Exit", Command.EXIT, 4};
5    MIDlet midlet;
6
7    public ExampleCommand (MIDlet mymidlet) {
8      midlet = mymidlet;
9      setCommandListener(this);
10     addCommand(save);
11     addCommand(delete);
12     addCommand(exit);
13     }
14
15    public void commandAction (Command c, Displayable d) {
16      if (c == save) {
17        \\ Save data
18        }
19
20      else if (c == delete) {
21        \\ Delete data
22        }
23
24      else if (c == exit) {
25        \\ Exit the application
26        midlet.notifyDestroyed();
27        }
28      }
29 }
```

Listing 4.4: Implementing Commands for MIDlets.

4.4.1 Lists, Text Boxes, Forms, and Alerts

The Displayable class has two subclasses, the Canvas and the Screen subclasses. The Canvas subclass contains objects that allow the developer to have precise control of what is drawn on the display. This is particularly useful for those applications that need precise placement and control of graphic elements. The `Canvas` subclass will not be described here any further.

The `Screen` subclass contains high-level objects that implement complete user interface components such as lists, alerts, text boxes, and forms. The `List` class is a `Screen` that displays a list of choice *elements*. Each element includes a string and may have an icon. `Lists` can be *implicit, exclusive*, and *multiple choice*. An implicit list is a list of items from which the user can select only one of the elements. The system automatically handles the scrolling of the selection as the user moves through the list. An exclusive list also allows the user to select one element; however, it is presented as a list of radio buttons that unselect any previously selected button when a new one is selected. A multiple choice list allows the user to select one or more elements from the list. Normally, check boxes are utilized in this list type.

Available methods to manipulate the list elements are the `append()`, `delete()`, `insert()`, `set()`, `getString()`, and `getImage()` methods. The type of list is selected using the interface class `Choice`, as follows:

```
List list = new List (String title, int listType, String[]
    stringElements, Image[] imageElements);

where listType can be IMPLICIT, EXCLUSIVE, or MULTIPLE; stringElements
    (imageElements) is the initial array of elements(images)

e.g., List list = new List (''Email list'', Choice.IMPLICIT, ''
    labrador@cse.usf.edu, ajperez@cse.usf.edu, pedrow@cse.usf.edu'',
    null);
```

The `TextBox` class is a `Screen` that allows the user to input and edit text. The maximum number of characters is defined by the application, which can use the methods `setMaxSize()` and `getMaxSize()` to set and obtain the maximum size. The application can also set *input constraints* to make sure the user includes allowed characters. Available constraints are ANY, NUMERIC, DECIMAL, PHONENUMBER, URL, and EMAILADDR. A `TextBox` *must* have `Commands` associated with it; otherwise, the user will not be able to go anywhere else. The following example code shows how a text box is created with an editable email address:

```
TextBox tb = new TextBox (String title, String text, int maxSize, int
    constraints);

e.g., TextBox tb = new TextBox (''Enter Email'', ''labrador@cse.usf.
    edu'', 30, TextField.EMAILADDR);
```

A `Form` is a `Screen` that may contain `StringItems`, `ImageItems`, `DateFields`, `TextFields`, `Gauges`, and `ChoiceGroups`, i.e., any of the subclasses of class `Item`, as shown in Figure 4.3. The `Form` can be manipulated using the `insert()`, `append()`, `delete()`, `set()`, `get()`, `size()`, and `deleteAll()` methods.

`Alerts` are `Screens` that can inform the user about errors and other exceptions, or as short informational notes and reminders. `Alerts` are displayed for a certain amount of time given by the `setTimeout()` method, or *modal*, which requires the user input to close the message. There are five `AlertTypes`: ALARM, CONFIRMATION, ERROR, INFO, and WARNING. The following code shows an example that creates an `Alert`.

```
Alert alert = new Alert (String title, String alertText, Image
    alertImage, AlertType.XXX);
where XXX can be any of the alertType

e.g., Alert alert = new Alert (''Warning'', ''Delete all?'', null,
    AlertType.WARNING);
```

4.5 The Media API

The *Media API* was designed to support sound in resource-constrained devices. It is a subset of the *Mobile Media API (MMAPI)*, which is an optional package intended for Java ME devices with advanced sound and multimedia capabilities, such as PDAs, smartphones, and the like. The Mobile Media API was created under the Java Specification Request 135. The rest of this section focuses on the Media API.

The Media API was designed to support tone generation and media flow controls with a low footprint audio playback. It is implemented in two packages, the `javax.microedition.media` package that contains a fully compatible subset of the classes included in the Mobile Media API, and the `javax.microedition.media.control`, which defines the specific `Control` types that can be used with a `Player`.

The Media API consists of three main components: `Manager`, `Player`, and `Controls`. The class `Manager` is used by the applications to request `Players` and supported content and protocols. The `Player` plays the media. A `Control` is an interface utilized to implement the controls of the `Player`.

The `createPlayer()` method of the `Manager` class can create a `Player` in two different ways. The first manner is shown in the following code:

```
Player Manager.createPlayer (String url)
where url specifies the protocol and content of the data as follows:

<protocol>:<content location>

e.g., Player p = Manager.createPlayer(''http://hello.wav'');
```

A `Player` can also be created to playback media from an `inputStream`, as follows:

```
Player Manager.createPlayer (InputStream stream, String type);
```

```
e.g., InputStream istream = getClass().getResourceAsStream(``hello.wav
    '');
      Player p = Manager.createPlayer(istream, ``audio/X-wav'');
      p.start();
```

where **type** can be any of the following:

- Wave audio files: `audio/x-wav`.

- AU audio files: `audio/basic`.

- MP3 audio files: `audio/mpeg`.

- MIDI files: `audio/midi`.

- Tone sequences: `audio/x-tone-seq`.

The `start()`, `stop()`, and `close()` are `Player` methods to start, stop, and close the `Player`.

The `Manager` class can also be used to generate tones, very useful for many applications given that sound is the only media supported by the Media API. A single tone can be generated using the following code:

```
Manager.playTone (int note, int duration, int volume)
```

where `volume` is a value from 0 to 100 in which 100 represents the highest volume supported by the hardware; `duration` is the duration of the tone in milliseconds; and `note` defines the tone of the note. A note is given by a number from 0 to 127. The formula to calculate a MIDI note given the frequency in Hz is given by the following Equation:

$$note = (12 \times log_2(f/440)) + 69 \tag{4.1}$$

so, for example, frequency 440 Hz corresponds to note 69, which is MIDI note A.

4.6 The Record Management System API

The Record Management System (RMS) is a simple record-oriented storage space that allows MIDlets to persistently store and retrieve data in the mobile device. The API is included in the package `javax.microedition.rms`.

The RMS uses the concept of *record store*, which is a collection of persistent *records*. Records are arrays of bytes of different lengths and types within the record store. Records are automatically identified by a `recordId` assigned by a monotonically, increasing-by-one mechanism with no wrap-around provision. Adjacent records in a record store do not necessarily have subsequent record

IDs. Record stores, on the other hand, are uniquely named using the name of the MIDlet suite plus the name of the record store. MIDlet suites at the same time are identified using the attributes MIDlet-Vendor and MIDlet-Name of the application descriptor (JAD) file.

MIDlets within a MIDlet suite can create multiple record stores and access one another's record stores directly. MIDlets in different MIDlet suites can share record stores using accessibility rules and authentication mechanisms. These access controls are defined at the time the record store is created.

The RMS API ensures that record store operations are atomic, synchronous, and serialized but does not include locking mechanisms. Therefore, the API implementation guarantees no corruption of the data but the serialization mechanism might give MIDlets access to the record in an undesired sequence, producing unexpected results. As a result, it is the programmer's responsibility to design MIDlets appropriately, so they coordinate access when multiple threads within the same MIDlet attempt to access the same record simultaneously.

4.6.1 Working with Record Stores and Records

The RMS API has several methods to manipulate record stores and records. The following list includes the methods available to work with record stores:

- `listRecordStores()`: This method returns a `String` with an array of the names of record stores owned by the MIDlet suite.

- `deleteRecordStore()`: This methods deletes a record store. MIDlet suites can only delete their own record stores. If the record store is currently open by a MIDlet when this method is called, or if the named record store does not exist, a `RecordStoreException` will be thrown. The method needs the `recordStoreName` as a parameter.

- `openRecordStore()`: This method allows to open a record store. The method takes a `String` and a `boolean` parameters indicating the name of the record store and whether the record should be created if it does not exist, and returns an object of the type `RecordStore`. Once the record store is opened, with this object the methods that provide information about the record store can be used.

- `closeRecordStore()`: Closes the record store.

- `getName()`: This method returns a `String` with the name of the opened or created record store.

- `getNumRecords()`: This methods returns an `int` with the number of records in the record store.

- `getSize()`: This method returns an `int` with the number of bytes in the record store.

- `getSizeAvailable()`: This methods returns an `int` with the number of additional bytes that the record store could use. It is worth mentioning that this number represents a memory snapshot given by the system to the requesting MIDlet but not a guarantee, as other MIDlets may occupy memory as well.

- `getNextRecordID()`: This method returns an `int` with the `recordId` of the next record to be added to the record store.

- `getVersion()`: This method returns an `int` with the version of the record store. Each time a record store is modified (record added, modified, deleted), its version is incremented.

- `getLastModified()`: This methods returns a `long` with the time of the modification made to the record store.

The methods available in the RMS API to manipulate individual records are the following:

- `addRecord()`: This method adds a new record to the record store and returns the new `recordId`. This is a blocking atomic operation; therefore, the method will not return until the record is written to persistent storage.

- `deleteRecord()`: This method deletes the record with `recordID` from the record store.

- `getRecordSize()`: This methods returns the number of bytes of the data available in record `recordID`.

- `getRecord()`: This methods returns the data stored in the record `recordID`.

- `setRecord()`: This method overwrites the data in record `recordID` with the data provided here.

Before finalizing this section, it is important to emphasize the fact that records are arrays of bytes; therefore, different data types must be converted into and out of byte arrays. CDLC classes such as `DataInputStream`, `DataOutputStream`, `ByteArrayInputStream`, and `ByteArrayOutputStream` can be used for such purpose.

4.7 Security

This section provides an overview of the security mechanisms included in the Java ME platform. In particular, this section lists the main security goals and the available mechanisms available to achieve them, and includes a brief description of MIDlet and networking security.

4.7.1 Information Security Goals and Mechanisms

Security is a very important aspect in any networked application, and LBS applications are not the exception. Security is guided by the following goals or principles:

- **Confidentiality:** Confidentiality is about the disclosure of information only to authorized individuals or systems. *Encryption* is a common mechanism used to provide confidentiality. An encryption mechanism transforms the original data before being sent using a secret code or secret key combination. Only the authorized receiver, with the appropriate key, can decrypt the message back to its original form upon its reception. There are *symmetric* and *asymmetric* encryption mechanisms. Symmetric mechanisms use the same secret key to encrypt and decrypt the message. Asymmetric mechanisms use a public and a secret key. The public key, which is publicly known, is used to encrypt the message by anyone who desires to communicate with the owner of the secret key.

- **Integrity:** Integrity means that data cannot be modified without proper authorization; it is keeping the information intact. Integrity is usually achieved by cryptographic methods plus additional information appended to the original message.

- **Authenticity:** Authenticity is about making sure that the message is authentic, that it comes from the real source. Digital signatures using asymmetric encryption are commonly used to provide authenticity.

- **Availability:** Availability means that information must be available when needed. Availability considers physical as well as logical attacks to the infrastructure such as failures of the electric power and denial of service attacks, among others.

4.7.2 MIDlet Security

Let us start by saying that Java is a programming language designed with security in mind. First of all, Java utilizes the "sandbox" model, which limits the execution of untrusted applications to a closed area where they cannot affect the system if they do not behave as expected. Second, Java enforces language semantics and eliminates programming errors at compilation time. Further, the compiled bytecode is verified to make sure the application follows all Java standards and was compiled correctly. Third, Java also has security policies to ensure safe access to sensitive resources. These policies are enforced by the Java security manager and the access controller. Finally, Java includes authentication, authorization, and encryption mechanisms to guarantee integrity, privacy, and confidentiality.

Unfortunately, all these good features together cannot be offered in resource-constrained devices; they occupy more memory space than the space available in the device. As a result, a simplified security platform has been developed for Java ME applications. Security mechanisms in Java ME are included in the Connected Limited Device Configuration (CLDC) and the Mobile Information Device Profile (MIDP) layers of the Java ME platform. They include a thorough off-line verification process and an in-device fast verification algorithm, a simplified sandbox model in which applications only have access to the classes supported by the device, and simplified security mechanisms such as authentication to trust signed MIDlets, protection domains, security policies and enforcement, and the use of HTTPS (only available in MIDP 2.0) to secure connections with remote machines. For the interested reader, a comprehensive presentation of Java ME CLDC/MIDP security is included in [27].

The MIDP 1.0 specification utilized the *sandbox* model in which all MIDlets or MIDlet suites (more than one MIDlet packaged together) are run in a sandbox, or a tightly controlled and separate environment where MIDlets in separate MIDlet suites have access to restricted resources and do not interfere with one another. The MIDP 2.0 specification expands this model and includes the concepts of *trusted* MIDlet and *protection domains*.

An untrusted MIDlet suite is a MIDlet suite whose authenticity and integrity of the JAR file cannot be trusted by the device. Untrusted MIDlet suites, such as those suites complying with the MIDP 1.0 specification, execute in the untrusted domain, which is a restricted environment where MIDlets have access to security sensitive APIs only if they have explicit user permission. The following APIs are not security sensitive and can be used by untrusted MIDlets without the explicit confirmation from the user (with the exception of the last two):

- javax.microedition.rms.

- javax.microedition.midlet.

- javax.microedition.lcdui.

- javax.microedition.lcdui.game.

- javax.microedition.media.

- `javax.microedition.media.control`.

- `javax.microedition.io.HttpConnection` (need user confirmation).

- `javax.microedition.io.HttpsConnection` (need user confirmation).

The MIDP 2.0 specification includes mechanisms to identify and trust a MIDlet suite and introduces the concept of protection domains for trusted MIDlet suites. A protection domain is a set of permissions associated with a root certificate in the device. A specific domain can be defined in the device using the public key of the domain entity, e.g., a software development company. Then, a MIDlet signed by the company, upon its verification in the device, will be given access to all those resources included in the permissions of the domain.

Digital signatures and authentication methods based on the Internet X.509 Public Key Infrastructure standard included in RFC 2459 [33] and the Internet RFC 2437 "PKCS #1: RSA Cryptography Specifications, Version 2.0" [34] are utilized to decide whether to trust or not a MIDlet suite. First, the MIDlet suite is signed; then, at downloading time, it is authenticated. The entire process consists of the following steps:

1. The sender creates a signing certificate. For this, the signer must know the root certificates used in the device for authenticating MIDlet suites. Thus, the sender needs to send its Distinguished Name (DN) and public key to a Certificate Authority (CA) to obtain a RSA X.509 certificate.

2. The sender encodes and inserts the certificate or certificates, if more than one CA is involved, into the application descriptor (JAD file) (See Section 4.2).

3. The sender signs the JAR file with its private key according to the encoding method included in RFC 2437. The signature is base64 encoded and included in the application descriptor as a single `MIDlet-Jar-RSA-SHA1` attribute without line breaks. The signature includes the JAR file but not the JAD file. By signing the entire JAR file, the signature provides MIDlet integrity.

4. The developer uploads the signed JAR file and the JAD file in a Website where clients can download the application from.

5. The receiver (client) downloads the MIDlet suite over-the-air and checks if the `MIDlet-Jar-RSA-SHA1` attribute exists in the application descriptor. If so, the device must verify the signer certificates and JAR signature; otherwise, the application is categorized and invoked as an untrusted MIDlet suite.

6. The receiver verifies the signer certificates by looking at the certificate authorities involved in the certificates included in the JAD file and the

root certificate authorities included in the device. The device first extracts the certificates from the MIDlet suite and validates them using the process defined in RFC 2459. If the authentication fails, the JAR installation is rejected.

7. The receiver now needs to verify the JAR signature. First, it gets the signer's public key from the verified signer certificate determined in the last step. Second, it gets the `MIDlet-Jar-RSA-SHA1` attribute from the application descriptor. Third, the attribute is decoded from base64 to a PKCS #1 signature, as specified in RFC 2437. Finally, the device uses the signer's public key, the signature included in the JAD file, and the SHA-1 digest included in the JAR file to verify the signature. If the verification fails, the receiver rejects the MIDlet suite and does not install it.

As described before, certificates are utilized in MIDP 2.0 security for authentication. The `javax.microedition.pki` package included in the basic specification provides applications with the `Certificate` interface to work with certificates through the following methods:

- `getIssuer()`: Returns the name of the issuer of the certificate.

- `getNotAfter()`: Returns the time in milliseconds after which the certificate is no longer valid.

- `getNotBefore()`: Returns the starting time of the certificate's validity.

- `getSerialNumber()`: Returns the serial number of the certificate.

- `getSigAlgName()`: Returns the name of the algorithm used to sign the certificate, as specified in RFC 2459.

- `getSubject()`: Returns the name of the certificate's subject.

- `getType()`: Returns the type of the certificate, e.g., "X.509."

- `getVersion()`: Returns the version number of the certificate.

4.7.3 Network Security

Security is very important for networked applications, like the ones included in this book. In addition to the authentication and integrity features provided in the MIDP 2.0 specification described before for MIDlet suites, the specification also includes protocols to provide integrity and confidentiality to networked applications, such as the Transport Layer Security (TLS) and its predecessor the Secure Socket Layer (SSL) protocols commonly used over the Internet. Both TLS and SSL encrypt the transport layer segments, i.e., UDP and TCP segments, so they work on an end-to-end basis. TLS is described in RFC 5246 [28].

The MIDP specification 2.0 defines the `HttpsConnection` and the `SecureConnection` interfaces, which are extensions of the `HttpConnection` and `SocketConnection` interfaces defined in Chapter 8. These interfaces are used by client devices to exchange security information with the server and establish a secure link between them.

The method `getSecurityInfo()` can be applied to an open connection to fill a `SecurityInfo` object and obtain the protocol name and version, cipher suite, and certificate of the connection. These can be obtained by calling the `getProtocolName()`, `getProtocolVersion()`, `getCipherSuite()`, and `getServerCertificate()` methods on the `SecurityInfo` object.

4.8 Privacy

Along with information security, privacy is of great concern to users of location-based information systems. Imagine the users of our LBIS tracking system example. The users are constantly sending their coordinates to the server of the service provider! This means that the service provider knows about all the places you have been into, the day of the week, the time of the day, etc. Although a good service provider could use this information to provide you with enhanced services, a bad service provider could used it against you somehow. Therefore, unless approved by the user, the service provider should not gather private information.

There are mechanisms available to provide privacy in location-based applications. Some of them are based on the idea of a *trusted third party (TTP)* that acts as an *anonymizer* hiding the location and identity of the user to the service provider. More recently, TTP-free schemes have appeared in the literature given the weaknesses of this approach in terms of guaranteeing the privacy of the user and the fact the the user now has to trust the TTP, which may not act as he or she expects. TTP-free schemes work based on the idea of *perturbation* or *obfuscation*. These schemes modify the real location of the users in such a way that do not allow the service provider to know where they exactly are while being able to obtain the service with desirable accuracy. More detailed information about privacy, current methods, and types of attacks can be found in [22, 49].

It is important to realize that different applications have different privacy and security requirements. For example, a real-time tracking application to protect individuals needs to know the location of the users. In this case, users must agree on being part of this service. At the same time, security is very important because you do not want others to know where you are. A participatory sensing application meant to collect noise samples does not need to know who is sending the samples but needs to know the exact (or almost exact) location of the users. Similarly, this application might need to have security mechanisms in place not to allow a stranger to change the noise level transmitted from a particular location. Finally, a location-based service meant to tell you the location of a restaurant close to you does not need to know your exact location nor your identity. Further, security might not be a big concern.

4.9   MIDlet Development and the LBIS Tracking System Example

This chapter presents some of the most important APIs for the development of MIDlets that require user interaction. However, the MIDlet running in the cellular phones of the clients of our LBIS tracking system example do not necessarily need to interact with the user. Some LBS will only need the MIDlet to acquire the location of the device and transmit it to the service provider's server for storage, processing, and visualization. As such, this MIDlet could run in the cellular phone's background without the knowledge of the user. As a result, the APIs to create graphical user interfaces, generate tones and play media, and store information locally are not as useful in our case as for other MIDlets. However, the section on security is extremely important.

The signature and verification procedure described in the security section is the standard way of delivering and downloading applications in a secure manner utilized by most companies and carriers. It guarantees the authenticity of the application (developer) and its integrity. The client application of our LBIS tracking system goes through the same uploading and downloading signature and verification procedure. It is worth mentioning, though, that this procedure might be slightly different from service provider to service provider, and even non-existent in other platforms and carriers. The chapter ends with a description of the mechanisms available to provide confidentiality over network connections, which can also be used by our LBIS tracking system client, and a brief note on privacy.

Chapter 5

Other Important Programming Aspects

5.1 Introduction

This chapter covers other important concepts in the development of applications for resource-constrained devices. In particular, it touches on memory management, concurrency, dynamic linking, and energy management concepts in Java ME applications. Although these are important concepts to consider in any application development, they are particularly important when programming applications for cellular devices. The restricted availability of resources makes programming less forgiving to certain errors and requires the efficient use of those resources, so they can be shared by all applications.

5.2 Memory Management

Memory is a very limited resource in cellular phones, and therefore, it must be managed and used appropriately. In terms of RAM memory, mobile devices usually have two memory areas where variables and execution information are stored, the *stack* and the *heap*. The stack is a data structure normally associated with threads, as it is used to store information about the methods called by the thread, such as the method's local variables, the return address and return value, and other information. As such, the stack is a very well structured memory. On the other hand, the heap is a pool of non-structured portion of memory for general use. One key difference between the stack and the heap is that, while the memory allocated from the stack is managed by the system, memory allocations from the heap are the responsibility of the programmer.

The use of memory in resource-constrained devices can be improved following several programming guidelines, such as the following:

- **Release memory as soon as possible; allocate memory as late as possible:** By releasing memory early, more memory is available for additional objects. At the same time, if the allocations are performed as late as possible, chances are that memory space is available, as most deallocations have been executed.

- **Run programs from ROM when possible:** In place execution saves RAM memory.

- **Select the right structure:** Variables can be stored in native types or inside other structures, such as objects. Using native structure saves considerable amount of memory as the overhead around the object is not needed.

- **Declare variables in best order:** Declaring variables in groups according to the word alignment may also save some space, as the memory can be more efficiently allocated.

- **Use arrays instead of vectors:** Vector uses objects, and therefore, it needs more resources since it needs memory space for the variables and for the object itself. The use of vector can be optimized if the vector is initialized with the appropriate size and not using the system's default size.

- **Consider using StringBuffer instead of String:** Concatenating data using String and the + operator consumes more memory than StringBuffer and the append method, as it creates temporary objects.

- **Use as few objects and classes as possible:** Both reduce the memory consumption.

- **Deference objects:** Set objects to null when they are no longer needed, so they are garbage collected.

- **Use the -g:none switch:** Compiling without debugging information increases performance and reduces the application footprint.

- **Obfuscate code:** Reduce names of packages, classes, methods, variables, etc. Some obfuscators can do this automatically.

- **Less fragmentation:** Use linear data structures and avoid creating/destructing objects very frequently. Both reduce heap fragmentation, which reduces the ability to create further objects.

5.3 Concurrency

Users take it for granted that computers can perform several tasks at the same time. While this is true regardless of the computer, it is more so in cellular phones given the real-time nature of the operations it has to perform.

Users expect the cellular phone to display images of the caller on the screen while ringing the phone, check for keyboard to accept or dismiss the call, and maybe consult your list of contacts while talking on the phone. Simultaneous tasks can be accomplished by using multitasking and/or multiprocessing. Multiprocessing means that the computer has more than one processing unit and therefore can assign tasks to different processors at the same time. This is not usually the case in cellular phones. Multitasking, on the other hand, is the time sharing of the processing unit. The operating system scheduler assigns a time slice of the processing unit to a particular task and then switches to another task, and so forth, so the computer gives the impression of working on all the tasks at the same time.

Multitasking is achieved by means of *processes* and *threads*. A process is considered as a self-contained execution environment, as the operating system assigns processes their own resources, in particular, their own memory space. Applications may run in a single process or multiple collaborating processes, which communicate among them by means of inter-process communication resources, such as sockets. For example, the Java virtual machine usually runs as a single process. In this book, processes are not considered any further.

Threads are the fundamental units of program execution. Every application runs in at least one process with at least one thread. However, in order to perform multiple tasks at the same time, a process may create more than one thread, each in charge of the execution of a sequential stream of instructions. Threads also have their own execution environment or *context*, which utilizes the process's memory space and shares it with other threads. The context has information about the thread, such as the content of the program counter to know which instruction is being executed, the local variables, and the state of the thread.

Ideally, a program executes multiple threads in parallel, each in charge of executing one piece or one task of the entire program. Since the cellular phone has one processor for code execution, the thread scheduling mechanism switches from thread to thread so they all get a piece of the processor's time. This process, known as *context switching*, is performed by the scheduler, which is part of the operating system or the Java virtual machine.

Threads can be in any of the following four states [57]:

- **Running:** The thread is executing code.

- **Ready:** The thread is allocated and ready to execute code.

- **Suspended:** The thread is waiting for an external event.

- **Terminated:** The thread finished execution.

Threads in Java are associated with an instance of the `java.lang.Thread` class. The `Thread` class provides a large list of available methods [56]; however, the following subset includes the methods available in the Java ME platform [30]:

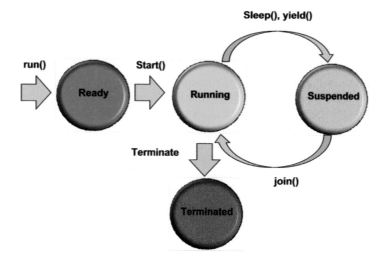

FIGURE 5.1: Threads' state machine.

- Methods related to information about the threads:

    - activeCount(): Returns the number of active threads.
    - currentThread(): Returns a reference to the currently executing thread object.
    - getPriority(): Returns the priority of the current thread.
    - setPriority(): Sets the priority of the current thread.
    - isAlive(): Tests if the thread is alive.

- Methods to change the state of the threads:

    - join(): Allows one thread to wait for the completion of another.
    - run(): Starts a new thread.
    - interrupt(): Interrupts the thread.
    - sleep(): The currently executing thread ceases execution for a specified amount of time.
    - start(): The Java virtual machine invokes the run() method and the thread begins execution.
    - yield(): The currently executing thread object temporarily pauses and allows other threads to execute.

Figure 5.1 shows a state diagram of the methods available in Java ME that take the threads from one state to another.

5.3.1 Defining and Starting Threads

There are two ways to create a thread. The first way is to declare a class that extends the **Thread** class. Listing 5.1 provides an example of how to create a thread extending the **Thread** class.

```
1  public class MyWorkProcess extends Thread {
2      public void run() {
3      ... // Here goes the thread's work
4      }
5  }
6
7  ...
8  Thread MyThread = new MyWorkProcess();;
9  MyThread.start();
10 ...
```

Listing 5.1: Creating a thread extending the **Thread** class.

In the first part of the code, since the **Thread** class implements the **Runnable** interface itself, **MyWorkProcess**, a subclass of **Thread**, overrides the run() method. In the second part of the code, the thread is started by creating an instance of the subclass and invoking its start() method.

A thread can also be created using the **Runnable** interface. First, a class that implements the **Runnable** interface must be defined. The runnable interface defines a run() method that includes the work to be performed by the thread. Then, an instance of the new class is created and used to start the new thread. Listing 5.2 shows this two-step process.

```
1  public class MyWorkProcess implements Runnable {
2      public void run() {
3      ... // Here goes the thread's work
4      }
5  }
6
7  ...
8  MyWorkProcess MyWork = new MyWorkProcess();
9  Thread MyThread = new Thread (MyWork);
10 MyThread.start();
11 ...
```

Listing 5.2: Creating a thread using the **Runnable** interface.

Either way of starting a thread is functionally similar. However, in resource-constrained devices, the second option may be preferable if the class that implements the **Runnable** interface has already been defined and used for other purposes. In this case, the overhead of defining an entirely new class is avoided.

The **Runnable** interface can also be used as shown in Listing 5.3.

```
1  Runnable theInvoker = new Runnable(){
2      public void run() {
3      ... // Here goes the thread's work
4      }
5  }
6  ...
```

```
7  Thread  t = new  Thread( theInvoker );
8  t.start();
9  ...
```

Listing 5.3: Creating a thread using the `Runnable` interface.

5.3.2 Stopping Threads

The old `stop()` and `suspend()` methods to stop and suspend threads have been deprecated because the former was shown to be unsafe when it unlocked all the monitors that it had locked before, and the latter was shown to be deadlock prone. One way to terminate a thread is to use a boolean variable that will force the thread to exit the `run()` method by itself. Listing 5.4 shows this operation, which includes the method `quit()` to change the value of the boolean variable.

```
1  public class MyWorkProcess implements Runnable {
2      private boolean flag = false;
3
4      public void run() {
5          while (!flag){
6              ... // Here goes the thread's work
7          }
8      }
9
10     public void quit(){
11         flag = true;
12     }
13 }
```

Listing 5.4: Terminating a thread.

5.3.3 Joining, Interrupting, and Sleeping Threads

If one thread uses the `quit()` method to stop another thread, it can use the `isAlive()` method to make sure that the first thread actually stopped. Further, the terminating thread can use the `join()` method to wait for the terminated thread to actually terminate before proceeding, as shown in Listing 5.5.

```
1  ...
2  MyWorkProcess.quit();   // tell it to quit
3  MyWorkProcess.join();   // wait until it does
4  ...
```

Listing 5.5: Using the `join()` method.

The `interrupt()` method is available since CLDC 1.1 and can be used to interrupt a thread. The `sleep()` method of the `Thread` object causes the current thread to suspend execution for a specified period of time and makes the processor available to other threads. Listing 5.6 prints the numbers from 0 to 3 five seconds apart using the `sleep()` method.

```
1  public class SleepExample implements Runnable {
2      public void run () {
3          for (i=0; i<=3; i++) {
4              Thread.sleep(5000);
5              System.out.println(i);
6          }
7      }
8  }
```

Listing 5.6: Putting a thread to sleep.

5.3.4 Monitors and Locks

Multithreading allows for the parallel execution of tasks, which reduces the overall execution time and makes a better utilization of the hardware resources. However, it also introduces new problems, the most important being *thread interference* and *memory consistency errors*. Thread interference may happen whenever multiple step operations coming from different threads act on the same data. If the operations *interleave* or overlap, there is the chance that the data may be changed in an erroneous order, producing unexpected, wrong results. This effect is even possible in single statement operations as those statements may be implemented in several steps by the virtual machine. *Memory consistency errors* occur when different threads have inconsistent views of what should be the same data. A common example of memory consistency errors is as follows: imagine that threads A and B are running and thread A has a statement to modify the content of a string and thread B has a statement to print the string out in the screen. Since thread B is never notified of the write operation of thread A, the value of the variable to be printed out by thread B may well be the original string or the modified one.

Thread interferences and memory consistency errors can be avoided by means of *thread synchronization*. Thread synchronization utilizes a construct called a *monitor* to control which thread can read or write data at any given time. Thread synchronization can be applied to both, objects and methods. Objects are synchronized by using the **synchronized** keyword and they lock the object in the entire block of code, as shown in Listing 5.7.

```
1  Object MyObject = new Object();
2  void MyFunction () {
3      synchronized (MyObject){ // Here the thread locks MyObject
4          ... //operations on the object; Here the thread holds the lock on
               MyObject
5          ... // Here the thread continues to hold the lock
6      } // Here the thread releases the lock
```

Listing 5.7: Thread synchronization.

Similarly, the **synchronized** word can be used to synchronize methods. In this case, the lock includes the entire code within the method, as shown in Listing 5.8.

```
1  void synchronized MyFunction () { // Everything inside this block is
       locked
2      ... // Code implementing MyFunction ()
3      } // Lock is released
```

Listing 5.8: Synchronizing methods.

The use of synchronized methods solves thread interference and memory consistency problems by 1) blocking or suspending all other threads invoking the same synchronized object until the current one is finished changing it; and 2) guaranteeing that changes to the state of the object are visible to all other threads. Listing 5.9 shows a simple example of synchronized methods. If two threads call any of these methods at the same time, one of them will be forced to wait until the other finishes modifying the synchronized object.

```
1  public class Counter {
2      private int counter = 0;
3
4      public synchronized int increment () {
5          counter++;
6      }
7
8      public synchronized int decrement () {
9          counter--;
10     }
11
12     public synchronized int result () {
13         return counter;
14     }
15 }
```

Listing 5.9: Example of synchronized methods.

Thread synchronization is not free and creates other problems. First, synchronization does not guarantee the order in which the threads invoke the methods; it just guarantees that only one thread at a time will be executing the method. Second, thread synchronization introduces overhead, as locking and unlocking data take time. Finally, thread synchronization can introduce another problem: *deadlocks*. A deadlock occurs if two threads attempt to lock objects that have been already locked by the others. The effect is that the two threads are blocked forever, waiting for one another. Listing 5.10 shows a deadlock example in which one thread using MyFunction1 locks MyObject1 but waits forever trying to lock MyObject2 because another thread using MyFunction2 already locked MyObject2. Similarly, the second thread is also in deadlock because it tries to lock MyObject1, which had already been locked by the other thread.

```
1  Object MyObject1 = new Object();
2  Object MyObject2 = new Object();
3
4  void MyFunction1 () {
5      synchronized (MyObject1){ // Here the thread locks MyObject1 (
           locked by MyFunction2)
6          synchronized (MyObject2){ // Here it tries to lock MyObject2
7          }
```

```
 8|    }
 9| }
10|
11| void MyFunction2 () {
12|     synchronized (MyObject2){ // Here the thread locks MyObject2
13|         synchronized (MyObject1){ // Here it tries to lock MyObject1 (
                locked by MyFunction1)
14|         }
15|     }
16| }
```

Listing 5.10: Deadlock example.

A simple technique to avoid deadlocks is to lock objects in the same order every time. For example, in Listing 5.10, the deadlock could have been avoided if MyFunction2 had synchronized MyObject1 first. In general, it is recommended to be careful about performing any operation that might take a long time to execute while holding a lock.

5.3.5   Waits and Notifications

Sometimes the programmer wants one thread to wait for a particular event before accessing the data, i.e., lock the synchronized object after the desired event takes place. One appropriate solution is to suspend the thread until the event occurs. One important aspect about suspending threads using regular locks on objects in resource-constrained devices continue to consume CPU cycles while the thread is suspended, and therefore drain the device's battery.

The Java java.lang.Object class defines three methods to suspend and wake up threads without spending energy. These are the wait(), notify(), and notifyAll() methods. Listing 5.11 shows the use of the wait() and notify() methods. The first part of the code shows one thread locking the object MyObject before executing the wait() method. This is a requirement; the thread must lock the object before invoking its wait() method. Once the thread suspends itself, it implicitly releases the object, so it can be locked by any other thread, and waits until a notification occurs or until a predefined amount of time has elapsed (wait (time in milliseconds)), if it does not want to wait indefinitely. The second part of the code shows another thread that 1) locks the same object, 2) performs some operation on the object, and 3) invokes the notify() method when finished. The notify() method produces two actions. First, it makes the second thread to release the object, and second, it notifies the other thread that the object was released. Upon receiving this notification, the first thread wakes up and continues.

```
1| Object MyObject = new Object();
2|
3| synchronized (MyObject) {
4|     try {
5|         MyObject.wait();
6|     }
7|     catch (InterruptExeption e) {
8|     }
9| }
```

```
10
11
12 synchronized (MyObject) {
13     ... /Some operations on object
14     MyObject.notify(); // or notifyAll()
15 }
```

Listing 5.11: Suspending threads.

5.4 Dynamic Linking

Dynamic linking is another important topic for Java ME programmers. With dynamic linking a programmer can develop libraries and provide services to many applications. Libraries provide many benefits. For example, libraries reduce application development time, as they are coded once but used many times; libraries reduce programming errors, as they are very well developed and tested before being used; libraries support the development of modular applications; finally and very important, libraries can save plenty of memory since many applications using the same library simultaneously only need one copy of the library loaded in memory.

Most libraries are not executable programs though. Executables and libraries reference to each other by *links* through the process known as *linking*, which is performed by the linker. Libraries can be linked either statically or dynamically. In *static linking* libraries are instantiated at the starting time of the calling program and stay in memory for as long as the program runs. On the other hand, in *dynamic linking* libraries are loaded and unloaded as needed, in a dynamic fashion. As explained in Section 2.3.1.4, for security reasons, the Java ME platform supports dynamic linking of those libraries and classes that are included in the application's JAR file only.

5.5 Energy Management

Energy is another precious resource in cellular phones. Unfortunately, there are no standardized APIs to manage energy-related properties and resources in Java ME. For example, developers lack APIs to query and set properties such as remaining battery level and screen brightness (e.g., off, dim, on, etc.), or set the device or parts of the device in different energy modes such as "off," "Hibernate," and "Sleep," according to the application needs. For the most part, the Java ME platform gives the responsibility of general energy management of the processor, I/O, radio, and other components that might affect general energy consumption of the device to the programmer.

The application developer for resource-constrained devices needs to make appropriate decisions not to drain the device's battery unnecessarily while meeting the application's requirements. For example, it has been shown that the most expensive function in terms of energy consumption in resource-constrained devices is communications [35]. Therefore, application developers need to pay close attention to this aspect when developing applications. Consider our LBIS tracking system example described in Chapter 1. Real-time tracking requires continuous transmissions of GPS fixes. One important question is: from the energy consumption point of view, which communication protocol would be more adequate for the transmission of continuous GPS fixes, TCP or UDP? The extra overhead of TCP plus the real-time nature of the fixes makes UDP to be the protocol of choice. This simple choice can make a big difference in terms of energy consumption. The authors of [19] analyzed this aspect and compared the time TCP and UDP spent transmitting while sending GPS fixes at different intervals. While they did not find a major difference while transmitting fixes every second, the energy savings were demonstrated using longer intervals. For example, Figure 5.2 shows the behavior of TCP and UDP when transmitting GPS fixes every 10 seconds. The energy savings by using UDP versus TCP are evident from the figure, as TCP spends more time transmitting than UDP. While at 4-second transmission intervals TCP and UDP have similar energy consumption (left part of the figure), at 10-second transmission intervals the experiment reveals that TCP consumes around 38% more energy than UDP. This is graphically shown in the right part of the figure as shorter periods of UDP transmissions overlap with those of TCP.

The question now is: how often is it necessary to send the fixes so that the object can be tracked and the number of transmissions be reduced to the minimum? In order to optimize the number of transmissions, it may be better to include another application in the mobile device to decide when to transmit the fixes. This is based on the fact that computing is considerably less expensive in terms of energy consumption than transmitting, especially if the extra CPU computations will also save some transmissions [35]. Chapter 12 treats this topic of processing the raw data to provide enhanced services or increase the system's performance further. In the same chapter, the Critical Point Algorithm [16] is described in detail, which is a simple application meant to reduce the number of GPS transmissions to reduce energy consumption while allowing the system to track the mobile device in real time.

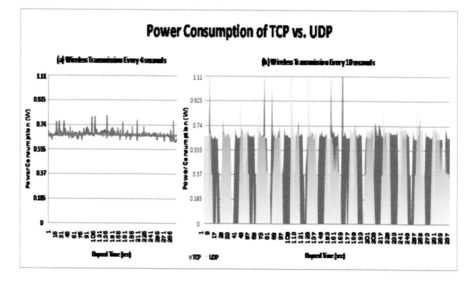

FIGURE 5.2: Energy consumption of UDP and TCP. Reproduced from [19] © 2003 IEEE, Inc. Included here by permission.

5.6 Other Important Programming Aspects and the LBIS Tracking System Example

This chapter touches on several programming aspects that are particularly important when programming applications for cellular phones. As such, theses aspects need to be considered when programming the client-side code for the cellular phones of our LBIS tracking system example.

Chapter 6

Obtaining the User's Position

6.1 Introduction

Obtaining the position of the end user's device is fundamental to Location Based Information Systems and Location-Based Services. This chapter describes the most important positioning techniques available to localize end devices in outdoor and indoor environments, with emphasis on the former. It starts with the Global Positioning System (GPS) since this is the primary system utilized by our LBIS tracking system example. Then, it continues with the most important positioning technologies utilized in cellular networks, using a GSM cellular network as an example. Finally, the chapter closes with a brief description of the most important positioning mechanisms for indoor applications and a description of the Java ME Location API 2.0.

6.2 The Global Positioning System (GPS)

The Global Positioning System (GPS) is perhaps the most widely used and ubiquitous system to obtain users' positions. It is a complex and expensive system made of three major segments: the Space Segment (SS), the Control Segment (CS), and the User Segment (US). These three segments together enable GPS receivers to determine their location, speed, direction, and time.

The Space Segment (SS) consists of the orbiting GPS satellites. A total of 24 satellites, four satellites in six orbital planes centered on the Earth, are needed so that at least six satellites can be detected by a GPS receiver from almost anywhere on Earth. Currently, the constellation of GPS satellites consists of 31 satellites; seven more have been added to provide redundant signals and improve the precision of GPS receivers and the reliability and availability of the system.

The Control Segment (CS) consists of several ground stations that track and monitor the space segment and a main control station, located in Colorado Springs, Colorado, that monitors and maintains the entire system. The main control station is in charge of updating the on-board atomic clocks of the satellites and their *ephemerides*, or a table with the exact position of the satellites in the sky. The ephemerides is later broadcast by the satellites and used by GPS receivers to calculate their own positions.

The User Segment (US) is made up of all GPS receivers. A high-level architecture of a GPS receiver consists of the receiving part, with an antenna tuned to the frequencies of the GPS satellites, a main processor, and a crystal oscillator. Depending on the receiver, they can monitor anywhere from 4 to 20 channels. The calculated position along with additional information derived from the satellite signal may then be further processed to build other systems such as stand-alone navigational systems or tracking applications like the one described in this book.

6.2.1　The Format of the GPS Navigation Message

GPS satellites continuously broadcast a 1500-bit-long *Navigation Message*. The message is broken down into five subframes 300 bits long, and each subframe is divided into ten words 30 bit long each. As shown in Figure 6.1, words 1 and 2 of every subframe always contain the same information. Word 1 is the *Telemetry Word (TLM)*, which is used by the GPS receiver for synchronization purposes. Word 2, the *Hand-Over Word (HOW)*, also for synchronization purposes, enables the receiver to identify the subframe. Words 3 to 10 of each subframe contain the rest of the navigation message as follows:

- **Subframe 1:** Contains the satellite clock, week number, and clock correction data.

- **Subframes 2 and 3:** Include the ephemeris of the satellite, which contains the satellite orbit.

- **Subframes 4 and 5:** Contain GPS system information and the *almanac*. The almanac contains information about every satellite in the constellation, ionospheric data to correct ionospheric errors, and information to translate the GPS time into the international time standard, the Coordinated Universal Time (CUT). Each navigation message contains 1/25th of the almanac (2 subframes), so a receiver needs 12.5 minutes to receive the entire almanac. The almanac is very important because it helps GPS receivers to locate satellites.

GPS satellites transmit navigation messages at the very low transmission rate of 50 bps, meaning that they transmit one navigation message every 30 seconds. This low transmission rate is one of the reasons why it takes so long to obtain the first GPS fix, or *Time to First Fix (TTFF)*. Regardless of how fast the GPS receiver is able to lock onto the satellite signals, it takes 30 seconds in the worst case to receive the navigation message.

All GPS satellites use Code Division Multiple Access (CDMA) technology to transmit the navigation messages. They all use the same two frequencies of

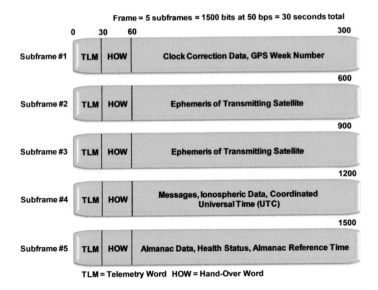

FIGURE 6.1: The GPS frame structure.

1.57542 GHz (L1 signal) and 1.2276 GHz (L2 signal) and encode the messages using a high-rate pseudo-random code that is unique to each satellite. The same codes are known to all GPS receivers, so they can decode the messages. More detailed information about the GPS system can be found in [32].

6.2.2 Lateration

Lateration is the process of calculating the user's position using distances between entities. Figure 6.2 shows three lateration examples in which the user's position (x, y) is determined using one, two, and three anchors in a two-dimensional system. Figure 6.2(a) shows the case in which the user only knows the distance r_1 to one anchor (X_1, Y_1). As it can be seen, the user can be located anywhere around the perimeter of the circumference with center (X_1, Y_1) and radius r_1. Of course, the error with respect to the real position of the user may be big, as the user may be located anywhere in the circumference. With the introduction of a second anchor, the error is reduced, as shown in Figure 6.2(b). Now, it is known that the user is located in either of the two intersecting points, and the idea is to eliminate the incorrect point using other methods, which is normally easy to do. However, the introduction of a third anchor eliminates the ambiguity of the last method since the intersecting point is unique. The position of the intersecting point can be found using Pythagoras' Theorem establishing the following system of equations

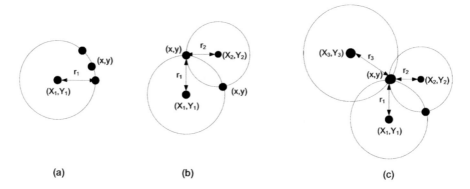

FIGURE 6.2: 2D circular lateration.

$$\sqrt{(X_1 - x)^2 + (Y_1 - y)^2} = r_1$$
$$\sqrt{(X_2 - x)^2 + (Y_2 - y)^2} = r_2 \qquad (6.1)$$
$$\sqrt{(X_3 - x)^2 + (Y_3 - y)^2} = r_3$$

and solving the system for (x, y). After some math manipulations, the same system can be rewritten in matrix form as follows:

$$2 \times \begin{bmatrix} X_3 - X_1 & Y_3 - Y_1 \\ X_3 - X_2 & Y_3 - Y_2 \end{bmatrix} \begin{bmatrix} x \\ y \end{bmatrix} = \begin{bmatrix} (r_1^2 - r_3^2) - (X_1^2 - X_3^2) - (Y_1^2 - Y_3^2) \\ (r_2^2 - r_3^2) - (X_2^2 - X_3^2) - (Y_2^2 - Y_3^2) \end{bmatrix}$$
$$(6.2)$$

Extending this method to a three-dimensional space involves including the third axis in the equations, as follows:

$$\sqrt{(X_1 - x)^2 + (Y_1 - y)^2 + (Z_1 - z)^2} = r_1$$
$$\sqrt{(X_2 - x)^2 + (Y_2 - y)^2 + (Z_2 - z)^2} = r_2 \qquad (6.3)$$
$$\sqrt{(X_3 - x)^2 + (Y_3 - y)^2 + (Z_3 - z)^2} = r_3$$

In the case of the GPS system, r_i is the distance between the GPS receiver and satellite i, (X_i, Y_i, Z_i) is satellite's i position coordinates, which can be calculated from the ephemerides, and (x, y, z) is the unknown position of the user. Therefore, in its simplest form, finding the position of the GPS receiver in a three-dimensional space consists of finding the distance between the GPS receiver and the satellites and solving the system of Equations in 6.3.

The problem with this method is in the calculation of the distance between the GPS receiver and the satellites. This distance is calculated by measuring the time it takes the satellite signal to reach the receiver and multiplying that time by the speed of light. The satellite navigation message contains clock information that can be used by the GPS receiver to know exactly the time at which the message was sent. The word exactly comes from the fact that the satellites are equipped with very precise atomic clocks to set these time stamps. However, in order to make GPS receivers affordable to common users, they are not equipped with such precise clocks, and the time at which the navigation message is received is measured using the GPS receiver's clock. Unfortunately, these two clocks are not synchronized and thus errors are introduced in the distance estimation. Further, given the high speed of light, small clock shifts can introduce large errors in the estimation. For example, a 1 μs clock shift introduces an error of 300 meters in the distance calculation.

In order to eliminate the error introduced by the lack of clock synchronization between the satellites and the GPS receiver, this error is included as an additional unknown variable in the system of equations. Now, the system calculates a *pseudo range p*, which is equal to the real distance r plus an error given by $c\delta t$, where c is the speed of light and δt is the time offset between the receiver's clock and the GPS system time. With four unknown variables, four equations are needed to solve the problem; therefore, a fourth measurement from a fourth satellite is included. This is the reason why four satellites is the minimum number of anchors needed by a GPS receiver to calculate its position in a three-dimensional space without synchronized clocks, or better said, with GPS receivers equipped with inexpensive clocks. Therefore, the new system of equations is as follows:

$$
\begin{aligned}
\sqrt{(X_1 - x)^2 + (Y_1 - y)^2 + (Z_1 - z)^2} + c\delta t &= p_1 \\
\sqrt{(X_2 - x)^2 + (Y_2 - y)^2 + (Z_2 - z)^2} + c\delta t &= p_2 \\
\sqrt{(X_3 - x)^2 + (Y_3 - y)^2 + (Z_3 - z)^2} + c\delta t &= p_3 \\
\sqrt{(X_4 - x)^2 + (Y_4 - y)^2 + (Z_4 - z)^2} + c\delta t &= p_4
\end{aligned}
\tag{6.4}
$$

This system of non-linear equations can be solved by an iterative approximation process of least squares using Taylor series to convert the non-linear equations into a system of linear ones. The mathematical procedure used here to calculate the user position with errors follows the approach presented in [55]. Other approaches can be found in [32, 37, 35].

The iterative method calculates estimated pseudo ranges $\widehat{p}_i$ as follows:

$$
\begin{aligned}
\sqrt{(X_1 - \widehat{x})^2 + (Y_1 - \widehat{y})^2 + (Z_1 - \widehat{z})^2} + c\widehat{\delta t} &= \widehat{p}_1 \\
\sqrt{(X_2 - \widehat{x})^2 + (Y_2 - \widehat{y})^2 + (Z_2 - \widehat{z})^2} + c\widehat{\delta t} &= \widehat{p}_2 \\
\sqrt{(X_3 - \widehat{x})^2 + (Y_3 - \widehat{y})^2 + (Z_3 - \widehat{z})^2} + c\widehat{\delta t} &= \widehat{p}_3 \\
\sqrt{(X_4 - \widehat{x})^2 + (Y_4 - \widehat{y})^2 + (Z_4 - \widehat{z})^2} + c\widehat{\delta t} &= \widehat{p}_4
\end{aligned}
\tag{6.5}
$$

Then, it calculates the difference between the estimated pseudo ranges and the exact ranges, and the following equations are obtained:

$$
\begin{aligned}
(a_{x1} - \Delta X)^2 + (a_{y1} - \Delta Y)^2 + (a_{z1} - \Delta Z)^2 - c\Delta t &= \widehat{p}_1 - p_1 \\
(a_{x2} - \Delta X)^2 + (a_{y2} - \Delta Y)^2 + (a_{z2} - \Delta Z)^2 - c\Delta t &= \widehat{p}_2 - p_2 \\
(a_{x3} - \Delta X)^2 + (a_{y3} - \Delta Y)^2 + (a_{z3} - \Delta Z)^2 - c\Delta t &= \widehat{p}_3 - p_3 \\
(a_{x4} - \Delta X)^2 + (a_{y4} - \Delta Y)^2 + (a_{z4} - \Delta Z)^2 - c\Delta t &= \widehat{p}_4 - p_4
\end{aligned}
\tag{6.6}
$$

where

$$a_{xi} = \frac{X_i - \hat{x}}{\hat{r}_i}$$
$$a_{yi} = \frac{Y_i - \hat{y}}{\hat{r}_i}$$
$$a_{zi} = \frac{Z_i - \hat{z}}{\hat{r}_i}$$

(6.7)

and

$$\hat{r}_i = \sqrt{(X_i - \hat{x})^2 + (Y_i - \hat{y})^2 + (Z_i - \hat{z})^2}$$

(6.8)

for $i = 1, 2, 3, 4$, which results in a systems of equations of the form:

$$\begin{bmatrix} \hat{p}_1 - p_1 \\ \hat{p}_2 - p_2 \\ \hat{p}_3 - p_3 \\ \hat{p}_4 - p_4 \end{bmatrix} = \begin{bmatrix} a_{x1} & a_{y1} & a_{z1} & -c \\ a_{x2} & a_{y2} & a_{z2} & -c \\ a_{x3} & a_{y3} & a_{z3} & -c \\ a_{x4} & a_{y4} & a_{z4} & -c \end{bmatrix} \times \begin{bmatrix} \Delta x \\ \Delta y \\ \Delta z \\ \Delta t \end{bmatrix}$$

(6.9)

which can be solved for Δx, Δy, Δz, and Δt. Finally, the new position considering errors is calculated using Equations 6.10 and the procedure is repeated until the desired precision is obtained.

$$\begin{aligned} x &= \hat{x} + \Delta x \\ y &= \hat{y} + \Delta y \\ z &= \hat{z} + \Delta z \\ \delta t &= \hat{\delta t} + \Delta t \end{aligned}$$

(6.10)

Since the lateration method relies on distance estimates to the anchors, in order for the method to provide good accuracy, it is desirable to have non-collinear anchors. In other words, if the anchors are very close to one another and far from the user's location, it will be necessary to have very precise estimates of the distances for the trilateration method to give good results since the range measurements will yield almost equal values. In this case, the equations are not linearly independent anymore and the combination of satellites cannot be used to calculate the GPS receiver's position. This effect, which is known as *Dilution of Precision (DOP)*, is also calculated by the GPS receiver in order to select the most appropriate satellites. The method followed by the GPS receiver to calculate the DOP is very similar to the one just explained for the calculation of the position. The details of these calculations can be found in [32]. In general, when the satellites are close to one another, the geometry is said to be weak and the DOP calculations result in a high value. On the other hand, when the satellites are far apart, the geometry is strong and the calculations provide a low DOP value. Therefore, geometries with lower DOP values are better to calculate the GPS receiver's position.

6.3   The GSM Cellular Network

Cellular networks are an essential component in LBIS. As shown in Figure 1.4, cellular networks play an important role in the architecture of our LBIS tracking system example, as they are used as a transport network connecting the end user to the Internet an vice versa. In addition, cellular networks can also play an important role in the estimation of the user's position. For these two reasons, this chapter briefly explains cellular networks using the Global System for Mobile communications (GSM) network as an example, and some of the most important mechanisms to estimate the user's position.

Figure 6.3 depicts the main building blocks of the GSM cellular network architecture. On the left side, there is the Radio Subsystem (RSS), which includes the Base Station Controller (BSC), the Base Transceiver Station (BTS), and the mobile users or Mobile Stations (MS). Each BTS consists of what is commonly known as a cell, and they provide the radio access interface to the MS located within the area of coverage of each particular cell. The BSC is a device that manages a group of BTSs and provides connectivity to those users who are roaming from one of its cells to another. The MS or cellular phone, consists of hardware and software and the Subscriber Identity Module (SIM) that contains all the information related to the user and the GSM services subscribed.

The second part of the architecture is the Network and Switching Subsystem (NSS), which consists of Mobile Services Switching Centers (MSC), the Gateway MSC (GMSC), the Home Location Register (HLR), and the Visitor Location Register (VLR). The MSC controls a group of BSCs in a geographical region; they build the backbone of the GSM network. A MSC sets up connections between the BSCs under its control and handles those connections that require the participation of BSCs outside its geographical region. The GMSC, as it name implies, is a gateway that connects the GSM network to other communication networks, such as the Public Switched Telephone Network (PSTN). The HLR is the database of the GSM system that contains all user information, such as the MS number, subscribed services, current location area, current MSC and VLR, and others. This information is needed in order to localize a MS in the entire GSM network. The VLR is a data base associated with each MSC that stores information of those users who are being served by that particular MSC.

This particular architecture only provides channels for voice connections as the network is not connected to any other data-oriented network. In order to satisfy this requirement, GSM networks have been modified to offer data connections through the General Packet Radio Service (GPRS). The GSM network architecture, including the GPRS service is depicted in Figure 6.4. As it can be seen, changes are included in the NSS with the introduction of the Serving GPRS Support Node (SGSN) module, the Gateway GPRS

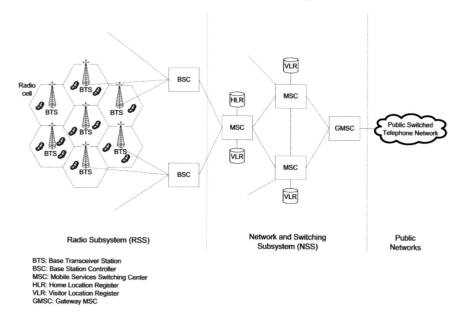

FIGURE 6.3: The GSM cellular network architecture.

Support Node (GGSN) and the HLR/GR database that now also contains the GPRS register (GR). As it can be seen, the BSCs direct voice calls to the appropriate MSC so the calls follow the voice path and data calls to the appropriate SGSN module so that they follow the data path. The mobile device of our LBIS tracking system sends GPS fixes to the system server in real time using the data path of the cellular network, or the GPRS service in the case of a GSM-based network.

In addition to voice and data transport services, cellular networks also utilize positioning technologies to know the whereabouts of the mobile users. These cellular positioning mechanisms are described next.

6.3.1 Cell Identification or Cell ID

The Cell ID is the simplest localization method available in cellular networks. The HLR contains enough information to locate a mobile user in the GSM network, such as the location area and MSC, and therefore the BSC and final BTS serving the user. As a result, a query to the cellular network looking for the location of a particular user using the Cell ID method returns the position of the BTS.

The accuracy of the Cell ID method therefore depends on the known range of the particular BTS serving the user at the time of the query. It can range from a few hundred meters in urban areas to several kilometers in rural ar-

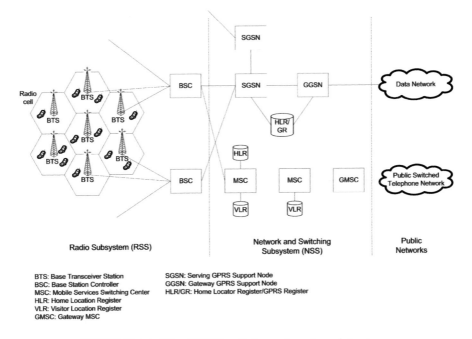

FIGURE 6.4: The GPRS cellular network architecture.

eas. This method, although fast and useful for some applications, is not very accurate for the type of applications considered in this book.

6.3.2 Enhanced Cell Identification

The accuracy of the Cell ID method can be easily enhanced if the BTS measures the time it takes a message to reach the user and come back, or the round trip time (RTT). The round trip time can then be used to estimate the distance at which the mobile user is from the BTS.

6.3.3 Enhanced Observed Time Difference (E-OTD)

This method is based on the broadcast of signals that that are periodically generated by the BTSs and the constant monitoring of those signals performed by the mobile stations. Upon receiving signals from enough BTSs, the mobile terminal uses lateration to discover its position. This is, therefore, a terminal-based positioning mechanism.

6.3.4 Uplink-Time Difference of Arrival (U-TDoA)

The Uplink-Time Difference of Arrival method is similar to the E-OTD but more complicated because the calculations are performed by the BTSs based on signals transmitted by the mobile station. The main problem with this method is that the mobile station does not transmit any signals while in idle; therefore, the network has to 1) wait for the mobile station to begin a transmission, i.e., a phone call, or 2) generate some signals that will make the mobile station to respond. Even if the mobile station is in transmission mode, the other problem is that only one BTS, the serving one, is capable of listening to this particular mobile station. In order to support this method, the network provider includes several *Location Measurement Units (LMU)* to compile measurements from the mobile station and surrounding BTSs and perform the calculations.

In reality, the U-TDoA and E-OTD methods are more complicated than they look. LMUs need to make time offsets measurements between the BTSs and mobile stations, and apply hyperbolic lateration techniques. Providing more details about these two methods is out of the scope of this book. The interested reader can find more information in [37].

6.3.5 Assisted GPS (A-GPS)

Contrary to E-OTD and U-TDoA, Assisted GPS is easier and cheaper to implement in a GSM network. A-GPS is a combined solution whereby a GPS-enabled mobile station and the cellular network collaborate to find the user's position. This collaboration translates into an improved accuracy over the GPS system alone, better indoor coverage, shorter time to first fix, and less power consumption at the receiver, all of them critical aspects in LBS applications like the tracking application being used as an example in this book.

The A-GPS method relies on assistant servers located in several parts of the GSM network. The assistance provided by these servers is of two types. Either the server provides information that the mobile station needs to perform the calculations, or the server performs the calculations using information provided by the mobile station. In the former case, the server provides the mobile station with information that the mobile station cannot obtain, such as the almanac of the GPS satellites, more accurate clock information, and accurate coordinates of the server or BTS. All this information can be used by the mobile station to calculate its position, calculate it faster, and improve the accuracy of the calculation. For example, almanac information allows the MS to lock to the GPS satellites faster, reducing the TTFF. In the later case, the server receives partial information from the MS and uses its computational power and good satellite signals to compute the position on behalf of the MS.

6.4   Indoor Positioning Systems

Cellular phones using the GPS system rely on the good reception of the radio signals from the GPS satellites. This is particularly challenging in indoor environments where the satellite signals, because of obstructions, are of very poor quality, if received at all. Under these conditions, some GPS-enabled cellular phones might not be able to calculate their position. Although indoor positioning systems have been designed to fill this gap, the integration and collaboration between outdoor and indoor positioning systems so that the mobile station can determine its position at any time in any place, is still an active area of research.

This section briefly lists the most commonly known indoor positioning systems and techniques. Then, it briefly describes Skyhook's hybrid positioning system (XPS) as an example of a successful positioning system that may seamlessly work in indoor and outdoor environments. Systems like Skyhook's complement the GPS system and provide an entire positioning solution for LBS applications.

6.4.1   Indoor Positioning Techniques

Indoor positioning systems came about to solve the problem of weak GPS signals and innacurate cellular positioning methods inside buildings. Although many LBS applications have been designed for outside environments, there are many applications that are confined within buildings, such as finding employees in large corporation buildings, inventories in warehouses and supermarkets, security applications, and others. Among the most important indoor solutions are those based on wireless local area networks (WLANs), fingerprinting, ultrasound, and RFIDs.

WLANs indoor systems utilize 802.11 WLAN access points as reference points for localization. Access points transmit periodic beacon signals that can be used by a mobile station to identify the access point with the best signal quality, its location, and the distance from it. This information can be used to calculate the position of the mobile device with different degrees of accuracy. In **proximity sensing**, the mobile device adopts the position of the closest access point as its position. This is a very simple indoor positioning system but suffers from accuracy problems, in particular for those applications that require precise location information, such as security and inventory. WLAN access points may cover an area of approximately 100 meters. Proximity sensing is based on the cellular identification idea described in Section 6.3.1.

Another WLAN solution is based on lateration, similar to outdoor positioning systems but using WLANs access points instead of BTSs. Mobile devices can estimate their distances from the access points using the received signal strength of the beacons and apply lateration techniques, like the one described in Section 6.2.2.

Fingerprinting is another solution to the indoor localization problem. It is based on off-line measurements of the received signal strength in very specific reference points within the space of interest. These measurements and reference points are saved in a local database and utilized by the system to find the location of the mobile device. The calculation of the position can be done in the mobile device, in the server, or in the server but assisted by the mobile device [37].

Ultrasound-based systems have also been utilized in indoor environments. These systems utilize radio frequency (RF) and ultrasound signals to estimate the distance between a reference device and the mobile node. This is based on the fact that ultrasound signals travel at a very different speed than RF signals (approximately 1,243 Km/h versus 300,000 Km/s). Reference devices installed in specific points in the area of interest transmit simultaneous RF beacons and ultrasound pulses periodically. Mobile devices equipped with RF and ultrasound receivers estimate the distance of the mobile device with respect to the reference device by time stamping the time at which each signal is received. If you assume that the RF signal arrived at time t_1 and the ultrasound pulse arrived at time t_2, with $t_2 > t_1$, using the concept of the propagation delay of a signal, Equation 6.11 shows how to calculate the distance between the reference device and the mobile node.

$$P_d(RF) = \frac{D}{SoL}$$

$$P_d(US) = \frac{D}{SoS}$$

$$t_2 - t_1 = P_d(US) - P_d(RF) \tag{6.11}$$

$$t_2 - t_1 = D\left(\frac{1}{SoS} - \frac{1}{SoL}\right)$$

$$D = \frac{t_2 - t_1}{\left(\frac{1}{SoS} - \frac{1}{SoL}\right)}$$

where $P_d(RF)$ is the propagation delay of the RF signal, $P_d(US)$ is the propagation delay of the ultrasound signal, SoL is the speed of light, SoS is the speed of sound, and D is the distance between the devices.

One advantage of this system is that it eliminates the problem of clock synchronization since it only uses the receiver's clock. On the down side, although ultrasound signals are able to go through walls and other obstacles, they do not travel very far. One example of an ultrasound-based system is the Cricket system developed by researchers at MIT [47].

There are many other indoor positioning systems. For example, the article in [45] describes a positioning system that utilizes a mobile robot along with RFID technology and Wi-Fi to track the location of items in a warehouse. In [36], the MIT Cricket, Ekahau [3], Intel Place Lab [4], AeroScout [1], and other indoor positioning systems are described in detail.

6.4.2 Skyhook's Hybrid Positioning System (XPS)

XPS is a software-based positioning system that combines Wi-Fi access points locations, GPS data, and cellular tower locations to provide 10-20 meter accuracy positions in indoor and outdoor environments. XPS software consists of two main components, the Mobile Location Client (MLC) and the XPS Location Server. The MLC is a thin layer of software installed in the cellular phone that lies between the applications running in the cellular phone and the location service. Upon the application request, the MLC uses the signals and location information of nearby Wi-Fi access points, cellular towers, and the GPS system, and calculates the cellular phone's position. In addition, the MLC performs power management functions that optimize the amount of energy needed to perform location estimations and the transmission of data to the XPS Location Server. This autonomous model corresponds to the mobile-based location provider architecture described in Section 1.2 and shown in Figure 1.2.

The MLC can also off-load the calculation of the cellular phone's position on the XPS Location Server. Upon a location request from an application, the MLC transmits the location information collected from the available positioning sources to the XPS Location Server where these data are processed. Specialized algorithms and databases in the server combine this information to provide fast and accurate positions to the mobile phones. This model corresponds to the location provider-based architecture described in Section 1.2 and shown in Figure 1.3, where Skyhook Wireless would play the role of the location provider.

Skyhook Wireless possesses a massive databases of Wi-Fi access points and cell towers and their real positions. Further, they have a procedure in place to add access points to the database. As a reference, Apple's iPhone and iPod Touch utilize Skyhook's positioning system. For more information about the system, its coverage, security features, software, etc., the reader is referred to the company's Website at `http://www.skyhookwireless.com/`. Other companies providing location data are Loc-Aid Technologies [5], Where [11], Veriplace [10], Useful Networks [9], and TechnoCom [8].

6.5 The Location API 2.0

The Java ME Location API 1.0 (JSR 179) included the basic support to obtain the position of the mobile device through the `LocationProvider`, `Criteria`, and `Location` objects. The `LocationProvider` object, as its name implies, is the provider of location data to the application. All interactions with the underlying positioning technology are handled through this object. Since there may be several positioning technology options through which a location may be obtained, several location providers may exist. `Criteria` contains the requirements of the application, such as the accuracy of the location, if the speed and course of the mobile phone are also needed, and the like. The cellular phone will return a `LocationProvider` that typically is able to meet these criteria, or null if a `LocationProvider` meeting these criteria does not exist. This process allows the mobile phone to return the "best" positioning technology based on the applications needs. Finally, `Location` is the object that contains the location data. The `Location` object contains important information about the current location, including an encapsulated `QualifiedCoordinates` class that contains information about the estimated latitude, longitude, and altitude of the current position as well as estimated horizontal and vertical accuracies associated with the calculated position. This accuracy information is important, as it provides a mean to estimate how far the calculated position is from the true geographic location of the device. The `Location` object also includes information about the speed and course of the mobile device, the time at which the position was calculated, and the positioning method utilized in the calculation.

Listing 6.1 shows how to use these objects and the `getLocation()` method to obtain the current location of the cellular phone using the Java ME location API 1.0. The first part of the code sets the criteria needed by the application and requests a `LocationProvider`. Once a `LocationProvider` is obtained, the application can get information about the real-time location of the device using the `getLocation()` method, which is shown in the second part of the code.

```
1  try {
2  // Create a Criteria object to define desired selection criteria
3  Criteria cr = new Criteria();
4  cr.setHorizontalAccuracy(20);//Requests an estimated accuracy of 20
       meters
5  cr.setSpeedAndCourseRequired(true);//Requests speed and course of
       mobile device
6
7  //Requests a LocationProvider that meets these Criteria
8  LocationProvider lp = LocationProvider.getInstance(cr);
9  // Get the location, 60 seconds timeout
10 Location loc = lp.getLocation(60);
11 Coordinates coord = loc.getQualifiedCoordinates();
12 if (coord != null) {
13 // Include code that uses coordinates here
14 // ...
15 }
16 }
17 catch (LocationException e) {
18 // Could not retrieve location
19 }
20 catch (InterruptedException e) {
21 // Location retrieval interrupted
22 }
```

Listing 6.1: Obtaining the location.

The `getLocation()` function works well for applications that require location information once. However, many location-based applications, such as our real-time tracking application example, require a continuous knowledge of the current location. For these applications, the `LocationListener` class allows an application to obtain positioning data at a defined interval. As an example, Listing 6.2 shows how to trigger the `locationUpdate()` method of `LocListener` every 4 s.

As shown in the listing, the `locationListener()` method takes three parameters. The `interval` is the time between updates required (4 s in the example). The `timeout` is the amount of time that the update is allowed to be late, once the interval has elapsed. Therefore, an update is expected at maximum every `interval` + `timeout` seconds. Finally, the `maxAge` value sets how old the last location result can be in order to be used when a new location request is made, which allows the implementation to reuse recent location results. So, for example, a value of 0 implies that the implementation will calculate new locations every time they are requested by the application and will not reuse past location results.

```
1  public class LocListener implements LocationListener {
2
3  LocListener locListener = new LocListener();
4  int interval = 4;// Interval between location updates is 4 s
5  int timeout = 2;// Timeout after location request is 2 s
6  int maxAge = 2;// Maximum age allowed for a duplicate location value
       to be returned is 2 s
7  lp.setLocationListener(locListener, interval, timeout, maxAge);
8  . . .
9  public void locationUpdated(LocationProvider provider, Location
       location) {
10 // This code will be triggered with updated location data at the
       defined interval
11 }
12 . . .
13 }
```

Listing 6.2: Obtaining the location at defined intervals.

On October 15, 2008, the final version of the Location API 2.0 was released. The specification was produced by the JSR 293 expert group, which consisted of representatives from companies like IBM, Ericsson, Motorola, Research in Motion, Nokia, Sony Ericsson, and others, telecommunication carries like Sprint, SBC, Telecom Italia, Orange France, and China Mobile Communications, and the University of South Florida.

The JSR 293 improves the original JSR 179 Location API for the Java ME specification and adds new features such as geocoding, mapping, navigation services, and landmark exchange, while maintaining backward application compatibility. The new API consists of two major packages:

- **javax.microedition.location:** Contains the classes needed to request and obtain a location, such as `Location`, `LocationProvider`, `LocationListener`, `ProximityListener`, `GeographicArea`, and the like. This is the same package defined in JSR 179, but improved.

- **javax.microedition.location.services:** Contains the classes and interfaces related to location-based services, such as geocoding, maps, and navigation. This is a completely new package.

6.5.1 Improvements from Version 1.0

This section describes some of the most important modifications included in version 2.0 of the Java ME Location API.

6.5.1.1 Criteria and LocationProvider

Although the `Criteria` in version 1.0 was good in terms of hiding the complexities of the different location technologies from the application developer, the `LocationProvider` returned the "best" positioning technology available that met such criteria, which in some circumstances led to ambiguous behaviors on different devices. For example, if the application included conflicting values in the `Criteria` object such as setting the PREFERRED_POWER_CONSUMPTION to LOW and the HORIZONTAL_ACCURACY to 5 meters, the `LocationProvider` of one implementation could give preference and choose A-GPS, while another implementation could give higher priority to power consumption and choose Cell-ID. This ambiguity put the burden on the application developer who needed to construct software that handled a variety of cases on different devices based on the technology type returned by that platform. This task was exacerbated by the large number of permutations of criterion settings compounded by new permutations for different platforms and the increasing number of available positioning technologies on cellular phones, which defeated the desired simplicity of hiding implementation details from the developer.

Version 2.0 of the Java ME Location API includes two solutions to this problem. First, the `Criteria` object now supports priorities, from 1 to N, for each criterion, with the lowest-numbered criterion (1) having the highest priority. This reduces ambiguity since it allows the application developer to clearly communicate to the device what criterion is the most important for the application. Second, an array of prioritized location method constants, or technology types defined in the `Location` object, can be used to specify the desired fallback order of positioning technologies to be used by the `LocationProvider`. For example, a tracking application may wish to use GPS as its preferred method and use cell signal-based positioning if GPS is not available. Similarly, it can then use cell ID if cell signal-based positioning is not available, and so forth. Listing 6.3 shows how to select this order of positioning technologies.

```
1  int [] preferredLocationMethods = new int [3];
2  preferredLocationMethods [0] = MTE_SATELLITE;//First preference of
       positioning technology
3  preferredLocationMethods [1] = MTE_TIMEDIFFERENCE;//Second preference
4  preferredLocationMethods [2] = MTE_CELLID;//Third preference
5  LocationProvider lp = LocationProvider.getInstance(
       preferredLocationMethods, parameters); //Get the LocationProvider
```

```
6 | for given preferred location technologies
```

Listing 6.3: Setting the order of positioning technologies.

With this new feature application, developers can easily create their own optimized application-specific positioning request sequences. This is a very nice feature for those smart applications running on powerful devices equipped with several wireless interfaces, as the application could switch positioning technologies according to the user position, best networking technology available, and so forth.

6.5.1.2 ProximityListener

The ProximityListener included in version 1.0 also needed improvement in several areas. First, when the ProximityListener was registered for a particular circular area, defined by a point and a radius, there was no method to set or discover the periodic refresh rate used to check the real-time position of the user against the registered position, or any other kind of communication from the implementation, if the proximity was not detected. Instead, the application had to wait until the implementation fired the proximityEvent() method before taking action. Therefore, if the method did not fire when expected while testing on a real device, debugging the application was extremely difficult. Causes for failure could vary from a momentarily dropped GPS signal, to a temporary loss in GPS accuracy, to a low refresh rate that could not capture the devices entrance into the circular area prior to its exit. Secondly, the ProximityListener lacked the ability to detect an exit from a particular area, as it only allowed the detection of an entrance into the area. Lastly, the only geographic shape supported by the ProximityListener was a circle, represented by a point and a radius. There are many cases where the use of a long rectangle area or an irregular polygon defined by multiple points is desired.

Proximity detection has been greatly enhanced in version 2.0 of the Java ME Location API. For example, an interval and timeout value can be defined by the application when the ProximityEnterAndExitListener, which has replaced the ProximityListener of version 1.0, is registered. Now, a new locationUpdated() method is called at a particular interval, so that the application can tell how frequently the device is checking proximity to the registered location. Further, the specification now supports the detection of departure from a specific area through the same ProximityEnterAndExitListener. Finally, the new specification allows the registration of different types of geographic areas, including CircularGeographicAreas, RectangleGeographicAreas, and PolygonGeographicAreas. With this modification, any polygon that is represented in a server-side GIS database can now be directly transferred to a mobile phone, constructed into a PolygonGeographicArea, and registered with the ProximityEnterAndExitListener.

6.5.1.3 Landmark and LandmarkStore

The `Landmark` and `LandmarkStore` also received an overhaul in version 2.0 to lend better support for future LBS applications. The `Landmark` now features new fields such as author, identifier, and timestamp, and the `LandmarkStore` has methods to search the store based on these properties. Wildcard searches are also allowed. This expanded search ability should make it much easier for applications to synchronize on-device landmarks with a database server and keep track of record updates.

The new specification also supports a large on-device database that may be accessed by multiple applications simultaneously. Further, it includes a `LandmarkStoreListener` that can inform the application when the contents of the `LandmarkStore` are modified by another thread or application. Privacy and security concerns are improved allowing `LandmarkStores` to be declared as "private," which can only be accessed by the application that created the `LandmarkStore`. In contrast, in version 1.0, `LandmarkStores` were always shared among all applications running on the device. Public `LandmarkStores` are still allowed and encouraged in version 2.0 for publicly available landmark datasets that can be shared among applications, such as a points-of-interest database.

6.5.2 New Features

Version 2.0 also includes several completely new features that will significantly accelerate software development for handsets as well as improve interoperability between mobile devices and server-side systems. These features provide basic location-aware services to third-party application developers that would otherwise have to manually code.

6.5.2.1 Landmark Exchange Formats

The "Landmark Exchange Formats" is a new feature, implemented in an `ExchangeFormatFactory`, meant to improve the area of interoperability. In version 1.0, `Landmarks` existed primarily inside a single device and were created and accessed by the same single application. This approach made it difficult to share landmarks among other mobile phones or desktop applications, or downloaded from Websites. In version 2.0, the `ExchangeFormatFactory` supports multiple exchange formats that promote interaction between mobile phones and with desktop or server applications. This ability allows users to share favorite places via e-mail or text-messages and applications to share landmarks via communication on specific ports.

6.5.2.2 Geocoding

Location API Version 2.0 provides three categories of services derived from new `ServiceProvider` and `ServiceListener` superinterfaces: Geocoding, Maps, and Navigation. Geocoding, or the translation of address information into latitude and longitude, as well as reverse geocoding, or the translation of latitude and longitude information into an address, are both supported through a `GeocodingServiceProvider`. This is a very important feature for interactions with the user, since positioning technologies provide coordinate information (i.e., "Latitude = 28.058425, Longitude = 82.416170"), which is not meaningful to the end user, and users provide location information in the form of an address (i.e., "4202 E. Fowler Ave. Tampa, FL 33620"), which is not useful to software and positioning technologies. Geocoding and reverse geocoding bridge the gap between the end user and the positioning technology and enable fluid user interaction with applications.

6.5.2.3 Map User Interfaces

Another important new feature is the ability to display location information in the form of a map. Version 2.0 features a `MapServiceProvider` that allows software developers to rapidly build solutions that include rendering map information, including landmarks and routes, to the mobile phone screen. This feature has various levels of control. If the application simply wants to show something on a map to the user, a single function call will hand over control to the `MapServiceProvider`, which will then show the map to the user in its default format.

If the application wants more control over what is rendered to the screen, there is also an option to retrieve a `BaseMap` from the `MapServiceProvider` and then render this information, along with various `MapOverlays`, to a graphics object defined by the application. Through the manipulation of `MapOverlays`, the application can add or remove certain related features on a map, such as showing only restaurant or museum attractions to the user.

6.5.2.4 Navigation

Navigation is perhaps one of the most significant new features included in version 2.0. It relates to the ability to easily add real-time guidance and directions to any mobile application. The `NavigationServiceProvider` supports two primary modes of operation. If applications simply want to use a turnkey navigation solution, it can make a simple call and allow the service provider to take control of the user interface as well as application flow to navigate to a particular location. For applications that want to handle the navigation logic and have more control over the navigation process, the `NavigationServiceProvider` can act as a route planner that returns a new `Route` object that contains all the information an application needs to navigate. Both methods allow the use of `NavigationServicePreferences`, which can specify anything from a mode of transportation preference (including walking and public transit), a desire to obtain the route with the least traffic, certain geographic areas to avoid, and voice or text directions.

The `Route` object, which consists of `RouteSegments`, allows more queries, so that an application can determine whether it is suitable for its use, including whether costs such as toll roads are involved, total travel time, and total distance. If the application chooses to control the actual navigation process, the RouteSegments contain the instructions as well as the locations where the instructions should be given. These features allow application developers to focus on creating a better navigation application instead of worrying about the logistics of planning a route and getting the geographic data to the cellular phone.

More details and example code about versions 1.0 and 2.0 of the Java ME platform Location APIs can be found in [12, 13, 17].

6.6 Obtaining the User's Position and the LBIS Tracking System Example

This chapter is crucial for our LBIS tracking system example, and for that matter, to any location-based application. These systems are all about location. This chapter explains the different indoor and outdoor positioning systems available and how the mobile station's position can be determined. At the end, the chapter describes the Java ME Location APIs 1.0 and 2.0, of prime importance in the development of Java ME-based location-based applications. Through the use of these APIs, the GPS-enabled clients of our LBIS tracking system obtain their locations in real time. Chapter 8 includes a complete example of 1) a MIDlet that uses the location API to obtain the location of the mobile device and sends it to the server using the UDP protocol, and 2) a server UDP-based application that receives the locations.

Chapter 7

Storing and Retrieving the Data: The Database

7.1 Introduction

One of the key elements of any information system is the data and, more specifically, how it is structured, stored, accessed, and maintained, in order to offer a reliable, flexible, and fast service. The database management system (DBMS) plays a key role in all these aspects.

In this chapter, a brief introduction about databases and DBMSs is given, with an emphasis on the fundamental elements of relational databases. The basic commands of the Structured Query Language (SQL) to define, manipulate, and query the database are also described using Postgres 8.3's DBMS as an example. In addition, the chapter briefly explains on how to work with geographical information using PostGIS, Postgres' extension for managing geographic elements.

7.2 Background

Databases have been around since computer systems started to manage large amounts of data. Initial applications, most of them related to "deductive question-answering systems" [26], had very application-dependent data banks, tailored to work for specific programs and with not many reusable elements. This fact halted standardization for many years.

In general, a database is an integrated collection of logically related records. Some initial database approaches focused on the optimal physical representation of the data, using tree-like data structures or networks of data, which had the drawback that, sometimes, users had to navigate through a large portion of the dataset to obtain the desired information. It was not until the work of Edgar Codd [26] that the use of tables and the foundations for a very efficient way to search and retrieve data from the database were proposed. This database model, called the relational model, is still the most commonly used scheme to build databases.

However, it is important to notice that the definition of databases goes beyond the mere storage of data. Databases involve different layers that create and separate the user from the complex representation of the data in the actual storage hardware in order to work at a higher level of abstraction. This is the concept of a Database Management Systems (DBMS), defined as the set of applications and data that allows the definition, implementation, access, and maintenance of the data in a database.

More formally, a DBMS is the union of subsystems that support all the functionalities related to the administration and usage of a database. A DBMS usually consists of the following core elements [52]:

- **The "hard" database:** The set of files or data structures that contain the data. This element deals with the internal data structure and the physical representation of the data in the database.

- **The model:** The definition of the structure and nature of the data to be stored in the system. There are different models for designing databases: networks, relational, object-oriented, etc. As mentioned before, this chapter focuses on the relational model.

- **The database engine:** All the programs that have direct access to manipulate the database. This element executes all the operations requested by the users and also maintains the physical structure of the database in optimal conditions in order to guarantee the integrity of the data and the rapid access to it.

- **The data definition and manipulation languages:** The programming languages that provide the communication channel between the user and the database engine to implement the database model and have access to the stored data. This chapter focuses on the SQL language, including its sub-languages, the Data Definition Language (DDL) and Data Manipulation Language (DML).

- **The data administration system:** The group of applications that allow the database manager to control the accessibility, security, backup, and all administrative operations that a DBMS needs in order to provide an effective service to its users.

- **The user application program:** The interface that facilitates all the operations that the user can perform via "wizards," menus, automated tasks, visual representation of the data or models, etc.

Database management systems offer a robust solution for storing and retrieving large amounts of data in a very efficient way. Databases differentiate from data storage in plain files in several key aspects. For example, files alone neither structure the data being stored in any way nor guarantee relationships across files, leaving the door open for data inconsistency, duplication of data, etc. Also, most of the major DBMS platforms, offer far more ways to access and protect the data from unauthorized users.

7.2.1 Design of the LBIS Tracking System Database

The design of a database depends exclusively on the requirements of the information system being implemented. These requirements define the nature and use of the stored data and their relationships. The design of the database for our LBIS tracking system example will be general enough to cover the basic requirements of a system that stores geographical tracking data from a group of users. Next, a more detailed description of the scenario:

- There is a group of users that will be geographically tracked via GPS-enabled mobile devices.

- Each user corresponds to a single individual. Each mobile device is also unique.

- The system must maintain basic information about the users: name, address, date of birth, social security number, and identification number.

- The system must maintain basic information about the devices: serial number, model, manufacturer, and year.

- The devices are not used exclusively by a single user.

- The period of time in which a user is being tracked is not predefined or slotted, and its duration is variable.

- The tracking data must include the different positions and the time of occurrences associated to a user and the device used.

This description is enough to define a database structure that models this scenario. First, it is evident that the lists of users and devices are not the same because a device can be used by different users; however, a single device can be used only by one user in a certain instant of time. The period of time in which a user makes exclusive use of a device will be defined as a *shift*. Second, based on the specifications, it can be concluded that the shifts do not have a constant length of time, so the initial and final dates and times must be registered. If a user changes devices, it will be considered a different shift for the user. Finally, it is clear that a single user cannot be doing two simultaneous shifts with the same device, but a single user may be carrying more than one device at the same time; however, there will be an individual shift per each device being used by the user.

The next section introduces the basic elements of a relational database and builds the database that models the example scenario, based on the previous requirements.

7.2.2 Structure of a Relational Database

Relational databases are the most commonly used databases nowadays. This term was defined for the first time in 1970 by Edgar Codd [26], who worked at IBM. The idea behind the design of relational databases is that all data with related parameters are grouped together. In addition, it considers that data in different groups can be related, and a relationship between groups can be established based on shared common parameters.

The following list includes the main elements of a typical relational database, contextualized with the terms used in the SQL language, which will be introduced later:

- Table.

- Column.

- Row or Register.

- Key and Foreign Key.

- View or Query.

A *table* is the structure that models and stores the data in the database. Ideally, each table contains related data, such as information about users, or information about the devices, and so on. A database can have as many tables as needed.

The data stored in a table usually have more that one dimension, or domains. Each domain is related to a specific piece of the data. For example, a user has several different pieces of information, such as name, date of birth, address, etc. Each one of these is a domain in the definition of an individual and has different data types. For example, the name and the address are strings of characters, and the birth date is a date with a defined format. A domain is commonly known as a *column*, making reference to a table representation of the data, as seen in Figure 7.1. The order of the columns on the table is very important in order to determine the meaning of that parameter in the definition of the individuals.

Another aspect of the columns is that, in order to define accurately each of the fields of the columns, constraints can be added to guarantee logically correct values within certain boundaries. For example, the gender of a person can only be male or female; any other value is not valid.

Once the columns of a table have been defined, the individual instances of information of this type that are stored in the table are called the *rows* of the table. For example, the information related to each individual in the system is contained in a single row in the users' table. A table can have as many rows as necessary in order to keep all the instances of information of that type. Each one of the rows must be unique in order to guarantee congruence on the database. For example, if a user is registered twice in the table, it is possible

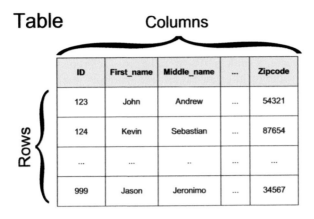

FIGURE 7.1: Rows and columns of the users' table.

that the shifts be assigned to one or the other row without distinction, losing consistency on the information.

Once the data are stored, a database must guarantee that each row can be accessed directly, without inconsistencies. For example, using the name of a person is not enough to identify the person in a unique way, or else imagine looking for a "John Smith" in the social security database. Each table must have a *primary key*, which is the minimal set of columns that allow the unique identification of each row. In the case of the social security database, the social security number would be the primary key given that each number belongs to one individual only. In some cases, more than one column might be necessary. For example, in order to identify a certain shift in our example database, you would need the identifier of the person, the device's serial number, and the date in which the shift started. None of these three columns alone would determine a unique shift, which turns these columns into the primary key of the shift table.

Despite the fact that in many cases a natural selection for a person's primary key would be the social security number, the use of this number for identification in a non-governmental database is a very critical topic for many people due to privacy concerns. If this number must be stored in the database, a recommended solution to avoid the access of this number is to create another unique valid identifier only for the specific application. For example, the unique identifier number that students have in a university database does not reveal their private information and the number is meaningless outside the context of the university.

All possible combinations of columns that identify, in a unique manner, a single row is called a *candidate key*. Just one of the candidates is selected to be the primary key, but the other candidates can also be used for querying information. For this example, if a user has both a unique company identifier and a social security number in the database, and the first one is the primary key, the social security number is a candidate key because it will produce a unique row if queried.

In some cases, a table needs to make cross-references to elements that exist in the same table or in other tables. For example, each shift requires the definition of the user working in that shift, which must be unique because each shift makes reference to a single person. In that case, the shift table must include all the columns that identify a person and a device in a unique manner, in other words, the person's identifier. The set of columns that contains the primary key of an element in another table is called a *foreign key*. It is important to mention that a foreign key cannot replace the primary key of the table because a foreign key is not necessarily unique in the table in which it is being used as a reference. For example, a person can perform many shifts, so a single one cannot be determined by the sole person's identifier, so it would violate the uniqueness requirement of a primary key.

The benefit of using a foreign key is that it avoids the repetition of data among tables. For example, the row with the information of a person may include a lot of information that is not relevant to the shifts table. If somebody's personal information is needed, it is enough to have the person's identifier to retrieve it. In addition, the foreign key controls congruence of the data. If the name of a person is stored in different tables, a misspelled name one time would make the registers different. Furthermore, if a person changes his or her name, this modification would need to be updated in every single table, making the administration of the system more cumbersome.

The process of updating a foreign key includes several options, which depend on the relationship between the key and the row where it is referenced. For instance, if a device is removed from the devices' table, do all the shifts related to that device need to be deleted as well? What about the tracking data if the device and shifts are deleted? The Data Definition Language (DDL) (more on this later) provides the following options when the foreign key of a table is updated or deleted:

- **RESTRICT:** Avoids the elimination of the row if it is an active foreign key.

- **NO ACTION:** Throws an error when it finds the cross-reference.

- **CASCADE:** Delete the original row and the one in which the foreign key is referenced.

- **SET NULL:** Changes the value of the foreign key to NULL in the row where the foreign key is referenced.

- **SET DEFAULT:** Changes the value of the foreign key to the DEFAULT value.

In the case of the last two options, the operation will not succeed if the foreign key does not support the value NULL or the default value, respectively.

Usually, when a user consults the database, not all columns of the table are required to answer the question. This subset of data from a table is called a *query* or a *view*. A single query may involve more than one table if the data for the desired view is spread across different tables, for example, the name of the persons, the serial numbers, and makers of all the devices that were used on shifts during the month of August. In this example, the name of the person is only in the users' table, and the maker of the devices is only in the devices' table.

Queries are definitely one of the most common operations over a database because they allow access to the stored data. The result of a query can be defined as a "virtual table" or view of the data, which shows only part of the total data stored in the tables, the data that satisfies a very specific need of information. More details about queries are included in the following section where the SQL language is introduced.

7.2.3   The Structure Query Language (SQL)

The Structured Query Language is the language for working with relational databases. This language was created in 1974 by Donald D. Chamberlin and Raymond Boyce [25] while working at IBM. The original name was SEQUEL (Structured English Query Language) and was created to provide a standard language for operations in relational databases. The complete language is formed by three sub-languages:

- **SQL:** Used for the definition of queries.

- **Data Manipulation Language (DML):** Allows the addition, modification, and deletion of data in the tables.

- **Data Definition Language (DDL):** Allows the creation, modification, and deletion of the tables.

The illustration of the different functionalities of the languages will be shown in the context of the database for the LBIS tracking system example and the functionality of the previously defined scenario. The structure of the database is shown in Figure 7.2. Depending on the system and the requirements of the problem to solve, more information can be included, or part of the example can be modified to match your own system. The intention is to provide a general structure that could be adapted to a wide spectrum of applications. All the scripts used in this chapter are valid for Postgres 8.3.

7.2.3.1   Data Definition Language (DDL)

The first step in the creation of a database is to define the structure of the information, which is the definition of the structure of the tables. This design depends entirely on the particular needs of the information system being developed. Listing 7.1 shows the script that creates the basic structure

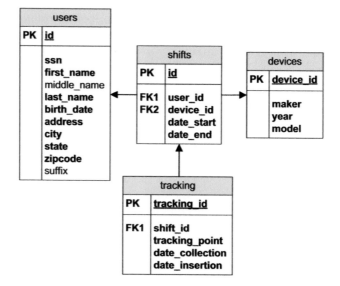

FIGURE 7.2: Design of the database of our LBIS tracking system example.

of a table that holds information about the users: unique identifier, social security number, full name (first, middle, and last name), date of birth, and full address.

```
1  CREATE TABLE users(
2    id INTEGER ,
3    ssn INTEGER ,
4    first_name VARCHAR(20)
5      CONSTRAINT first_name_not_null NOT NULL ,
6    mid_name VARCHAR(20) ,
7    last_name VARCHAR(20)
8      CONSTRAINT last_name_not_null NOT NULL ,
9    birth_date DATE ,
10   address VARCHAR(50)
11     CONSTRAINT address_not_null NOT NULL ,
12   city VARCHAR(20) DEFAULT 'TAMPA'
13     CONSTRAINT city_not_null NOT NULL ,
14   zipcode bigint DEFAULT 33620
15     CONSTRAINT zip_not_null NOT NULL ,
16   state VARCHAR(2) DEFAULT 'FL'
17     CONSTRAINT state_not_null NOT NULL
18     CONSTRAINT state_check
19     CHECK (state IN ('FL', 'GA', 'AL')),
20   CONSTRAINT users_pk
21     PRIMARY KEY (id),
22   CONSTRAINT user_city_fk
23     FOREIGN KEY (city, zipcode, state)
24     REFERENCES cities_table (city, zipcode, state)
25     ON UPDATE CASCADE ON DELETE SET DEFAULT
26 ) TABLESPACE pg_default;
```

Listing 7.1: Structure of the users' table.

Notice that the enumeration of the fields is not enough to define a person's row or register. This is because there are some constraints given by the nature of the data being stored. For example, most of the data needed cannot be null, like the first and last name of the person, or the name of the city, state, and zip code where the person was born. These last three fields are especially important because they are a foreign key for the cities_table, where these three items will be checked against to avoid a false statement. In addition, the table includes the restriction that the only valid states in a user's address are Florida, Georgia, and Alabama. The last line has the following dual effect. If a new user is being included in the database, upon the submission of the information, the ON UPDATE CASCADE part of the code goes to the cities_table table and checks whether the city, zip code, and state included in the submitted information are valid, i.e., are included in the cities_table, which it is assumed to be completely populated. If one or more of these three fields are deleted from the cities_table, the ON DELETE SET DEFAULT part of the code replaces those fields in the users table with the default information, which is "Tampa," "FL," and "33620."

The primary key of the users table is the *id* column, which is defined as an INTEGER data type. The value of this column contains a unique identification number for the user. This column is included based on the comment made in Section 7.2.2 about the privacy issue of using the social security number of a person in a database. Now, in order to avoid a manual assignment of this number and the extra work of looking for an unused number, it is recommended to assign that task to the database, which it can do automatically.

There are different ways to automatically assign unique numbers using the database. For example, Postgres includes a data type called SERIAL, which performs this mission. However, given that it is not an standard data type, it may bring compatibility problems if the database is changed to other platforms. In that case, the best way to do it is to use a SEQUENCE element, which performs a similar function and it is supported by all mayor database engines. The following script, Listing 7.2, shows how to create a sequence of unique numbers in Postgres.

```
1  CREATE SEQUENCE user_seq
2     INCREMENT 1
3     MINVALUE 0
4     MAXVALUE 9223372036854775807
5     START 1
6     CACHE 1;
7  ALTER TABLE user_seq OWNER TO postgres;
```

Listing 7.2: Creating unique sequence numbers in Postgres.

The script is very simple. It says that the sequence will start with the number 1, and will be incremented by 1 each time. The maximum value is a BIGINT. The CACHE parameter defines the number of values that the database will calculate a priori and will be ready for assignment. This accelerates the data insertion process. Another option not used in this example is CYCLE, which start the sequence again once the maximum or the minimum value is reached, depending on the direction of the increment. If the `CYCLE` option is not selected and the sequence reaches the final possible value, the database generates an error.

The next value of a sequence is obtained using the `nextval('user_seq')` function. Every time this function is used, the database returns the next value of the sequence, and the value of the sequence is modified, being either increased or decreased, depending on the sign of the increment.

Now let us assume that the table needs to be changed. The following examples illustrate the syntax of the functions available to modify an existing table:

- **Add a column:** Some users have a suffix on their name (Jr., II, etc.).

```
ALTER TABLE users
  ADD suffix VARCHAR(5);
```

- **Change data type:** There are some users whose last name is longer than 20 characters.

```
ALTER TABLE users
  ALTER last_name TYPE VARCHAR(30);
```

- **Add a new constraint:** The date of birth should be greater than June 1950.

```
ALTER TABLE users
  ADD CONSTRAINT date_constraint
  CHECK (birth_date > '1950-06-30');
```

- **Delete constraint:** The constraint on the states for the birthplace is not required anymore.

```
ALTER TABLE users
  DROP CONSTRAINT state_check;
```

- **Delete a column:** Middle name column is not needed.

```
ALTER TABLE users
  DROP COLUMN mid_name;
```

Finally, when a table is no longer necessary, it can be removed using the `DROP TABLE users;` command, which in this case deletes the users' table.

If a table to be deleted is being referenced by foreign key constraints, then the word `CASCADE` needs to be included in the script in order to tell Postgres that all the foreign key constraints must be dropped as well, such as in the case of the command `DROP TABLE cities_table CASCADE;`.

7.2.3.2 Data Manipulation Language (DML)

Once the tables are created, the next step is to insert data in them. List-ing 7.3 shows the SQL script to do just that.

```
1  INSERT INTO users
2    (id, ssn, first_name, last_name,
3     suffix, birth_date, address, city, zipcode,
4     state)
5    VALUES (nextval('user_seq'), 123456789, 'John', 'Smith',
6    NULL, '1980-01-01', '12345 W 1st.', 'Orlando', 32830,
7    DEFAULT);
```

Listing 7.3: Populating the database.

Notice that the identifier of the user is automatically generated by Postgres using the **nextval** function. In addition, this person does not have a suffix, so that field has no data. In that case, the reserved word **NULL** is used to represent a void field. Remember that the **NULL** cannot be inserted on those columns with a **NOT NULL** constraint. Also, note that the state where the person was born is defined as a default value, which is Florida, by using the **DEFAULT** reserved word.

The DML also allows for the modification of data already in a table, as shown in Listing 7.4. The following example updates the data of the register just inserted in the table, which now includes a suffix on the name and modifies the name of the city of birth.

```
1  UPDATE users u
2    SET u.suffix = 'Jr.', u.city = 'Tampa'
3    WHERE u.id = 321;
```

Listing 7.4: Modifying data.

In the previous script, the user had to provide the data to be included in the record. However, it is possible that the data already existed somewhere else in the database. In this case, it can be retrieved from another table and included in the updated register. The following example (Listing 7.5) updates the user identifier of a person in a certain shift. The identifier of the new user is obtained based on the social security number of the person, which is stored on the users' table.

```
1  UPDATE shifts s
2    SET s.user_id =
3      (SELECT u.id FROM users u
4       WHERE u.ssn = 123456789)
5    WHERE s.shift_id = 9001;
```

Listing 7.5: Querying and modifying data.

In previous examples, just one record was affected because the **WHERE** state-ment returns a single register. However, it is possible to modify more than one record. Let us assume that each user is assigned to a certain office location of the company, and that there is a certain device that is used exclusively by the people in that office. All the people who have used that device will be assigned to that specific office. The code in Listing 7.6 shows how to modify the office identifier of all those users who used the device 9876, which was assigned to another office. The code within parenthesis returns the user identifiers of those users who used device 9876, and the first part of the code sets the office identifier of all those users to 9002. This code assumes that the user_id in the shifts table is a foreign key to the users table and that the users table has an office_id item.

```
1  UPDATE users us
2    SET  us.office_id = 9002
3    WHERE us.id IN
4      (SELECT DISTINCT s.user_id
5        FROM shifts s
6        WHERE s.device_id = '9876');
```

Listing 7.6: Modifying multiple registers.

The DISTINCT parameter modifies the query in such a way that it only retrieves the different values stored in those columns despite the fact that there could be several repetitions of that value. In the example, a user may have had several shifts with a particular device, so obtaining the original list of users would include repetitions. The DISTINCT parameter would make sure that each different identifier just appears once in the query result. This is useful, for example, to reduce the number of users that will be updated in the previous script.

The final example covers the case in which the data are no longer required. In this case, the DML offers the option to delete a set of registers from a table. The following example shows how the city of Topeka, Kansas, is deleted from the table of cities in the database.

```
1  DELETE
2    FROM cities_table
3    WHERE city = 'Topeka' AND state = 'KS';
```

Listing 7.7: Deleting data.

As before, the WHERE clause is included to define a target set of registers based on the result of a query. If the deleted rows are being referenced as foreign keys in another table, the deletion policy already defined in the table will take care of the cross-referenced rows.

7.2.3.3 Data Retrieval

Once the database is populated with data, the most common operation is to consult it. As it was shown in some of the data manipulation examples before, data retrieval is used to define the target registers to perform the manipulation. This section focuses on the data retrieval process and provides basic script structures for consulting the database.

The SELECT clause is the command that allows data retrieval. For example, if a list of all users is required, the SELECT * FROM users command will retrieve all the columns of every row.

More specific queries can be performed since not all the retrieved data using this command might be needed. For example, Listing 7.8 shows the script used to retrieve the identifiers and full names of those users whose first name is John.

```
1  SELECT u.id, u.first_name, u.mid_name, u.last_name
2    FROM users u
3    WHERE u.first_name = 'John';
```

Listing 7.8: Querying the database for specific users.

Another interesting query is to obtain a list of the date, serial number, and maker of the device of all the shifts in which the user 'John Smith' participated. Assuming that his identifier number is known, this operation involves the users, shifts, and devices tables. From the first table, the personal information can be obtained. From the second table, the association between the user and the device and the date of the shift can be obtained. Finally, the third table provides the information about the maker of the device. The script is shown in Listing 7.9.

```
1  SELECT u.id, u.first_name, u.last_name, s.device_id, d.maker
2    FROM users u, shifts s, devices d
3    WHERE u.id = s.user_id AND s.device_id = d.id AND u.id = 321;
```

Listing 7.9: Querying from different tables.

SQL offers the option to create very complex SELECT clauses using the JOIN clause, which allows to select data from different tables. A good reference to look for more details on this command and the structure of the scripts, can be found in the Postgres's documentation at http://www.postgresql.org/docs/.

7.2.4 PostGIS and Geographical Databases

PostGIS is an extension of the PostgresSQL server that adds functionality to work with geographical objects. This product was developed by the company Refractions Research as part of a project in spatial databases. PostGIS is available to the public via the GNU-GPL open source license from the company's Website at http://www.refractions.net/products/postgis/.

The main advantage of PostGIS is that it implements OpenGIS very closely, which is an open standard for GIS systems created by the Open Geospatial Consortium, Inc. (OGC) (http://www.opengeospatial.org/). The OpenGIS standard defines basic geometric types and functions in both an abstract fashion and real implementations on actual languages in order to offer foundations for interoperability among different GIS applications. PostGIS has been certified to be compliant with the *"Typed and Functions"* specified in the *"Simple Features Specification for SQL"* documents that define the minimum specifications of an SQL implementation of the standard. The OpenGIS standards can be found in the OGC Website at `http://www.opengeospatial.org/standards/is`.

7.2.4.1   Structure of PostGIS

As mentioned before, PostGIS follows the OpenGIS standard, more specifically, the section called *"OpenGIS Implementation Specification for Geographic Information — Simple Feature Access — Part 2: SQL Option,"* which defines the basic structure and functionalities that an implementation of OpenGIS in SQL should have. This part of the standard can be found in the Web page `http://www.opengeospatial.org/standards/sfs`.

The document defines the basic SQL operations to store, retrieve, query, and update data with non-spatial and spatial attributes, or geometry-valued attributes, and the set of functions that can be applied to these objects. Furthermore, OpenGIS defines that any database with geometric data in any of its tables need to have extra metadata tables with information about the geometric type columns. The standard considers two cases: if the geometry data types have been predefined or not. In the second case, the structure of the new data types must be defined in new metadata tables, while in the first case, the database already has them defined natively. The metadata tables, as defined by OpenGIS, are the following:

- The `geometry_columns` table stores all the columns with geometric data in the database, including the geometry type.

- The `spatial_ref_sys` table contains the set of available coordinate systems and transformations for geometry objects. This is necessary to have a correct interpretation of the geometry, based on the selected model.

- The `feature_table` stores a collection of features or geometry types. The columns of the feature table represent geometric valued attributes while rows represent individual features. The geometry of a feature is one of its feature attributes. While logically a geometric data type, a column with geometric information in a regular table is implemented as a foreign key to a geometry table.

- The `geometry_table` stores the instances of geometric objects, which may be implemented using either standard SQL numeric types or SQL binary types.

PostGIS predefines all the geographical data types described in the standard and also includes 674 functions for geometric objects, which not only makes it compliant with the standard but also extends it considerably.

7.2.4.2   Creating a Table with Geographical Columns

Based on our LBIS tracking system example, the tracking table features a geometric type column that contains the GPS fixes (points) collected from the mobile devices in their respective shifts. Listing 7.10 shows how to create the tracking table, including the mentioned column.

```
 1  CREATE TABLE tracking(
 2    tracking_id INTEGER ,
 3    shift_id INTEGER
 4      CONSTRAINT shift_id_not_null NOT NULL ,
 5    date_collection date
 6      CONSTRAINT date_coll_not_null NOT NULL ,
 7    date_insertion date
 8      CONSTRAINT date_ins_not_null NOT NULL ,
 9    CONSTRAINT tracking_pk
10      PRIMARY KEY (tracking_id),
11    CONSTRAINT shift_id_fk
12      FOREIGN KEY (shift_id)
13      REFERENCES shifts (shift_id)
14      ON UPDATE CASCADE ON DELETE CASCADE
15  )TABLESPACE pg_default;
16
17  SELECT AddGeometryColumn( 'tracking', 'tracking_point',
18    32661, 'POINT', 2);
19
20  ALTER TABLE tracking
21    ADD CONSTRAINT tracking_point_valid_check
22      CHECK (isvalid(tracking_point));
```

Listing 7.10: Creating a table with a geometric type column.

The first section of the code works as a regular SQL table creation sentence. However, no geometric column has been included. This is because the geometric column has to be added using the PostGIS function `AddGeometryColumn()`, as shown in the second section of the code. The parameters of this function are the name of the table in which the new column will be added, the name of the new column, the reference number of the spatial reference system which, for the platform presented in this book, has been decided to be the *EPSG:32661 WGS 84/UPS North*, the type of geometry (a point), and the number of dimensions of the geometric object. The last part of the code adds a constraint that checks for the validity of the coordinates.

PostGIS will not only insert the new column on the destination table, but it will also create an entry on the metadata table `geometry_columns` with the data of the new column.

7.2.4.3   Inserting Geographical Data in a Table

Once the table has been created, including the geometric column, then the database is ready to be used. Listing 7.11 shows how to insert a point in the tracking table of the example.

```
 1  INSERT INTO tracking
 2    (tracking_id, shift_id, tracking_point, date_collection,
         date_insertion)
```

```
3   VALUES
4   (nextval('tracking_seq'), 999, GeomFromText('POINT(1.9845  49.8543)',
       32661),'2009-01-02', '2009-01-01');
```

Listing 7.11: Inserting a point in the tracking table.

The function `GeomFromText(..)` is the one in charge of generating the geometric object. It receives two parameters, the *"Well-Known-Text"* (WKT) description of the geometric object and the respective spatial reference system.

7.2.4.4 Retrieving Geographical Data

Retrieving geometric data from a table can be performed as shown in Listing 7.12, which is meant to obtain all the points and collection time from a certain shift.

```
1   SELECT AsText(t.tracking_point) AS  trackingpoint, t.date_collection
2   FROM tracking t
3   WHERE t.shift_id = 999;
```

Listing 7.12: Retrieving geometric data.

In this example, the function `AsText(..)` is used to transform the internal representation of the geometric object into a WKT format that can be easily read.

7.2.4.5 Useful Geometric Operators

The following list contains the operators used to perform basic operations between geometric objects:

- **&&** : This operator tells whether the bounding box of one geometry intersects the bounding box of another. The example in Listing 7.13 returns the identifier of the shift and the time of collection of all points contained in a defined polygon.

```
1   SELECT t.shift_id, t.date_collection
2   FROM tracking t
3   WHERE t.tracking_point && GeomFromText('POLYGON((...))',-1);
```

Listing 7.13: Use of the && operator.

- $\doteq$: This operator tests whether two geometries are geometrically identical. The example in Listing 7.14 returns all points that match the definition provided in the `GeomFromText()` function.

```
1   SELECT AsText(t.tracking_point) AS  trackingpoint, t.
       date_collection
2     FROM tracking t
3     WHERE t.tracking_point ~= GeomFromText('POINT((...))',-1);
```

Listing 7.14: Use of the $\doteq$ operator.

- = : This operator tests whether the bounding boxes of two geometries are the same, without taking into account the geometry of the elements.

More detailed explanation and additional operators can be found in [7].

7.3 Accessing the Database Using Java

Previous sections show how to create, modify, and query databases, and how to work with geometric objects using PostGIS. This section explains how to connect with the database and insert and retrieve data using Java. All of these operations are possible due to the Java Data Base Connectivity (JDBC) API, which allows communication between a Java application and a database. It is important to mention that the code that shows these operations in this section is implemented in the server part of the LBIS system, i.e., the application in the server connects, inserts, and retrieves data from the database, which is located in the same machine.

7.3.1 Connecting to the Database via JDBC

This section shows how to connect to the database using JDBC using the Java EE platform. Listing 7.15 shows the example code to accomplish this. The first two lines of code are the ones in charge of creating the connection with the database. The parameter in the second command is the one in charge of defining the source of the data. It is very important that the name provided be the same as the one defined for the database in the *JDBC resources* in the server. The third command declares and opens the connection. At this point, the connection is ready to perform common operations on the database, therefore the code to insert, retrieve, delete, etc., data must be inserted here. After all the operations on the database are executed, the connection must be closed. The last command performs this task. Finally, if any of the commands cannot be executed due to an error, an exception will be thrown. The exception can be caught using a try-catch block as shown in the example, or by declaring that the containing method be in charge of handling and returning any possible exception.

```
1  try{
2
3    javax.naming.InitialContext ic = new javax.naming.InitialContext();
4
5    javax.sql.DataSource dataSource =
6      (javax.sql.DataSource)ic.lookup("jdbc/lbsbook");
7
8    Connection lbs_book = dataSource.getConnection();
9
10   // All operations on the databases are defined here!
```

```
11
12   lbs_book.close();
13
14   }catch(Exception ex){ex.printStack();}
```

Listing 7.15: Connecting to the databse using JDBC.

7.3.2   Data Insertion

Once the connection has been opened, the application can perform all the necessary operations on the database. Listing 7.16 shows an example code to insert data in the database, more specifically, it includes a tracking point in the tracking table.

The first line creates a template script called preparedStatement in which the values of certain parameters are defined in the following lines. The preparedStatement has variable and fixed parameters. The variable parameters are defined by including a question mark ('?') in the definition of the script. The values are then assigned based on the order of appearance of the question marks in the statement. In this example, four columns are selected to be variable: the collection date of the coordinate, the identifier of the shift, the position collected, and the insertion date of this row in the database. The two fixed parameters are the identifier of the tracking point, which is generated based on a sequence element previously defined, and the geographical reference system.

```
 1   PreparedStatement   insertStatement =
 2     lbs_book.prepareStatement("INSERT INTO tracking
 3     (tracking_id, date_collection, shift_id, tracking_point,
           date_insertion)
 4     VALUES
 5     (nextval('tracking_seq'),?,?,ST_GeomFromText(?,32661),?)");
 6
 7   insertStatement.setTimestamp(1, new java.sql.Timestamp(timefix));
 8
 9   insertStatement.setLong(2, shift_id);
10
11   String coordinate = "POINT("+XLong+" "+YLat+")";
12   insertStatement.setString(3,coordinate);
13
14   insertStatement.setTimestamp(4, new java.sql.Timestamp(new Date().
           getTime()));
15
16   insertStatement.executeUpdate();
```

Listing 7.16: Inserting a tracking point in the database.

The executeUpdate() method is used for all commands that modify the database, like CREATE, INSERT, UPDATE, and DELETE. This method returns an integer value that represents the number of rows that were affected by the execution of the SQL statement in the database.

7.3.3 Data Queries

The third operation is data retrieval, which is executed using the `executeQuery()` method. Given that data retrieval brings data back from the database, they must be stored in a data structure, which in Java is called `ResultSet`. This structure automatically organizes the data in the columns defined on the query statement.

The code in Listing 7.17 illustrates how to define and execute a query, and how to access the data brought from the database. In this example a regular statement is used instead of the prepared statement already shown in the previous example. The result of the query will show the identifier, first, and last name of all the users whose identifier is less that 2001.

```
1  //Open the connection with the database
2
3  Statement stmt = lbs_book.createStatement();
4  ResultSet rs;
5
6  rs = stmt.executeQuery("SELECT id, first_name, last_name
7    FROM users WHERE id < 2001");
8
9  while (rs.next()) {
10   int id = rs.getInt(1);
11   String firstName = rs.getString("first_name");
12   String lastName = rs.getString("last_name");
13   System.out.println(id + '','' + firstName + '''' +
14     lastName + "\n");
15 }
16
17 //Close the connection with the database
```

Listing 7.17: Querying the database.

The first two lines create a statement object from the open connection `lbs_book` and the `ResultSet` object. The third line invokes the `executeQuery()` method, which receives the statement and returns the set of rows obtained from the query. These rows are stored in the `ResultSet` variable. The while statement will go over all the elements in the `ResultSet` object. Different methods can be used to access the data from each column of the row. For example, the method `getString(.)` returns a string, the method `getInt(.)` returns an integer value, and others for different data types. All these methods identify a column by the name of the column, as it was defined on the query statement, or by the column index, which is a range of values starting at 1. In the case where the query uses table name aliases (e.g., `SELECT u.id from users u`), it is recommended to assign aliases to the columns (e.g., `SELECT u.id users_id from users u`). For more information about the different methods to read the data from the `ResultSet` object, visit the documentation of the Java SE platform at `http://java.sun.com/javase/6/docs/api/java/sql/ResultSet.html`.

7.4 pgAdmin III: Postgres's Database Administration Tool

The default installation of Postgres includes pgAdmin III, an administration tool to manage and interact with the database. This section briefly describes this tool with three examples that show how to create a new database, how to add tables to it using the wizard interface, and how to use the SQL execution module to run SQL code.

7.4.1 Creating a New Database

The first step is to open the pgAdmin tool. This application can be found in the start menu folder of Postgres. Once the tool is open, the Postgres icon can be identified in the left-hand menu, which represents the database system as a whole. Although the example shows how to work with a local database server, the tool can also be used to manage remote databases.

The following step is to open a connection with the database server to have access to the databases. Double-click on the database server icon and wait until it connects to the server. Once the connection is made, the tool displays all the components of the database system: databases, users, groups, and tables.

In order to create a new database, click on *Databases* in the object browser. The system should respond displaying all the existing databases. Right-click on *Databases* and select the option *New Database*, as shown in Figure 7.3. A new window appears (see Figure 7.4) to define the parameters of the new database. In this example, three parameters are defined: name of the database, owner user, and the template of the database. As it can be seen from the figure, the name chosen for the new database is *lbsbook*. Remember that it is recommended to write the name of the databases in lowercase letters when working in Postgres. The owner of the database is defined as the *postgres* user, which is the administrator of the system. Finally, the *template_postgis* template is used. The selection of this option guarantees the use of geometrical information and its respective functions; it creates all spatial variables and the metadata tables.

7.4.2 Creating a New Table Using the Wizard

Once the database has been created, the following steps show how to create new tables:

1. Under *Databases* in the object browser window, select the database in which you want to add the new table. If a red "x" sign appears on the database name, it means that the server has no connection with that

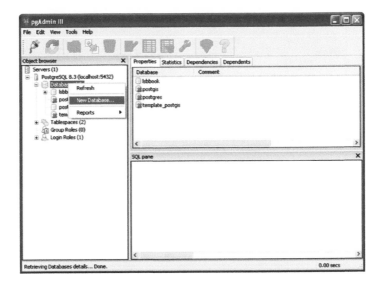

FIGURE 7.3: Creating a new database.

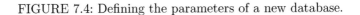

FIGURE 7.4: Defining the parameters of a new database.

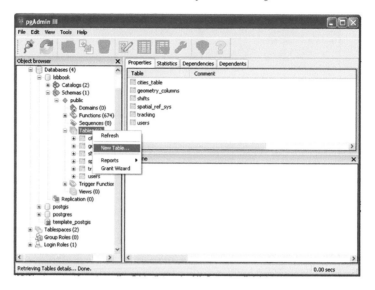

FIGURE 7.5: Selecting the option to create a new table in a database.

database. Click once on the name of the database of choice to start the connection with the database.

2. Under the database name of choice, click on the "+" sign next to *Schemas*. If you do not see *Schemas*, click on the "+" sign next to the database of choice.

3. Click on the "+" sign next to *Public*.

4. Right-click on *Tables* and select the *New table ...* option from the floating menu, as shown in Figure 7.5.

5. The new window asks for the general parameters of the new table. The table "devices" is created including this name in the *Properties* tab, as shown in Figure 7.6.

6. To define the columns, click on the *Columns* tab, as in Figure 7.7. Click on the *Add* button. In the new window, define the characteristics of the new column such as name, data type, and if the variable accepts NULL values or not. At the end of the process, all the columns will be listed in the *Columns* tab, as shown in Figure 7.8.

7. Table constraints are included using the *Constraints* tab. Select the type of constraint that you would like to add and click on the *Add* button. In the case of a primary key constraint being added, the new window has two tabs. The first one is to define the name of the constraint. The second tab is to define the columns that will be part of the primary key. The

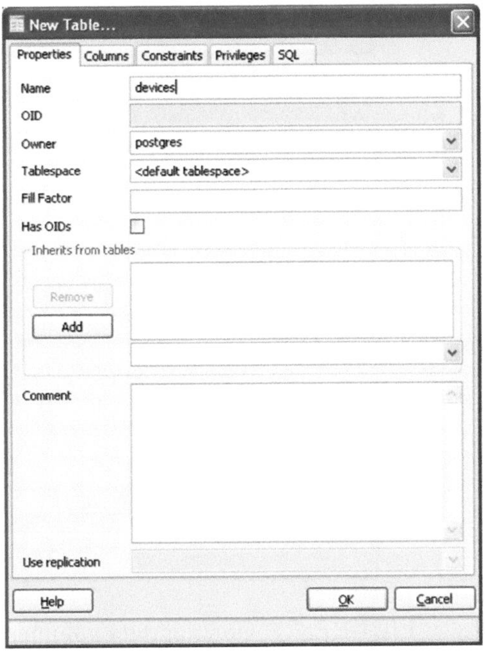

FIGURE 7.6: Defining the name of the new table.

first one receives the name of the constraint, as shown in Figure 7.9. Click on the *Columns* tab in order to define the columns. From the dropbox menu, select the columns, one at a time, and click on the *Add* button, as shown in Figure 7.10.

8. To define more general constraints, like the ones that define limits for values in certain columns, instead of adding a "primary key" constraint, select a "check" constraint and click on the *Add* button. A new window will ask you to define the name of the constraint and the logical evaluation of the constraint. For example, Figure 7.11 shows hot to limit the value of the "zipcode" column in the "cities_table" table to be less than 99999.

9. After creating all columns and constraints, pgAdmin allows you to see the resultant SQL script that would replicate a table with the exact same characteristics of the one the wizard just created. This code can be seen in the SQL tab in the *New Table* window, as shown in Figure 7.12.

The next section describes how to work directly with SQL scripts using the pgAdmin tool.

FIGURE 7.7: Creating new columns.

FIGURE 7.8: List of all columns.

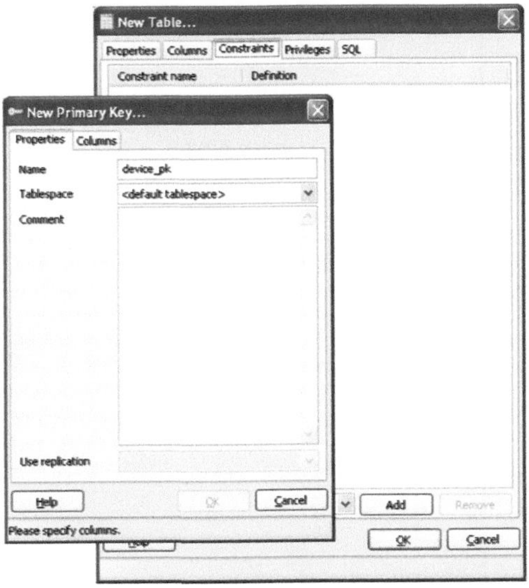

FIGURE 7.9: General information about a primary key constraint.

FIGURE 7.10: Including the columns that are part of the primary key.

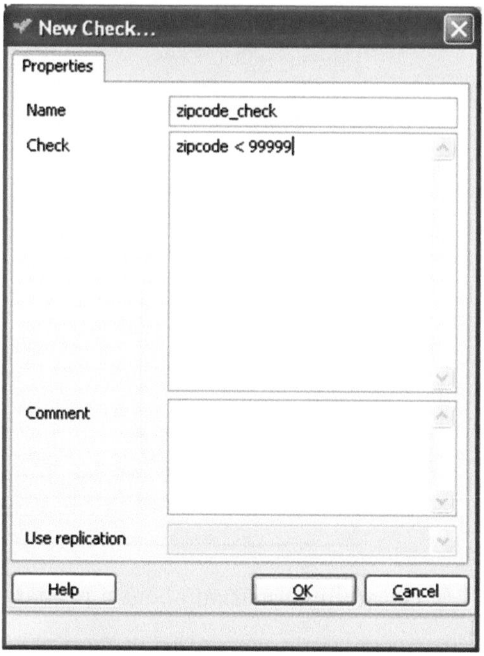

FIGURE 7.11: Including a constraint for the zipcode column.

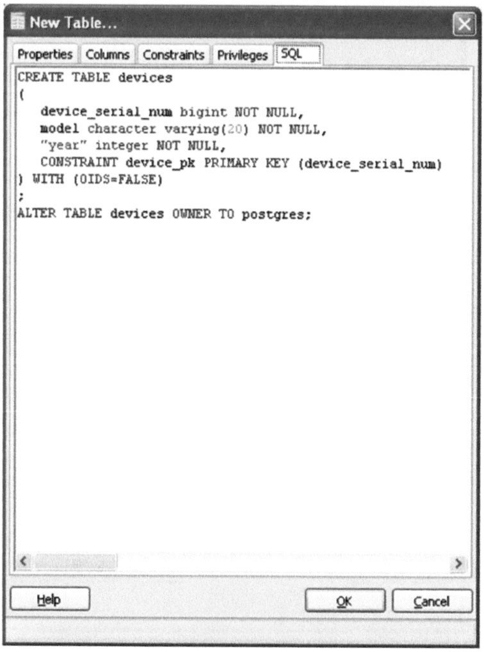

FIGURE 7.12: Obtaining the SQL script for the creation of the table.

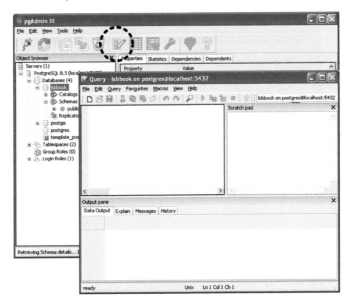

FIGURE 7.13: Opening the SQL execution module.

7.4.3 Using the SQL Execution Module

In order to execute SQL code using the pgAdmin tool, the first step is to select the database on which the operations will be executed. Select a database by clicking on the database icon. Once the database has been selected, the icon marked in Figure 7.13 will turn active. That icon will open the SQL execution module of the pgAdmin tool. Once you click on it, a new window with the execution module appears, showing in the title of the window the selected database and the server in which the database is located.

The upper left-hand section of the window is the one in which the SQL code is written and executed. The upper right-hand section works as a scratch paper to copy, paste, and modify SQL code without affecting the one to be executed. The lower section of the window is dedicated to show the results of the execution of the SQL code. Figure 7.14 shows the results of executing the SQL code on the right hand section. In order to execute the code, click on the green arrow icon in Figure 7.15.

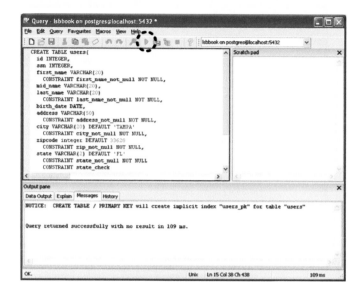

FIGURE 7.14: Executing SQL code to create a new table.

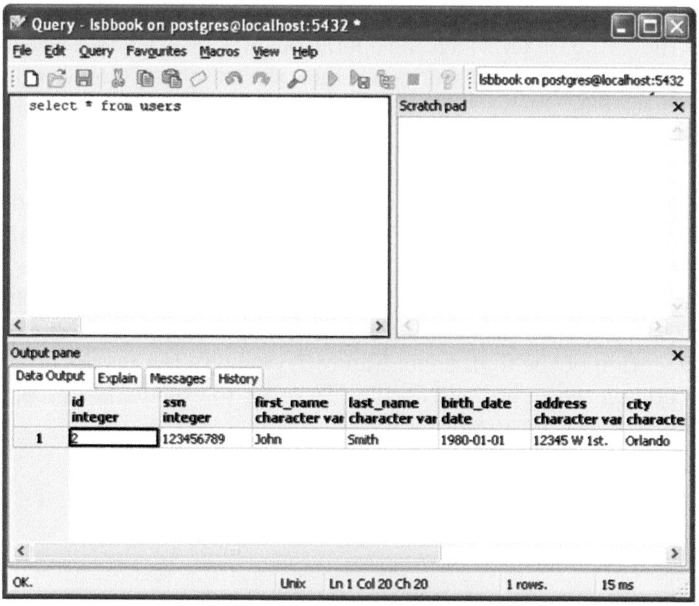

FIGURE 7.15: Executing a SQL query.

7.5 The Database and the LBIS Tracking System Example

This chapter describes how to design, create, modify, manipulate, and query a database in support of a LBIS. It shows how to perform these tasks using the command and graphical user interface of the Postgres DBMS. The database used to store all the information related to the LBIS tracking system example is used as an example.

Chapter 8

Sending and Receiving Data: Communications

8.1   Introduction

Communications is a critical aspect in most of todays' systems, and location-based information systems are not the exception. Applications (and users) need to send queries and receive responses in real-time, update data, interact with other machines and databases, etc. Today's applications are networked applications; they send and receive data over wired and wireless networks.

In order to offer a common ground for the diverse group of existing devices, Java ME defines a layered stack of libraries that are directly related to the capabilities of the devices. This chapter describes these libraries along with the most important objects and functionalities offered by the Java ME platform in support of data communications: The Connected Limited Device Configuration (CLDC), the Mobile Information Device Profile (MIDP), and the Wireless Messaging API (WMA).

8.2   The Generic Connection Framework (GCF) of the CDLC

As noted in Chapter 3, general and extensible classes are defined in the Generic Connection Framework (GCF) of the CLDC specification to support networking capabilities. The GCF, which is included in the `javax.microedition.io` package, includes the `Connection` interface, which is the foundation object for all other communication interfaces defined within the framework. The `Connector` object acts as a "factory" of connections, i.e., instead of using different abstractions for specific forms of communications, a general abstraction is defined that does not define any type of network connection. Instead, the static method `open()` of the class `javax.microedition.io.Connector` is used to create all connections using

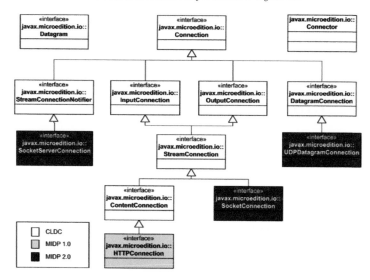

FIGURE 8.1: Hierarchical tree of inheritance of the `Connection` interface.

a string as an input parameter that describes the target. The string, which must conform to the URL format as described in RFC 2396 [21], is used as follows:

```
{scheme}:[{target}][{params}]
{scheme}://{user}{:password@}{host}{:port}{/url-path}{;parameters}
```

where *scheme* defines the communication protocol, for example, datagram, HTTP, TCP, etc.; *user* and *password* are used when the connection requires the verification of the user; *host*, *:port*, and */url-path* identify the exact address of the destination of the communication, like an IP address, a certain communication port, and a path to reach the desired resource; and *params* allow for the definition of parameters and their values in a format `";param=val"`, where `param` is the name of the parameter and `val` is the value.

Figure 8.1 shows the inheritance tree of all objects that are related to communication operations that depend directly on the `Connection` interface implemented at the CLDC level. The following list briefly describes the functionalities of all these elements [59]:

- **InputConnection:** This interface includes the `openInputStream()` and `openDataInputStream()` methods that return the `InputStream` and `DataInputStream` of the device from which data can be read. These methods allow for serial communication between the devices.

- **OutputConnection:** This interface includes the `openOutputStream()` and `openDataOutputStream()` methods that return the `OutputStream` and `DataOutputStream` of the device to which data can be written. These methods allow for serial communication between the devices.

- `StreamConnection:` This connection type combines the `InputConnection` and `OutputConnection` interfaces to implement two-way communication interfaces.

- `ContentConnection:` This connection type is an interface based on the `StreamConnection` interface and provides basic information contained in HTTP connections such as the content type, encoding, and metadata length.

- `StreamConnectionNotifier:` This interface provides the method `acceptAndOpen()` that waits for other devices, or clients, to request a stream connection. Once the request is received, it starts a new `StreamConnection` to establish the connection between the devices. The connection must be closed once the communication link is no longer needed.

- `DatagramConnection:` This interface provides several methods to handle the input/output of datagrams such as `receive` (`Datagram datagram`), `send` (`Datagram datagram`), `getMaximumLength()`, and methods to create new datagrams. The `Datagram` data type contains the data buffer and the address associated with it.

8.3   The Mobile Information Device Profile (MIDP)

The MIDP provides a second level of communication in the Java ME hierarchy with a more specific set of functionalities according to the individual capabilities and resources of the mobile devices. The protocols implemented in these libraries support the most important transport layer protocols used in the Internet, the Transport Control Protocol (TCP) and the User Datagram Protocol (UDP), which allow the devices to establish direct connections with resources available in any network.

The MIDP also includes specific support for HTTP connections but with more functionalities than the ones provided by the `ContentConnection` interface. Figure 8.1 shows the updated hierarchy of the `Connection` interface with the new objects.

The following list includes the new elements introduced in the MIDP and a short description of their function:

- `SocketConnection:` This interface, based on the `StreamConnection`, provides the functionality of a full-duplex TCP connection between two devices.

- **ServerSocketConnection**: This interface provides the functionality of a TCP server waiting for TCP connection requests from clients and creating a **StreamConnection** when the request is accepted. It is based on the **StreamConnectionNotifier**.

- **UDPDatagramConnection**: This interface provides the methods for communication using the UDP protocol. It is based on the **DatagramConnection**.

- **HTTPConnection**: This interface, based on the **ContentConnection**, provides the methods that allow HTTP connections.

Listing 8.1 shows the usage of the **Connector** class including examples with different protocols.

```
1  //HTTP Connection
2     HTTPConnection client =
3        (HTTPConnection)Connector.open("http://www.wikipedia.com/
           Topology_control");
4
5  //Socket Connection
6     SocketConnection client =
7        (SocketConnection)Connector.open("socket://131.131.2.149:5555");
8
9  //Datagram Connection
10    DatagramConnection client =
11       (DatagramConnection)Connector.open("datagram://131.131.2.149:5556"
           );
12
13 //Server Socket Connection
14    ServerSocketConnection server =
15       (ServerSocketConnection)Connector.open("socket://:2500");
```

Listing 8.1: Use of the **Connector** class to create connections with different protocols.

Please notice that when creating a server socket connection, the **Connector** class needs to define the type of protocol and the port in which the application will be listening for incoming connections.

The following sections provide specific examples that show how to use these interfaces. In particular, examples are included to show how to implement TCP and UDP clients and servers and how to use the HTTP protocol. The examples are based on a mobile device that sends data to a server periodically and a server that receives such data. Code is included to implement one TCP and one UDP client, and a server application that implements both TCP and UDP listeners. As expected, the mobile device clients will be using the libraries available in Java ME while the server applications will use the libraries available in the Java Enterprise Edition (Java EE) platform.

8.3.1 A TCP Client Example

The Transport Control Protocol (TCP) is the transport layer protocol of choice for data-oriented transactions in which the reliability of the data are more important than the delay within which the data need to be received. TCP has embedded mechanisms to guarantee the reception of the segments as well as flow and congestion control mechanisms. Acknowledgment packets and sequence numbers are included in the protocol to detect and retransmit missing segments. While TCP's flow control mechanism guarantees that a fast transmitter does not overwhelm the receiver, its congestion control mechanism dynamically changes the sender's transmission rate according to network conditions so network resources are used more efficiently. TCP is a connection-oriented protocol meaning that before sending user's data the sender and the receiver need to agree on the communication parameters to use and establish a connection. This connection establishment process is accomplished by the well-known three-way handshake procedure. More on TCP can be found in [39].

Listing 8.2 shows the implementation of the TCP client. The most important parts of the code are

- The creation of the SocketConnection sockConn using the method Connector.open(). Notice that the connection is only established once, which is controlled by the conditional statement if(sockConn == null).

- The creation of the output stream outstream. The output stream object is used to send the data through the socket.

- Formatting the information that will travel through the socket. TCP sockets receive information contained in an array of bytes.

- Sending the data using the write() method of the output stream.

- For most communication operations, it is necessary to define try-catch blocks to catch exceptions. In this example, all errors are printed on the default output device, which is usually the screen.

```
1  SocketConnection sockConn;
2
3  public void tcpSend() {
4
5        String serverName = "131.131.2.149";
6        String serverPort = "5555";
7
8        //Send data via TCP
9        if(sockConn == null){
10           try
11           {
12                sockConn = (SocketConnection) Connector.open("socket://"
                       + serverName + ":" + serverPort);
13
14           }catch(IOException ex){
15                System.out.println("Could not create connection: " +
                       ex);
16           }
17           try
```

```
18    {
19              sockConn.setSocketOption(SocketConnection.KEEPALIVE, 1);
20    }catch(IOException ex)
21    {
22              System.out.println("Could not set socket option: " +
                  ex);
23    }
24
25    try{
26
27          outstream = sockConn.openOutputStream();
28
29    }catch(IOException ex){
30          System.out.println("Could not open socket stream: " + ex)
              ;
31    }
32    }
33
34    // get the payload
35    byte[] data = getPayload().getBytes();
36
37    try
38    {
39
40          outstream.write(data);
41
42    }catch(IOException ex){
43          System.out.println("Could not write to socket stream: " + ex);
44    }
45 }
```

Listing 8.2: Example of a TCP client.

8.3.2 A UDP Client Example

Listing 8.3 shows the code corresponding to a UDP client. The following list comments on the most important statements:

- The creation of the socket **dc** using the `Connector.open()` method.

- Formating the data in an array of bytes.

- Preparing the datagram.

- Sending the data using the **send()** method of the connection class.

- Closing the socket.

- This client does not contain any individual try-catch blocks inside the code because it is defined to return any exception to the process that invoked this method. It is assumed that the invoking process will have this call inside a try-catch block.

```
1 UDPDatagramConnection dc;
2
3 public void udpSend() throws Exception {
4
```

```
 5    String serverName = "131.131.2.149";
 6    String serverPort = "5555";
 7
 8    //Send data via UDP
 9    if(dc == null){
10        dc = (UDPDatagramConnection) Connector.open("datagram://" +
              serverName +
11            ":" + serverPort);
12    }
13
14    byte[] data = getPayload().getBytes();
15
16    Datagram dg = dc.newDatagram(data, data.length);
17
18    dc.send(dg);
19
20    dc.close();
21    //You could leave the UDP socket open to avoid extra overhead
22  }
```

Listing 8.3: Example of a UDP client.

8.3.3 A Generic Server Example

This example shows the design of the `ListenerManager`, a server's general connection manager designed to handle both TCP and UDP connections running in the Sun Java Application Server. The idea is to define and control the listeners in a single class instead of having to start each service from a different class. Listing 8.4 shows the implementation of the `ListenerManager` while Listings 8.5 and 8.7 show the individual listeners for TCP and UDP connections.

The following list comments on the most important lines of the implementation of the `ListenerManager` included in Listing 8.4:

- The implementation of the `ServletContextListener` interface declares two methods: the `contextInitialized()` method and the `contextDestroyed()` method. When the Sun Java Application Server loads your server application and such application has a class implementing the `ServletContextListener` interface, the server executes the lines within the `contextInitialized()` method. Also, when the server unloads the application, it executes the `contextDestroyed()` method.

- The creation of an instance of a `TCPTestServer` accepts connection requests and starts threads; each of these threads manages the communication with a different single client. The parameter for the constructor of this class is the TCP port that the server uses to listen for incoming connections. All exceptions from the TCP server socket creation process are caught in the external try-catch statement.

- The creation of an instance of a `UDPTestServer` receives all the incoming messages from UDP clients. The parameters of this class are the UDP port that the socket uses to listen for incoming messages and a name (description) of the UDP socket. Remember that UDP is an unreliable protocol and there is no sense of connection, as in TCP.

- Given that this code runs on the server, the definition of a **Logger** object is useful to keep record of all errors that occur during the execution of the server application, instead of printing the errors on the screen.

```java
package cse.usf.edu.lbsbook.comm;

import java.io.IOException;
import java.util.logging.Level;
import java.util.logging.Logger;
import javax.servlet.ServletContextEvent;
import javax.servlet.ServletContextListener;


public class ListenerManager implements ServletContextListener{

    private static TCPTestServer theTCPServer;
    private static UDPTestReceiver theUDPReceiver;

    public ListenerManager()
    {
    }

    public void contextInitialized(ServletContextEvent sce)
    {
        try{
            theTCPServer = new TCPTestServer(31686);
            theTCPServer.start();
            try
                {
                theUDPReceiver = new UDPTestReceiver(2029, "lbsbook");
                theUDPReceiver.start();
                } catch (Exception ex) {
                    Logger.getLogger(ListenerManager.class.getName()).
                        log(Level.SEVERE, null, ex);
                }

            }catch(IOException ioex){
                Logger.getLogger(ListenerManager.class.getName()).log(
                    Level.SEVERE, null, ioex);
            }
    }

    public void contextDestroyed(ServletContextEvent sce)
    {
    if(theTCPServer != null && theTCPServer.isAlive())
        {
        theTCPServer.shutdown();
        theTCPServer = null;
        }

    if(theUDPReceiver != null && theUDPReceiver.isAlive())
        {
        theUDPReceiver.shutdown();
        theUDPReceiver = null;
        }
    }
}
```

Listing 8.4: Example of the generic server application for both TCP and UDP.

8.3.4 A TCP Server Example

A TCP listener needs two classes, the ServerSocket that waits for connection requests and the structure that contains the socket that is used to maintain the connection between client and server, which in this example is called ConnectionDump.

Listing 8.5 shows the example code of the class TCPTestServer, which instantiates the ServerSocket object, and the data structure that contains all the ConnectionDump objects. Notice that the TCPTestServer is a Thread, so it runs in the background because there is no way of knowing in advance when a user is going to ask for a connection; otherwise, this waiting process would block the process until a connection is received.

The constructor of the class creates the new ServerSocket and assigns the communication port defined in the parameter. The next line uses the method setSoTimeout() to trigger a java.net.SocketTimeoutException exception if the socket does not receive any incoming messages during the defined period of time; however, despite the exception, the socket continues to be active.

The run() method is the heart of the TCP server. The first line creates an auxiliary socket of which the only mission is to receive the new socket created by the method serv_socket.accept() when an incoming connection request is accepted. When a new connection is created, the socket is added to the dump_list data structure that holds all open connections. The finally block contains a piece of code that is always executed in case that an exception occurs, which in this example nullifies the temporary socket and terminates the cycle.

```
1  public class TCPTestServer extends Thread {
2
3      private final int port;
4      private ServerSocket serv_socket;
5      private LinkedList<ConnectionDump> dump_list;
6
7
8      public TCPTestServer(int port) throws IOException {
9          this.port = port;
10         this.serv_socket = new ServerSocket(port);
11         this.serv_socket.setSoTimeout(10*1000);// set blocking timeout
                for accept() call
12         this.dump_list = new LinkedList<ConnectionDump>();
13     }
14
15     public void run(){
16         Socket tmp_socket = new Socket();
17
18         while (this.serv_socket != null){
19             try{
20
21                 tmp_socket = this.serv_socket.accept(); // this blocks
                        for 10 seconds.
22
23                 if(tmp_socket.isConnected()){
24
25                     this.dump_list.add(new ConnectionDump(tmp_socket));
26
27                 }
```

```
28
29              }catch(IOException _){}
30
31              finally{
32                  tmp_socket = null;
33              }
34          }
35      }
36
37  public void shutdown(){...}
38
39  protected class ConnectionDump extends Thread{...}
40 }
```

Listing 8.5: Example of the listener class for TCP connections.

Inside the `TCPTestServer` the code includes the definition of the protected class called `ConnectionDump`. Listing 8.6 presents the main operations on this object.

Each `ConnectionDump` object has a `Socket`, an `InputStream`, and a boolean value `active` that keeps the main cycle running. In the constructor method, the socket is received as a parameter and is assigned to the local variable `sock`. After that, the input stream is obtained for that socket to allow the reception of incoming data from the sender device.

In the `run()` method, the main cycle runs while the value of the boolean variable is true. On each instance of the cycle, a new array of bytes is declared, which receives the data from the method `read()` of the `instream` variable. This example prints the data on the default output device just to show that it is now accessible for use in the application. If an exception is generated during this process, the cycle stops and calls the `shutdown()` method. The implementation of this method is not defined in this example.

```
1  protected class ConnectionDump extends Thread{
2
3      Socket sock;
4      InputStream instream;
5      boolean active;
6
7      public ConnectionDump(Socket sock){
8          this.sock = sock;
9          if (sock.isConnected()){
10             try{
11                 this.instream = sock.getInputStream();
12             }catch(IOException ioex){
13                 Logger.getLogger(ConnectionDump.class.getName()).log
                        (Level.SEVERE, null, ioex);
14             }
15         }
16         this.active = true;
17         this.start();
18     }
19
20     public void run(){
21         while(active){
22             try{
23                 byte[] b = new byte[124];
24                 this.instream.read(b); // bytes read from the stream
25                 Logger.getLogger(ConnectionDump.class.getName()).log(
```

```
                        Level.INFO, "TCPTestServer - incoming string:" +
                        new String(b));
26              }catch(IOException ioex){
27                  Logger.getLogger(ConnectionDump.class.getName()).log(
                        Level.SEVERE, null, ioex);
28                  this.shutdown();
29              }
30          }
31      }
32
33      public void shutdown() {...}
34 }
```

Listing 8.6: Example of the class that models individual TCP connections once accepted.

8.3.5 A UDP Server Example

The User Datagram Protocol (UDP) protocol is the transport layer protocol of choice for real-time applications such as voice and video-based applications in which the timeliness is more important than the reliability of the data. Real-time applications do not suffer much if a few segments are lost in their way to the destination; however, these packets need to reach the receiver within a certain period of time to maintain the real-time nature of the transmission. Contrary to the TCP protocol, UDP is connectionless, unreliable (no acknowledgment packets and sequence numbers), and does not include any flow and congestion control mechanism.

Because of its connectionless nature, the UDP protocol does not need any special structure to maintain a connection with any other device; UDP can receive segments from any source as long as those packets are addressed to the receiver in the defined communication port. This allows to have a simpler structure than the one needed for TCP connections.

Listing 8.7 presents the main method of the UDP server class, the UDPTestReceiver. This class uses a DatagramSocket and a temporary DatagramPacket that receives the message obtained by the receive() method of the datagram socket. In addition, this class also defines a temporary array of bytes that is only useful for defining the size of the longest possible payload of a datagram for this application, a boolean variable that keeps the main cycle running, and a string variable that represents the name of the server. This last one is useful in case there is more than one UDP socket running.

In the construction method, the new datagram socket is created using the communication port defined in the parameter of the function and a socket timeout is defined to notify the lack of activity from the clients. In addition, the name of the UDP server is received as a parameter.

In the run() method, the cycle keeps running while the boolean value of the variable active is true. Inside the cycle the method receive() blocks the thread until a new message arrives or when the timeout expires. Once the message is received, the payload is dumped into a string variable which makes the data accessible to the application. When the cycle ends, the socket is closed and nullified. The methods `isActive()` and `setActive()` return and assign values to the `active` variable, respectively.

```
1  public class UDPTestReceiver extends Thread
2  {
3      DatagramSocket myUDPReceiver;
4      boolean active = true;
5
6      byte[] recBytes = new byte[150];
7      DatagramPacket receptorPacket = new DatagramPacket(recBytes,150);
8
9      private String name;
10
11     public UDPTestReceiver(int port, String name) throws Exception
12     {
13         myUDPReceiver = new DatagramSocket(port);
14         myUDPReceiver.setSoTimeout(10*1000);
15         this.name = name;
16     }
17
18
19     public void run()
20     {
21        while(active)
22        {
23            try
24            {
25
26                myUDPReceiver.receive(receptorPacket);
27
28                String receivedData = new String(receptorPacket.getData
                       ());
29                Logger.getLogger(UDPTestReceiver.class.getName()).log(
                       Level.INFO, name+"UDP Received Data->"+receivedData)
                       ;
30            }
31            catch(SocketTimeoutException e)
32            {
33
34            }
35            catch(Exception e)
36            {
37                Logger.getLogger(UDPTestReceiver.class.getName()).log(
                       Level.SEVERE, null, e);
38            }
39        }
40
41        myUDPReceiver.close();
42        myUDPReceiver = null;
43     }
44
45     public boolean isActive() {...}
46
47     public void setActive(boolean active) {...}
48  }
```

Listing 8.7: Example of the server application for UDP.

8.3.6 A HyperText Transfer Protocol (HTTP) Example

The HTTP protocol is an application layer protocol that allows sharing hypermedia documents based on the client-server model. The main idea behind this protocol is to create a lightweight information system platform for accessing and managing the mixture of plain text, images, video, sound, and links to other hypermedia files that are now common in the Web. The only assumption that HTTP does is that it works over a reliable transport layer protocol, like TCP.

The protocol works based on a request-reply model. The most common case of use of HTTP is when the client sends a GET message requesting a certain element, and then it is delivered by the server. The most common example of this case is the use of an Internet browser in which each Web page is requested via GET messages. Another option is the POST message that allows the user to upload content into the HTTP server, like when filling an HTML form. The following example focus on the request of information.

The example included in this section (Listing 8.8) shows a very basic Web browser that obtains the context of plain HTML or text files from HTTP servers. The code, which is derived from an example found in `http://developers.sun.com/mobility/midp/articles/network/`, uses an HTTP connection to allow the application to download the content of a file, if the size of the file is available. The URL address is obtained from a text field in the GUI of the application; for example, `http://www.page.com/index.htm`. The code includes two methods: the `commandAction()` method that is invoked when the *ok* option is clicked on the cellular phone and the `getSimplePage()` method that creates the connection and obtains the content of the remote file. This last method is executed inside a thread in order to liberate the `commandAction()` method from waiting until the communication is finished.

In a HTTP connection, there is more information about the nature of the data being sent, like the size of the file or the type of content (MIME type), so the user can interpret it more accurately. In this example, the size of the file is obtained and the code reads that exact number of bytes from the server. If the size is not known, it reads data until the server closes the communication.

```
1  public class BasicBrowser extends MIDlet implements CommandListener {
2
3      private boolean midletPaused = false;
4
5      private Command exitCommand;
6      private Command okCommand;
7      private Form form;
8      private StringItem stringItem;
9      private TextField textField;
10
11     /**
12      * The HelloMIDlet constructor.
13      */
14     public HelloMIDlet() {
15     }
16
17  public void commandAction(Command command, Displayable displayable) {
```

```
18   if (displayable == form) {
19     if (command == exitCommand) {
20        exitMIDlet();
21     } else if (command == okCommand) {
22        try {
23           Thread t = new Thread(){
24              public void run(){
25                 try{
26                    getSimplePage(textField.getString());
27                 }catch(IOException ex){
28                    ex.printStackTrace();
29                 }
30              }
31           };
32           t.start();
33        } catch(Exception e) {
34           e.printStackTrace();
35        }
36     }
37  }
38 }
39
40 private void getSimplePage(String url) throws IOException {
41
42    StringBuffer buffer = new StringBuffer();
43    InputStream the_input_stream;
44    HttpConnection the_connection;
45
46    try {
47       int i = 0;
48       long tam = 0 ;
49       int a_byte = 0;
50       the_connection = (HttpConnection)Connector.open(url);
51       the_input_stream = the_connection.openInputStream();
52       tam = the_connection.getLength();
53
54       if( tam != -1) {
55          for(i = 0 ; i < tam ; i++ )
56             if((a_byte = the_input_stream.read()) != -1) {
57                buffer.append((char) a_byte);
58             }
59             stringItem.setText("\n The code of the webpage is:\n" + buffer
                   .toString());
60       } else {
61          stringItem.setText("\n Sorry but the entered URL is not
                   supported.");
62       }
63
64    } finally {
65       the_input_stream.close();
66       the_connection.close();
67    }
68 }
```

Listing 8.8: Example of an HTTP connection.

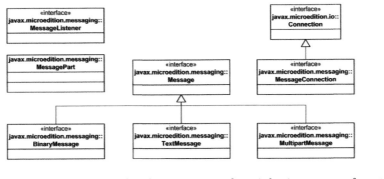

FIGURE 8.2: Hierarchical tree of inheritance of the `javax.microedition.messaging` package.

8.4 The Wireless Messaging API (WMA)

This section describes the Wireless Messaging API, which provides the messaging capability to mobile devices using the cellular network. This API, developed by the JSR 205 expert group, includes two widely used messaging services: the Short Messaging Service (SMS), which exchanges text-only messages, and the Multimedia Messaging Service (MMS), which extends the capabilities of the SMS messages by allowing embedded multimedia content in the message.

The WMA is based on the Generic Connection Framework specified in the CLDC, as it can be seen from Figure 8.2. The following list contains the main components of the messaging API, as defined in the `javax.microedition.messaging` package:

- **MessageConnection:** Interface based on the basic `Connection` interface. It creates the connection between two devices and allows the transmission of a message.

- **Message:** This interface is designed to model a basic message object. The WMA defines three types of messages:

  - **BynaryMessage:** This interface models a message with a binary array of data.

  - **TextMessage:** This interface models a text message.

  - **MultipartMessage:** This interface defines a message that can also carry multimedia content, or a MMS message.

- **MessagePart:** This class models a `MultipartMessage` object. This object contains the definition of the message content according to the

MIME standard and the data related to the content, either binary or text.

- **MessageListener:** This interface defines a mechanism to notify that a new message has arrived. The main idea behind this element is to acknowledge the independence between the notification of the arrival of a message and the actual reception of the message that includes bringing the information to the device in order to avoid blocking the **MessageListener** from other notifications.

Addressing in the messaging domain is different compared to the one used in TCP or UDP because it directly depends on the type of message. For example, the destination address in a SMS messages is identified by the number registered in the SIM card of the cellular phone, also known as the *Mobile Subscriber Integrated Services Digital Network Number (MSISDN)*. In the case of MMS messages, the destination address can assume multiple formats: an e-mail address, phone number, IPv4, or IPv6 IP addresses.

Listing 8.9 shows how to define addresses for SMS and MMS in WMA. In both cases, it is important to identify the communication port that will receive the message. In the case of SMS, a numeric port is required. It is recommended to use values from the 49152–65635 range because smaller values might have been reserved for other applications. In the case of MMS, the application identifier is a string of up to 32 characters that uniquely identifies your application.

```
1  String appID = getAppProperty("MmsAppID");
2  String address = "mms://+555123456:" + appID;
3  int sms_port = getAppProperty("SmsAppCommPort");
4
5  //SMS message
6  (MessageConnection)Connector.open ("sms://+555123456"+sms_port);
7
8  //MMS message
9  (MessageConnection)Connector.open (address);
```

Listing 8.9: Example of how to define addresses for SMS and MMS in WMA.

The **getAppProperty()** method obtains values from parameters of the applications, which are defined in the JAD file of the application. The following example shows how to define the application parameters:

```
SmsAppCommPort: 51234
MmsAppID: wma_example_app
```

8.4.1 A Multimedia Messaging Service Example

Listing 8.10 shows an application that sends MMS messages. The application opens a new connection before sending every message to avoid having an idle thread running when no messages are being sent. The sender sends a single-part multipart message as a basic example, which contains the location information of the mobile device. The code assumes that there is a method called `getLocationInfo()` that obtains the new location of the device from a location provider object.

The first step is to create the connection. It is assumed that the client opens a server connection that allows the device to send messages to different users. Then, a new multi-part message is created, specifying the address of the receiver, which in this case is an e-mail address. After that, the location of the node is included in the message. Finally, the message is sent and the connection is closed.

```
1  final public void sendMessage(
2    Thread th = new Thread() {
3    public void run(){
4           MessageConnection connection=null;
5           String appID = getAppProperty("MmsAppID");
6           try
7           {
8             String address="mms://lbsbook@mail.usf.edu";
9
10            //Establishing connection
11            connection=(MessageConnection)Connector.open("mms://:"+appID
                 );
12
13            //Create a multipart message
14            MultipartMessage message=(MultipartMessage) connection.
                 newMessage(MessageConnection.MULTIPART_MESSAGE, address)
                 ;
15
16            message.setSubject("LOCATIONUPDATE");
17
18            MessagePart locationPart=new MessagePart(getLocationInfo().
                 getBytes(),
19                 "text/html", "id:2", "text", null);
20
21            message.addMessagePart(locationPart);
22
23            connection.send(message);
24
25          }catch(Exception e){ //Handle exception}
26
27          if(connection!=null)
28          {
29              try {
30                  connection.close();
31                  }catch(Exception e){//Handle exception}
32          }
33      }
34    };
35    th.start();
36  }
```

Listing 8.10: Example of the construction and sending process of a MMS message.

The synchronous version of the receiver and more information about the WMA can be found in http://developers.sun.com/mobility/midp/ articles/wma2/.

8.5 Communications and the LBIS Tracking System Example

This chapter describes the different communication options available in Java ME to send and receive data over a network. It describes how to use the reliable TCP protocol, the unreliable UDP protocol, the HTTP application layer protocol, and the messaging service in a general way, i.e., to send and receive any type of data. In the case of the LBIS tracking system example, clients will use the UDP protocol to send the GPS fixes to the server. The following sections explain two projects: A Java ME project that obtains the mobile device's locations and sends them to the server via UDP, and a server application that receives the messages sent by the mobile device.

8.5.1 A Java ME Tracking MIDlet Using UDP

The first project is created using NetBeans in the following way. Open Net-Beans, go to the menu *File → NewProject* and on the left side of the dialog box (Categories list), click on *Java ME*. After this, click on *Mobile Application* in the Projects list. Click *Next* and in the following dialog box, and write down the project's name and location. In this example, the project's name and location are both `CommChapter`. Uncheck the *Create Hello MIDlet* option and click *Next*. In the next dialog box, select as Emulator Platform *Sun Java Wireless Toolkit 2.5.2 for CLDC*. Select *CLDC-1.1* in the Device Configuration option and *MIDP-2.1* in the Device Profile option. Click *Finish*.

Now create the package `cse.usf.edu.lbsbook.comm`. In order to do this, right click over the name of the project (`CommChapter`) in the Projects Window (in the upper left side of the screen, below the toolbox, if you don't see it, click on the menu *Window → Projects*). Create a new MIDlet inside the `cse.usf.edu.lbsbook.comm` package called `LocationUDPExample`. To create the MIDlet, right click on the package's name in the Projects Window and in the menu that is shown, click *New → MIDlet*. Now copy the code shown in Listing 8.11.

```
1  package cse.usf.edu.lbsbook.comm;
2
3  import javax.microedition.midlet.*;
4  import javax.microedition.lcdui.*;
5
6  //Packages for Location API
7  import javax.microedition.location.LocationException;
8  import javax.microedition.location.Coordinates;
9  import javax.microedition.location.Criteria;
10 import javax.microedition.location.LocationProvider;
11
12 //Packages for Communication
13 import java.io.OutputStream;
14 import javax.microedition.io.Connector;
15 import javax.microedition.io.Datagram;
```

```
16  import javax.microedition.io.SocketConnection;
17  import javax.microedition.io.UDPDatagramConnection;
18
19  public class LocationUDPExample extends MIDlet implements
        CommandListener {
20      private boolean midletPaused = false;
21      private boolean midletStopped = false;
22
23      private LocationProvider lp;
24      private Thread myThread;
25
26      private UDPDatagramConnection datagramConnection;
27      protected SocketConnection sockConn;
28      protected OutputStream outstream;
29
30      String serv_address = "127.0.0.1";
31      String serv_port = "2029";
32
33      private Command exitCommand;
34      private Command okCommand;
35      private Display display;
36      private TextField textField;
37      private Form form;
38
39      public LocationUDPExample(){
40          form = new Form("Send Location info via UDP");
41          String t = "This is a Test on Sending locations via UDP";
42          form.append(t);
43          display = getDisplay();
44          okCommand = new Command("Send", Command.SCREEN, 1);
45          exitCommand = new Command("Exit", Command.SCREEN, 2);
46
47          textField = new TextField("Information Sent","",30,TextField.
                ANY);
48
49          form.addCommand(okCommand);
50          form.addCommand(exitCommand);
51          form.setCommandListener(this);
52
53          form.append(textField);
54      }
55
56      private void initialize(){
57        // Include these lines inside the initialize method
58        Criteria cr = new Criteria();
59        cr.setHorizontalAccuracy(30);
60        try {
61          lp = LocationProvider.getInstance(cr);
62        }
63        catch (Exception ex)
64        {
65            java.lang.System.out.println("Error getting Location Provider
                : " + ex);
66        }
67      }
68
69      public void commandAction(Command command, Displayable displayable
            ){
70          if(displayable == form){
71              if(command == exitCommand){
72                  destroyApp(false);
73                  notifyDestroyed();
74              }
75              else if(command == okCommand){
76              myThread = new Thread(){public void run(){
77                  try {
78                      updateLocation();
```

```
79                        }
80                        catch (Exception ex){
81
82                        }
83                 }};
84              myThread.start();}
85          }
86      }
87
88      public Display getDisplay () {
89          return Display.getDisplay(this);
90      }
91
92      public void exitMIDlet() {
93        destroyApp(true);
94        notifyDestroyed();
95      }
96
97      public void startApp() {
98          if (midletPaused) {
99             resumeMIDlet ();
100         } else {
101            initialize ();
102            startMIDlet ();
103         }
104         midletPaused = false;
105     }
106
107     public void resumeMIDlet(){
108         midletPaused = false;
109     }
110     public void startMIDlet(){
111         display.setCurrent(form);
112     }
113     public void pauseApp() {
114         midletPaused = true;
115     }
116
117     public void destroyApp(boolean unconditional) {
118         midletStopped = true;
119     }
120
121     public void udpLocationSend(String location) throws Exception {
122         //Sending the location data using UDP
123         if(datagramConnection == null){
124             datagramConnection = (UDPDatagramConnection) Connector.
                    open("datagram://" + serv_address + ":" + serv_port);
125         }
126         byte [] data = location.getBytes();
127         Datagram dg = datagramConnection.newDatagram(data, data.length
                );
128
129         datagramConnection.send(dg);
130         datagramConnection.close();
131         datagramConnection = null;
132     }
133
134     public void updateLocation() throws Exception
135     {
136        try {
137            javax.microedition.location.Location l = lp.getLocation(30)
                  ;
138            Coordinates c = l.getQualifiedCoordinates();
139            if(c != null)
140            {
141             try
142             {
```

```
143        String sentString = ""+c.getLatitude()+"-"+c.
               getLongitude()+"-"+ System.currentTimeMillis()+"-"
               ;
144        udpLocationSend(sentString);
145        textField.setString(sentString);
146      }
147      catch (Exception ex)
148      {
149      }
150    }
151  }
152  catch (LocationException ex)
153  {
154      ex.printStackTrace();
155  } catch (InterruptedException ex)
156  {
157      ex.printStackTrace();
158  }
159  }
160 }
```

Listing 8.11: A tracking MIDLet example using the UDP protocols

When the user selects the *Send* command, the application obtains the last location from the `LocationProvider` and sends it along with the current time of the device in the `updateLocation()` method. The information sent to the server is also shown in a textfield. In order to test this, run the emulator and load a location file by clicking in the menu *MIDlet → External* events and then in the window that appears, go to the Location tab and click on the Browser button. Select the `xml` file with the locations and click *Open*. Then in the location tab click the green play button. Now every time the user presses the *Send* command (lower right side of the emulator's phone screen), the location sent should appear in the text field. This code assumes that the UDP server is in the same machine (listening in the local address 127.0.0.1) and uses the UDP port 2029.

8.5.2 Server-Side Application

This section explains the server side project to be deployed in the Sun Java Application Server. It is assumed that the reader has installed the Sun Java Application Server and registered it with the NetBeans IDE. Specific information on how to perform these tasks can be found in Appendix A.

The first step is to create an application to be deployed in the Sun Java Application Server. To do this, open NetBeans and go to the menu *File → NewProject*. In the dialog box, on the left side of the dialog box (Categories list), click on *Java Web* and after this, click on *Web Application* in the Projects list. Click *Next* and in the dialog box write the name of the project as `ServerExample`, choose the registered Sun Java Application Server to deploy the project, and click *Next* and *Finish*.

Create a new package called `cse.usf.edu.lbsbook.comm` and create in this package three classes with the code shown in Listings 8.4, 8.5, and 8.7.

Please remember that the code shown in Listing 8.5 is complete when you write the protected class shown in Listing 8.6.

The last step involves the registration of the `ListenerManager` class in the application's descriptor. To do this, double-click on the `web.xml` file in your NetBeans' project (it should be under Configuration files in the Project's tree). Then on the General Tab, look for Web Application Listeners and click on the *Add* button. Look for the `ListenerManager` class and click *Ok*. Click now on the *Save* button in the toolbox to save the changes to the `xml` file.

A Web listener is needed because in these types of projects there are no `main()` methods. When the Web application loads/unloads, the `ServletContextListener` interface allows you to initialize and start the TCP and UDP server classes. At this point, build and deploy your application.

Now, run your Java ME client and start sending locations to the server. If everything works as expected, you should see the incoming data in the server's log, which is visible in NetBeans in the output window or inside the server console (in your Web browser).

Chapter 9

Java ME Web Services

9.1   Introduction

This chapter provides an overview of Web services and describes the Java Platform Micro Edition (Java ME) Web Services API (WSA) to support Web services in resource-constrained devices, such as cellular telephones, PDAs, and the like.

9.2   An Overview of Web Services

Web services were created to allow any networked client find applications located anywhere in the Internet and use them as if they were locally installed applications, regardless of the platform and architecture where these applications were created and deployed. In order for this concept to be a reality, several rules were put in place so that a client application located in Tampa could actually access and use a Web service in a machine located in Spain. These rules pertain to the following four critical aspects:

1. **Web service application development and deployment:** Application developers need to develop and deploy their applications (services) in such a way that they can be accessed and used by all clients. The nature of the Java language and the use of the Java Platform Enterprise Edition (Java EE) for the development and deployment of applications address this aspect.

2. **Describing Web services:** This second aspect defines how remote services are described, which is included in the *Web Services Definition Language (WSDL)* specification 1.1. For example, a WSDL file describes the service itself, what it does, how to use its methods, and where it can be found in the Internet.

3. **Finding Web services:** The third aspect has to do with finding services over the Internet. This aspect was solved by the creation of the *Universal*

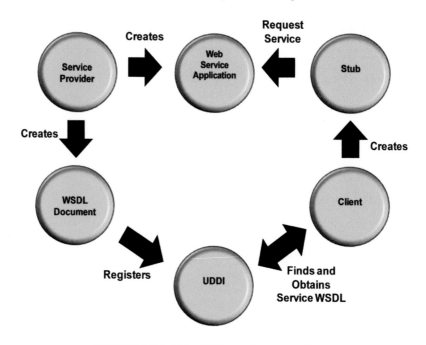

FIGURE 9.1: The Web services paradigm.

Description, Discovery, and Integration (UDDI) registry, a centralized registry used by developers to post their services and by clients to find them.

4. **Connecting and using Web services:** This fourth aspect includes the use of specific protocols and markup languages to connect clients to Web services providers and exchange information. Among them are the *HTTP* protocol, the *Simple Object Access Protocol (SOAP)*, the *Remote Procedure Call (RPC)*, and the *eXtensible Markup Language (XML)*.

Figure 9.1 shows the steps and entities involved in the creation and use of Web services. The entire process begins when the service provider or developer who designs the Web service application creates the XML-based WSDL document, registers the Web service in the UDDI registry, and finally makes the service available in its Web server. The UDDI registry, as explained before, is a repository of WSDL files that clients use to find Web services. The client goes to the registry and downloads the WSDL file of the Web service that provides the functionality of interest. The developer of the client uses the WSDL file to generate a stub that contains the code needed by the client application to make calls to the remote Web service. This code, which is added to the client application, handles all messaging details between the client and the server as well as the response to the client application. The stub is a very important piece of the application because it hides all communication details from the programmer. For example, the stub sets up an HTTP connection with the remote server and sends a remote procedure call over the HTTP connection using the Simple Object Access Protocol (SOAP). Normally, the stub code is automatically generated by a stub generator.

Two of the most important features of Web services is that 1) they use standard protocols and mechanisms that are currently in use in the Internet, and 2) the fact that the stub code hides from the programmer all the complexities of connections and data transmissions between client and server. On the down side, Web services introduce several inefficiencies since XML and SOAP require respectable processing power and memory and extra bandwidth due to excessive protocol overhead. This is particularly important for resource-constrained devices sending data over bandwidth-limited communications channels.

9.3 The Web Services API (WSA)

Given the success of Web services in powerful, wired computers, the JSR 172 expert group also developed an API to support Web services on resource-constrained devices using the Java Platform Micro Edition (Java ME) based on the Connected Device Configuration (CDC) and the Connected Limited Device Configuration (CLDC 1.0 and CLDC 1.1).

The WSA includes two optional packages to the Java ME platform. The first one is the *Java API for XML-based RPC (JAX-RPC)* package, which allows mobile devices to access remote XML-based Web services. JAX-RPC is a Java API for interacting with SOAP-based Web services. This package, which is a subset of the JAX-RPC specification for the Java SE platform, is a remote procedure call implementation in the Java programming language.

The second package, *Java API for XML Processing (JAXP)*, adds XML parsing capabilities to the platform. Given the widely use of XML-structured data for clients to interact with servers over the Internet, it makes sense to include an optional package that provides this parsing capability for all applications instead of adding the same code in each application. This package is a subset of the JSR 063 Java API for XML Processing (JAXP) that meets platform size and performance requirements.

The entire process and components of the WSA are shown in Figure 9.2. A MIDlet running on top of the MIDP and CLDC makes use of the JAXP API to handle XML documents. The same application uses the JAX-RPC API to access a Web service over the network utilizing the stub and the *Service Provider Interface (SPI)* of the runtime. It is worth mentioning that the application only interacts with the stub; the stub interacts with the SPI and runtime on behalf of the application.

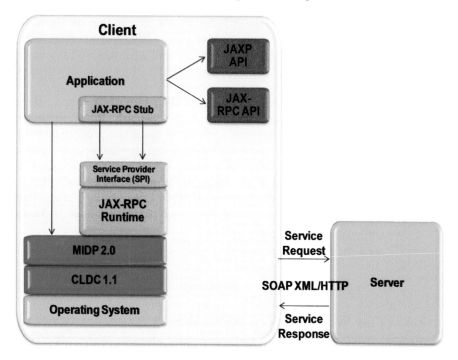

FIGURE 9.2: The entire process and components of the Web services API.

9.3.1 The JAX-RPC Package

This API includes the `javax.microedition.xml.rpc`, `javax.xml.rpc`, `javax.xml.namespace`, and `javax.rmi` subset of packages, which contain all the classes and interfaces that make up the stub, SPI, and runtime.

The stub makes requests to the runtime and receives service responses through the service provider interface. Once the stub is generated from the WSDL description of the service, the application has to instantiate an instance of the stub by creating a new instance of the stub class generated by the stub generator. This instance of the stub is then used to perform the following functions:

- Set the properties of the stub to invoke an RPC. The stub calls the `setProperty()` method of the `Operation` class to set property values for an RPC invocation. The stub is also responsible to make appropriate format conversions of the values. The following property values are defined:

  - `Stub.ENDPOINT_ADDRESS_PROPERTY`: Address of the service endpoint.
  - `Stub.PASSWORD_PROPERTY`: Password for authentication purposes.

- Stub.USERNAME_PROPERTY: Username for authentication purposes.

- Stub.SESSION_MAINTAIN_PROPERTY: Indicates if a client wants to participate in a session with a service endpoint.

- Operation.SOAPACTION_URI_PROPERTY: Uniform Resource Identifier (URI) to use for HTTP SOAPAction header

- Create objects describing the input and return parameters. The classes Type, Element, and ComplexType are used by the stub to describe the input and return parameter of an operation with the runtime.

- Create an Operation object representing an invocation of an RPC. The stub uses the Operation class to describe an RPC invocation to the runtime.

- Encode the input parameter values. The parameters being passed to the runtime are encoded in an array of Object.

- Invoke the RPC. The invoke method is utilized by the stub to execute an RPC. The Object array contains the parameter values of the call.

- Decode the return parameter values. The return values received in the Object array are decoded and passed back to the calling application.

The runtime contains all the functionality needed to transfer data to and from the server in a completely transparent manner. In other words, the method and its arguments are encoded and sent, and then received and decoded by the stub and the runtime on behalf of the application. Normally, the MIDlet and the stub reside in the device's memory, but the runtime, all JSR 172 components, and Java ME platform components, are embedded in the device.

9.3.2 The JAXP Package

This API includes the javax.xml.parsers, org.xmal.sax.helpers, and org.xmal.sax subset of packages that are used to parse XML documents.

9.4 A Web Service Example

This section describes how to develop and deploy a simple Web service that makes simple calculations. The idea is to develop a client application for the mobile device that will ask the user to enter two parameters and the type of operation to perform. The parameters are integer numbers and the valid operations are sum, subtraction, multiplication, and division. Upon receiving the inputs from the user, the client application will invoke a Web service that resides in a specific server and pass the input parameters and operation. The Web service will perform the calculation and send the result back to the client, which will be shown in the screen.

The Web service development process is very much automated in Net-Beans. The calculator Web service example described above will be developed in two parts. First, the Web service will be created; then, the MIDlet.

9.4.1 Web Service Creation

The first step is to create a new project in NetBeans. Open NetBeans and click on *File→NewProject...* From the *Categories* list, select *Web*, and from the *Projects* list, select *Web Application*. Write in the name of your project, and click *Next* and *Finish*. The second step is to create a package for the project. For this, select the project just created from the list of projects in the Project's tab and right click on it. Select *New→Java Package*, write in the name and click *Finish*. Once the project and package are created, the third step is to create the Web service. For this, select the project, right click on it, and select *New→Web Service*. Write in the name of the Web service, select the package just created, and click *Finish*. In our example, the name of the project is LbsBook and the name given to the Web service is ServerCalculatorService. After that, the default configuration page appears to define the operations of the Web service. In our example, these operations are sum, subtraction, multiplication, and division, and the input and output parameters are of type integer. Click on the *Add Operation* button to define the operations and parameters. At the end, you should have a screen like the one shown in Figure 9.3.

Once the operations and parameters are set, you can click on the *Source* button to leave the design screen and see the code that NetBeans automatically creates for you. As you can see from Figure 9.4, NetBeans creates almost all the code for you; further, it indicates where you need to include the additional code needed to implement your functions (sum, subtract, multiply, divide). The figure shows only the code needed to implement the sum function.

Once the code of your functions is included, save the changes, and right click on the service to *Clean and Build* your project and then repeat it to *Undeploy and Deploy* it. As part of these processes, NetBeans creates the WSDL file automatically for you. Listing 9.1 shows part of the WSDL file of the calculator Web service. The WSDL file is automatically saved in the http://IPadd:port/ProjectName/WebServiceName?wsdl link, where IPadd is the IP address of the machine, port is the port number defined for Glassfish, ProjectName of your project, and WebServiceName is the name of your Web service. The entire path can be found in NetBeans by right clicking on the service and choosing Properties. In our case, the entire path is http://localhost:12796/LbsBook/ServerCalculatorService?wsdl.

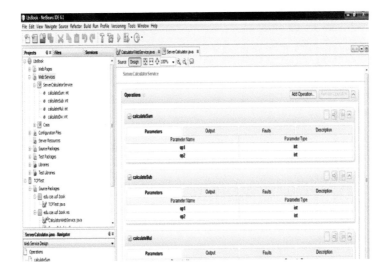

FIGURE 9.3: Definition of Web service operations and parameters.

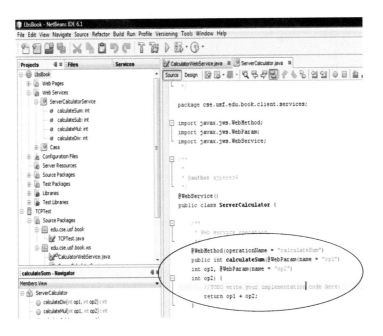

FIGURE 9.4: The Web service implementation code.

This ends the Web service creation process. Now, it is the time to develop the MIDlet that will be installed and run in the mobile device, the client of the Web service calculator.

```
1  <?xml version="1.0" encoding="UTF-8" ?>
2  <!-- Published by JAX-WS RI at http://jax-ws.dev.java.net. RI's
       version is
3  JAX-WS RI 2.1.3.1-hudson-417-SNAPSHOT.
4  -->
5  <!-- Generated by JAX-WS RI at http://jax-ws.dev.java.net. RI's
       version is
6       JAX-WS RI 2.1.3.1-hudson-417-SNAPSHOT.
7  -->
8  <definitions xmlns:wsu="http://docs.oasis-open.org/wss/2004/01/oasis
       -200401-wss-
9  wssecurity-utility-1.0.xsd" xmlns:soap="http://schemas.xmlsoap.org/
       wsdl/soap/"
10 xmlns:tns="http://services.client.book.edu.usf.cse/" xmlns:xsd="http
       ://www.w3.org/2001/XMLSchema"
11 xmlns="http://schemas.xmlsoap.org/wsdl/" targetNamespace="http://
       services.client.book.edu.usf.cse/"
12 name="ServerCalculatorService">
13 - <types>
14 - <xsd:schema>
15 <xsd:import namespace="http://services.client.book.edu.usf.cse/"
16 schemaLocation="http://localhost:12796/LbsBook/
       ServerCalculatorService?xsd=1" />
17 </xsd:schema>
18 </types>
19 - <message name="calculateSum">
20 <part name="parameters" element="tns:calculateSum" />
21 </message>
22 - <message name="calculateSumResponse">
23 <part name="parameters" element="tns:calculateSumResponse" />
24 </message>
25 - <message name="calculateSub">
26 <part name="parameters" element="tns:calculateSub" />
27 </message>
28 . . .
```

Listing 9.1: The WSDL file of the calculator Web service.

9.4.2 MIDlet Creation

In order to create the MIDlet, create a new project using the *Mobility* option and the *MIDP Application* option in NetBeans. Write in the name and click *Finish*. As before, create a new Java package for the project just created. To do this, right click on the project name, select *New Java Package*, write in its name and click *Finish*. Now, select *Project* and right click on it to select *New Java ME Web Service Client*. In the same screen, provide the URL of the WSDL document that NetBeans created for you when you finished creating the server part (see last section). Based on this WSDL document, NetBeans maps the WSDL definitions to Java representation and the XML data types to Java types to create a skeleton application for you. The skeleton code, along with the additional code that needs to be included so that the MIDlet gets the data (operands) and command from the user and sends them to the service using the stub interface, is included in Listing 9.2.

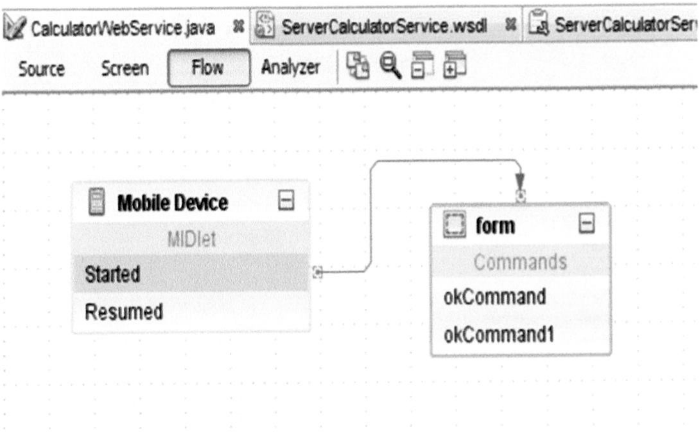

FIGURE 9.5: Design of the calculator MIDlet.

At this time, you should see a screen like the one shown in Figure 9.5, which shows the *Flow* screen in NetBeans to design the flow of tasks for the calculator example. As it can be seen, upon starting the MIDlet, it goes directly to show the form to the user, and the form has two commands, one that implements the Add operation and one for the Subtract operation. The form is shown in Figure 9.6. Once the MIDlet is ready and run, it should look like the one shown in Figure 9.7.

```java
package edu.cse.usf.book.ws;

import java.rmi.RemoteException;
import javax.microedition.midlet.*;
import javax.microedition.lcdui.*;

public class CalculatorWebService extends MIDlet implements
        CommandListener {

    private boolean midletPaused = false;

    //<editor-fold defaultstate="collapsed" desc=" Generated Fields ">
    private Form form;
    private TextField textField;
    private TextField textField1;
    private TextField textField2;
    private Command okCommand;
    private Command okCommand1;
    //</editor-fold>

    /**
     * The CalculatorWebService constructor.
     */
    public CalculatorWebService() {
    }

    //<editor-fold defaultstate="collapsed" desc=" Generated Methods
        ">
    //</editor-fold>
```

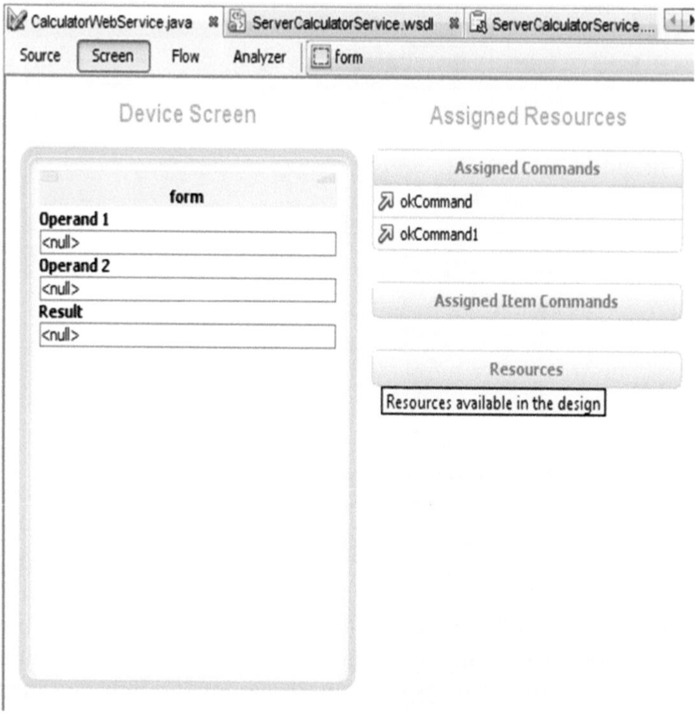

FIGURE 9.6: Design of the calculator form.

```
29   //<editor−fold defaultstate="collapsed" desc=" Generated Method:
          initialize ">
30   /**
31    * Initilizes the application.
32    * It is called only once when the MIDlet is started. The method
          is called before the <code>startMIDlet</code> method.
33    */
34   private void initialize () {
35       // write pre−initialize user code here
36
37       // write post−initialize user code here
38   }
39   //</editor−fold>
40
41   //<editor−fold defaultstate="collapsed" desc=" Generated Method:
          startMIDlet ">
42   /**
43    * Performs an action assigned to the Mobile Device − MIDlet
          Started point.
44    */
45   public void startMIDlet () {
46       // write pre−action user code here
47       switchDisplayable (null , getForm ());
48       // write post−action user code here
49   }
50   //</editor−fold>
51
```

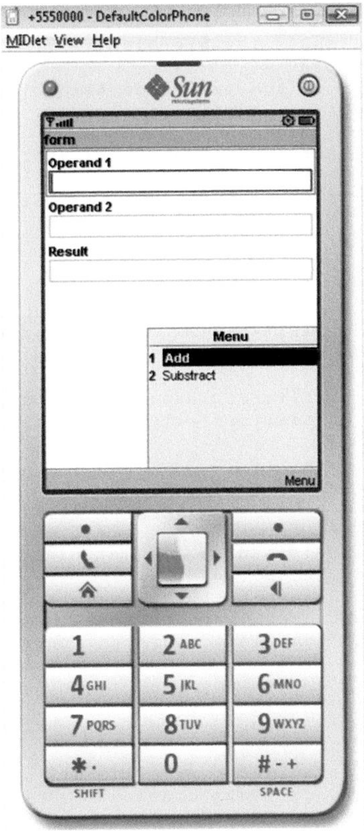

FIGURE 9.7: The calculator MIDlet.

```
52  //<editor−fold defaultstate=”collapsed” desc=” Generated Method:
       resumeMIDlet ”>
53  /**
54   * Performs an action assigned to the Mobile Device − MIDlet
       Resumed point.
55   */
56  public void resumeMIDlet () {
57      // write pre−action user code here
58
59      // write post−action user code here
60  }
61  //</ editor−fold>
62
63  //<editor−fold defaultstate=”collapsed” desc=” Generated Method:
       switchDisplayable ”>
64  /**
65   * Switches a current displayable in a display. The <code>display
       </code> instance is taken from <code>getDisplay</code> method
       . This method is used by all actions in the design for
       switching displayable.
66   * @param alert the Alert which is temporarily set to the display;
       if <code>null</code >, then <code>nextDisplayable</code> is
       set immediately
67   * @param nextDisplayable the Displayable to be set
```

```
68          */
69          public void switchDisplayable(Alert alert, Displayable
                nextDisplayable) {
70              // write pre-switch user code here
71              Display display = getDisplay();
72              if (alert == null) {
73                  display.setCurrent(nextDisplayable);
74              } else {
75                  display.setCurrent(alert, nextDisplayable);
76              }
77              // write post-switch user code here
78          }
79          //</editor-fold>
80
81          //<editor-fold defaultstate="collapsed" desc=" Generated Getter:
                form ">
82          /**
83           * Returns an initiliazed instance of form component.
84           * @return the initialized component instance
85           */
86          public Form getForm() {
87              if (form == null) {
88                  // write pre-init user code here
89                  form = new Form("form", new Item[] { getTextField(),
                        getTextField1(), getTextField2() });
90                  form.addCommand(getOkCommand());
91                  form.addCommand(getOkCommand1());
92                  form.setCommandListener(this);
93                  // write post-init user code here
94              }
95              return form;
96          }
97          //</editor-fold>
98
99          //<editor-fold defaultstate="collapsed" desc=" Generated Method:
                commandAction for Displayables ">
100         /**
101          * Called by a system to indicated that a command has been invoked
                on a particular displayable.
102          * @param command the Command that was invoked
103          * @param displayable the Displayable where the command was
                invoked
104          */
105         public void commandAction(Command command, Displayable displayable
                ) {
106             // write pre-action user code here
107             if (displayable == form) {
108                 if (command == okCommand) {
109                     // write pre-action user code here
110
111                     // write post-action user code here
112
113                     Runnable theInvoker = new Runnable(){
114                         public void run() {
115                             int op1 = Integer.parseInt(textField.
                                getString());
116                             int op2 = Integer.parseInt(textField1.
                                getString());
117                             ServerCalculatorService_Stub
                                remoteCalculator = new
                                ServerCalculatorService_Stub();
118                             int op3;
119                             try
120                             {
121                                 op3 = remoteCalculator.calculateSum(
                                    op1, op2);
122                                 textField2.setString(""+op3);
```

```
123                                    }
124                                    catch (RemoteException ex) {
125                                        ex.printStackTrace();
126                                        textField2.setString(ex.getMessage());
127                                    }
128                                }
129                            };
130
131                            Thread t = new Thread(theInvoker);
132                            t.start();
133                    } else if (command == okCommand1) {
134                        // write pre-action user code here
135
136                        // write post-action user code here
137                    }
138                }
139            // write post-action user code here
140        }
141    //</editor-fold>
142
143    //<editor-fold defaultstate="collapsed" desc=" Generated Getter:
             textField ">
144        /**
145         * Returns an initiliazed instance of textField component.
146         * @return the initialized component instance
147         */
148        public TextField getTextField() {
149            if (textField == null) {
150                // write pre-init user code here
151                textField = new TextField("Operand 1", null, 32, TextField
                    .ANY);
152                // write post-init user code here
153            }
154            return textField;
155        }
156    //</editor-fold>
157
158    //<editor-fold defaultstate="collapsed" desc=" Generated Getter:
             textField1 ">
159        /**
160         * Returns an initiliazed instance of textField1 component.
161         * @return the initialized component instance
162         */
163        public TextField getTextField1() {
164            if (textField1 == null) {
165                // write pre-init user code here
166                textField1 = new TextField("Operand 2", null, 32,
                    TextField.ANY);
167                // write post-init user code here
168            }
169            return textField1;
170        }
171    //</editor-fold>
172
173    //<editor-fold defaultstate="collapsed" desc=" Generated Getter:
             textField2 ">
174        /**
175         * Returns an initiliazed instance of textField2 component.
176         * @return the initialized component instance
177         */
178        public TextField getTextField2() {
179            if (textField2 == null) {
180                // write pre-init user code here
181                textField2 = new TextField("Result", null, 32, TextField.
                    ANY);
182                // write post-init user code here
183            }
```

```
184          return textField2;
185      }
186      //</editor-fold>
187
188      //<editor-fold defaultstate="collapsed" desc=" Generated Getter:
             okCommand ">
189      /**
190       * Returns an initiliazed instance of okCommand component.
191       * @return the initialized component instance
192       */
193      public Command getOkCommand() {
194          if (okCommand == null) {
195              // write pre-init user code here
196              okCommand = new Command("Add", Command.OK, 0);
197              // write post-init user code here
198          }
199          return okCommand;
200      }
201      //</editor-fold>
202
203      //<editor-fold defaultstate="collapsed" desc=" Generated Getter:
             okCommand1 ">
204      /**
205       * Returns an initiliazed instance of okCommand1 component.
206       * @return the initialized component instance
207       */
208      public Command getOkCommand1() {
209          if (okCommand1 == null) {
210              // write pre-init user code here
211              okCommand1 = new Command("Substract", Command.OK, 0);
212              // write post-init user code here
213          }
214          return okCommand1;
215      }
216      //</editor-fold>
217
218      /**
219       * Returns a display instance.
220       * @return the display instance.
221       */
222      public Display getDisplay () {
223          return Display.getDisplay(this);
224      }
225
226      /**
227       * Exits MIDlet.
228       */
229      public void exitMIDlet() {
230          switchDisplayable (null, null);
231          destroyApp(true);
232          notifyDestroyed();
233      }
234
235      /**
236       * Called when MIDlet is started.
237       * Checks whether the MIDlet have been already started and
             initialize/starts or resumes the MIDlet.
238       */
239      public void startApp() {
240          if (midletPaused) {
241              resumeMIDlet ();
242          } else {
243              initialize ();
244              startMIDlet ();
245          }
246          midletPaused = false;
247      }
```

```
248
249    /**
250     * Called when MIDlet is paused.
251     */
252    public void pauseApp() {
253        midletPaused = true;
254    }
255
256    /**
257     * Called to signal the MIDlet to terminate.
258     * @param unconditional if true, then the MIDlet has to be
             unconditionally terminated and all resources has to be
             released.
259     */
260    public void destroyApp(boolean unconditional) {
261    }
262
263 }
```

Listing 9.2: The entire Web service client.

As said before, the stub is automatically generated by a stub generator, which in this case is included in NetBeans. This stub handles the communication part with the server hiding all these details from the program developer. Listing 9.3 shows the stub for the calculator example.

```
1  import javax.xml.rpc.JAXRPCException;
2  import javax.xml.namespace.QName;
3  import javax.microedition.xml.rpc.Operation;
4  import javax.microedition.xml.rpc.Type;
5  import javax.microedition.xml.rpc.ComplexType;
6  import javax.microedition.xml.rpc.Element;
7
8  public class ServerCalculatorService_Stub implements
       ServerCalculatorService, javax.xml.rpc.Stub {
9
10     private String[] _propertyNames;
11     private Object[] _propertyValues;
12
13     public ServerCalculatorService_Stub() {
14         _propertyNames = new String[] { ENDPOINT_ADDRESS_PROPERTY };
15         _propertyValues = new Object[] { "http://localhost:12796/
             LbsBook/ServerCalculatorService" };
16     }
17
18     public void _setProperty( String name, Object value ) {
19         int size = _propertyNames.length;
20         for (int i = 0; i < size; ++i) {
21             if( _propertyNames[i].equals( name )) {
22                 _propertyValues[i] = value;
23                 return;
24             }
25         }
26         String[] newPropNames = new String[size + 1];
27         System.arraycopy(_propertyNames, 0, newPropNames, 0, size);
28         _propertyNames = newPropNames;
29         Object[] newPropValues = new Object[size + 1];
30         System.arraycopy(_propertyValues, 0, newPropValues, 0, size);
31         _propertyValues = newPropValues;
32
33         _propertyNames[size] = name;
34         _propertyValues[size] = value;
35     }
36
```

```
37    public Object _getProperty(String name) {
38        for (int i = 0; i < _propertyNames.length; ++i) {
39            if (_propertyNames[i].equals(name)) {
40                return _propertyValues[i];
41            }
42        }
43        if (ENDPOINT_ADDRESS_PROPERTY.equals(name) ||
              USERNAME_PROPERTY.equals(name) || PASSWORD_PROPERTY.equals
              (name)) {
44            return null;
45        }
46        if (SESSION_MAINTAIN_PROPERTY.equals(name)) {
47            return new Boolean(false);
48        }
49        throw new JAXRPCException("Stub does not recognize property: "
              + name);
50    }
51
52    protected void _prepOperation(Operation op) {
53        for (int i = 0; i < _propertyNames.length; ++i) {
54            op.setProperty(_propertyNames[i], _propertyValues[i].
                  toString());
55        }
56    }
57
58    public int calculateMul(int op1, int op2) throws java.rmi.
          RemoteException {
59        Object inputObject[] = new Object[] {
60            new Integer(op1),
61            new Integer(op2)
62        };
63
64        Operation op = Operation.newInstance(
              _qname_operation_calculateMul, _type_calculateMul,
              _type_calculateMulResponse );
65        _prepOperation( op );
66        op.setProperty( Operation.SOAPACTION_URI_PROPERTY, "" );
67        Object resultObj;
68        try {
69            resultObj = op.invoke( inputObject );
70        } catch( JAXRPCException e ) {
71            Throwable cause = e.getLinkedCause();
72            if( cause instanceof java.rmi.RemoteException ) {
73                throw (java.rmi.RemoteException) cause;
74            }
75            throw e;
76        }
77
78        return ((Integer )((Object[]) resultObj)[0]).intValue();
79    }
80
81    public int calculateSub(int op1, int op2) throws java.rmi.
          RemoteException {
82        Object inputObject[] = new Object[] {
83            new Integer(op1),
84            new Integer(op2)
85        };
86
87        Operation op = Operation.newInstance(
              _qname_operation_calculateSub, _type_calculateSub,
              _type_calculateSubResponse );
88        _prepOperation( op );
89        op.setProperty( Operation.SOAPACTION_URI_PROPERTY, "" );
90        Object resultObj;
91        try {
92            resultObj = op.invoke( inputObject );
93        } catch( JAXRPCException e ) {
```

```
 94                Throwable cause = e.getLinkedCause();
 95                if( cause instanceof java.rmi.RemoteException ) {
 96                    throw (java.rmi.RemoteException) cause;
 97                }
 98                throw e;
 99            }
100
101            return ((Integer )((Object[])resultObj)[0]).intValue();
102        }
103
104        public int calculateDiv(int op1, int op2) throws java.rmi.
               RemoteException {
105            Object inputObject[] = new Object[] {
106                new Integer(op1),
107                new Integer(op2)
108            };
109
110            Operation op = Operation.newInstance(
                   _qname_operation_calculateDiv, _type_calculateDiv,
                   _type_calculateDivResponse );
111            _prepOperation( op );
112            op.setProperty( Operation.SOAPACTION_URI_PROPERTY , "" );
113            Object resultObj;
114            try {
115                resultObj = op.invoke( inputObject );
116            } catch( JAXRPCException e ) {
117                Throwable cause = e.getLinkedCause();
118                if( cause instanceof java.rmi.RemoteException ) {
119                    throw (java.rmi.RemoteException) cause;
120                }
121                throw e;
122            }
123
124            return ((Integer )((Object[])resultObj)[0]).intValue();
125        }
126
127        public int calculateSum(int op1, int op2) throws java.rmi.
               RemoteException {
128            Object inputObject[] = new Object[] {
129                new Integer(op1),
130                new Integer(op2)
131            };
132
133            Operation op = Operation.newInstance(
                   _qname_operation_calculateSum, _type_calculateSum,
                   _type_calculateSumResponse );
134            _prepOperation( op );
135            op.setProperty( Operation.SOAPACTION_URI_PROPERTY , "" );
136            Object resultObj;
137            try {
138                resultObj = op.invoke( inputObject );
139            } catch( JAXRPCException e ) {
140                Throwable cause = e.getLinkedCause();
141                if( cause instanceof java.rmi.RemoteException ) {
142                    throw (java.rmi.RemoteException) cause;
143                }
144                throw e;
145            }
146
147            return ((Integer )((Object[])resultObj)[0]).intValue();
148        }
149
150        protected static final QName _qname_operation_calculateDiv = new
               QName( "http://services.client.book.edu.usf.cse/", "
               calculateDiv" );
151        protected static final QName _qname_operation_calculateSub = new
```

```
        QName ( "http://services.client.book.edu.usf.cse/", "
        calculateSub" );
152 protected static final QName _qname_operation_calculateSum = new
        QName ( "http://services.client.book.edu.usf.cse/", "
        calculateSum" );
153 protected static final QName _qname_operation_calculateMul = new
        QName ( "http://services.client.book.edu.usf.cse/", "
        calculateMul" );
154 protected static final QName _qname_calculateMulResponse = new
        QName ( "http://services.client.book.edu.usf.cse/", "
        calculateMulResponse" );
155 protected static final QName _qname_calculateDiv = new QName ( "
        http://services.client.book.edu.usf.cse/", "calculateDiv" );
156 protected static final QName _qname_calculateSub = new QName ( "
        http://services.client.book.edu.usf.cse/", "calculateSub" );
157 protected static final QName _qname_calculateSum = new QName ( "
        http://services.client.book.edu.usf.cse/", "calculateSum" );
158 protected static final QName _qname_calculateDivResponse = new
        QName ( "http://services.client.book.edu.usf.cse/", "
        calculateDivResponse" );
159 protected static final QName _qname_calculateMul = new QName ( "
        http://services.client.book.edu.usf.cse/", "calculateMul" );
160 protected static final QName _qname_calculateSubResponse = new
        QName ( "http://services.client.book.edu.usf.cse/", "
        calculateSubResponse" );
161 protected static final QName _qname_calculateSumResponse = new
        QName ( "http://services.client.book.edu.usf.cse/", "
        calculateSumResponse" );
162 protected static final Element _type_calculateDivResponse;
163 protected static final Element _type_calculateSum;
164 protected static final Element _type_calculateMul;
165 protected static final Element _type_calculateSubResponse;
166 protected static final Element _type_calculateDiv;
167 protected static final Element _type_calculateSub;
168 protected static final Element _type_calculateSumResponse;
169 protected static final Element _type_calculateMulResponse;
170
171 static {
172     _type_calculateMulResponse = new Element (
            _qname_calculateMulResponse , _complexType ( new Element [] {
173     new Element ( new QName ( "", "return" ), Type.INT )}), 1,
            1, false );
174     _type_calculateDiv = new Element ( _qname_calculateDiv ,
            _complexType ( new Element [] {
175     new Element ( new QName ( "", "op1" ), Type.INT ),
176     new Element ( new QName ( "", "op2" ), Type.INT )}), 1, 1,
            false );
177     _type_calculateSub = new Element ( _qname_calculateSub ,
            _complexType ( new Element [] {
178     new Element ( new QName ( "", "op1" ), Type.INT ),
179     new Element ( new QName ( "", "op2" ), Type.INT )}), 1, 1,
            false );
180     _type_calculateSum = new Element ( _qname_calculateSum ,
            _complexType ( new Element [] {
181     new Element ( new QName ( "", "op1" ), Type.INT ),
182     new Element ( new QName ( "", "op2" ), Type.INT )}), 1, 1,
            false );
183     _type_calculateDivResponse = new Element (
            _qname_calculateDivResponse , _complexType ( new Element [] {
184     new Element ( new QName ( "", "return" ), Type.INT )}), 1,
            1, false );
185     _type_calculateMul = new Element ( _qname_calculateMul ,
            _complexType ( new Element [] {
186     new Element ( new QName ( "", "op1" ), Type.INT ),
187     new Element ( new QName ( "", "op2" ), Type.INT )}), 1, 1,
            false );
```

```
188        _type_calculateSubResponse = new Element(
               _qname_calculateSubResponse , _complexType( new Element [] {
189            new Element( new QName( "", "return" ), Type.INT )}), 1,
               1, false );
190        _type_calculateSumResponse = new Element(
               _qname_calculateSumResponse , _complexType( new Element [] {
191            new Element( new QName( "", "return" ), Type.INT )}), 1,
               1, false );
192    }
193
194    private static ComplexType _complexType( Element [] elements ) {
195        ComplexType result = new ComplexType ();
196        result.elements = elements;
197        return result;
198    }
199 }
```

Listing 9.3: The stub of the Web service calculator example.

9.5 Web Services and the LBIS Tracking System Example

Web services are not very related to our LBIS tracking system example application. In fact, they are not used at all in the system. Web services are included in the book because they are very popular and important in many business applications, which are now extending the services to the very large population of mobile phone users.

Chapter 10

System Administration

10.1 Introduction

The LBIS tracking system example described in Chapter 1 includes a "main control station" connected to the Internet to administer the system and visualize the users' positions in real time. This chapter explains how to implement system administration functions such as including new users and devices in the system, deleting them, etc., using popular Web 2.0 tools. The chapter begins with a brief introduction of the World Wide Web (WWW) that explains the evolution of Web pages, which at the same time leads to the Google Web Toolkit (GWT). The following sections show the development process to add administrative functions using GWT. As an example, they show how to create (add) a device in the system from the main control station. This process implies software development for the client (i.e., the control station) and the server. Chapter 11 builds on top of this chapter showing how to visualize the data in the main control station using the same Web tools.

10.1.1 The World Wide Web (WWW)

The WWW, or Web, is a system of interlinked documents distributed throughout the Internet to share information in an automated manner. The Web has become one of the most successful applications in the Internet, and it has evolved from static hyperlinked documents to interactive applications, providing e-commerce, mapping, multimedia, and social networking services, among others. The Web is made of the following components:

- **Web page:** A document that consists of Web objects.

- **Web object:** A file that is available in a Web server. Each Web object is addressable by a single Uniform Resource Locator (URL).

- **Web server:** A computer that maintains Web objects and utilizes the HTTP protocol to transfer Web objects to Web clients.

- **Web client:** Any computer program that utilizes the HTTP protocol to obtain or provide Web objects. Web clients can be Web browsers but can also be any computer program that utilizes the HTTP protocol.

- **HyperText Transfer Protocol (HTTP)**: A request/response application layer protocol that interconnects Web clients to Web serves. HTTP is a stateless protocol, meaning that there is no concept of session in the protocol. The current version of the protocol is described in RFC 2616 [29].

- **HyperText Markup Language (HTML):** Defines the markup language for Web pages. A Web browser utilizes the HTML contained in a Web page to render the page and show it in the screen. HTML code can embed client-side scripting code that the Web browser executes when it loads the Web page. Normally, this code is JavaScript.

The Web has evolved considerably over the past years. The initial Web was specified by the components described above, and Web development was performed by simply writing Web pages using the HTML language. Web browsers for the first time presented HTML-based information in a very nice and simple way. However, the information presented in Web browsers was static and when electronic commerce became popular, it was clear that a more dynamic approach to generate content was needed. Then, technologies like PHP (Hypertext Preprocessor), Java Servlet Pages (JSP), Active Server Pages (ASP), and some others became popular. These new languages allowed the creation of scripting procedures that a Web server would utilize to generate pages upon HTTP requests, therefore supporting dynamic page generation. At the same time, software companies began producing technology to execute code on the client side (Web browsers). As a result of this effort, client-side scripting languages were developed. Examples of these languages and frameworks are JavaScript, Flash, and Java applets. Consequently, current Website pages are made of static and dynamic code in both client and server sides. One popular framework to create this class of interactive Web applications is the Google Web Toolkit, which will be utilized in this chapter to create system administration functions for our LBIS tracking system example.

10.2 Google Web Toolkit

The Google Web Toolkit (GWT) is a framework to create dynamic and interactive Web applications. Applications developed using the toolkit have the following major characteristics:

- Code is written using the Java programming language.

- Parts of a GWT application execute in the Web client and other parts in the Web server.

- The GWT compiles the Web client code written in Java to JavaScript.

GWT Development Process

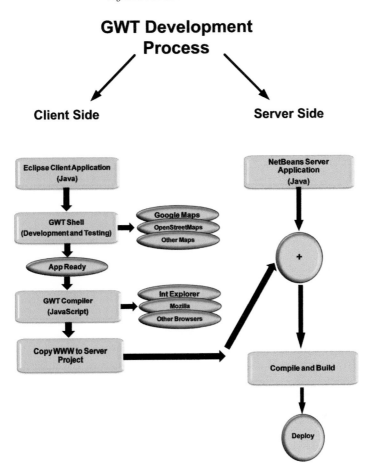

FIGURE 10.1: The GWT development process.

- The GWT code that executes in the Web client runs in JavaScript.

- GWT generates code that is compatible with most popular Web browsers.

A GWT-based application consists of client-side code and the server-side code. The client-side code is developed utilizing the Eclipse IDE and the GWT. The server-side code is developed in NetBeans. When both client and server-side codes are completed and tested, the client-side code is compiled using the GWT and copied to the server-side application so it can be deployed in the Internet. Figure 10.1 shows the GWT development process, which is the basis for the development of both system administration functions and data visualization. The following sections explains how to use this framework to implement a "create device" system administration function.

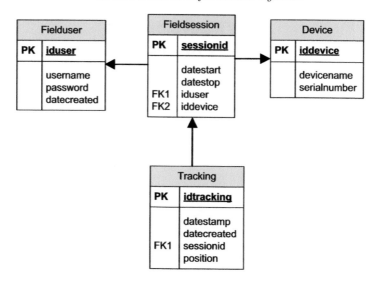

FIGURE 10.2: The database model.

In order to implement the "create device" function, a database needs to be designed and implemented. Figure 10.2 shows the relational database model utilized to support this application, which consists of the following tables:

- **Fielduser:** Stores information about the users of the system.

- **Device:** Stores information about the devices of the system.

- **Fieldsession:** Stores information about the sessions that are active/inactive in the system.

- **Tracking:** Stores information about a device's position in a field session.

10.3   Creating System Administration Functions

This part of the book guides the reader through the process shown in Figure 10.1 to create a system administration function. The example consists of the code that will run in the control station and the server of the system to add new devices into the database of the system. The implementation of similar administrative functions such as deleting and updating devices, creating, updating, and deleting users, etc., are left to the reader, as they can be implemented following the same procedure.

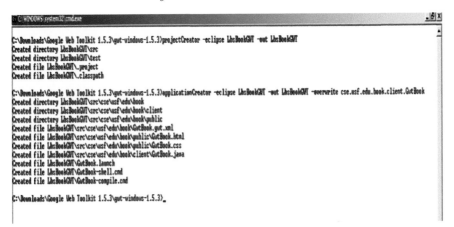

FIGURE 10.3: Creating a project for Eclipse using the GWT command line tool.

10.3.1 Client-Side Code

The goal of the client-side code is to create a GUI to enter the data of the new device using the Web browser in the main control station and submit the data to the server so the new information is stored. As shown in Figure 10.1, the client-side part of the application is developed using the Eclipse IDE. Therefore, the first step for the development of a client-side GUI is to create a project for Eclipse using GWT. This is accomplished by opening a Windows command line window in the directory where GWT 1.5.3 is installed and writing:

```
projectCreator —eclipse LbsBookGWT —out LbsBookGWT

applicationCreator —eclipse LbsBookGWT —out LbsBookGWT cse.usf.edu.
    book.client.GwtBook
```

The option -eclipse tells the applicationCreator tool that the files are going to be generated for Eclipse. LbsBookGWT is the project name. The -out option tells the tool to place the generated files in the LbsBookGWT directory. Finally, the cse.usf.edu.book.client.GwtBook is the name of the package that will contain all the standard classes of the application. Figure 10.3 shows the execution and results of the command.

Once the project is created, the next step is to import it into the Eclipse's workspace. In order to do this, open the Eclipse IDE, select your workspace location and click on the menu *File→Import*. In the next screen, select the root directory of the project (the path to the directory created by the applicationCreator). Make sure the checkbox that says *Copy projects into workspace* is checked. This option copies the project's directory into your cur-

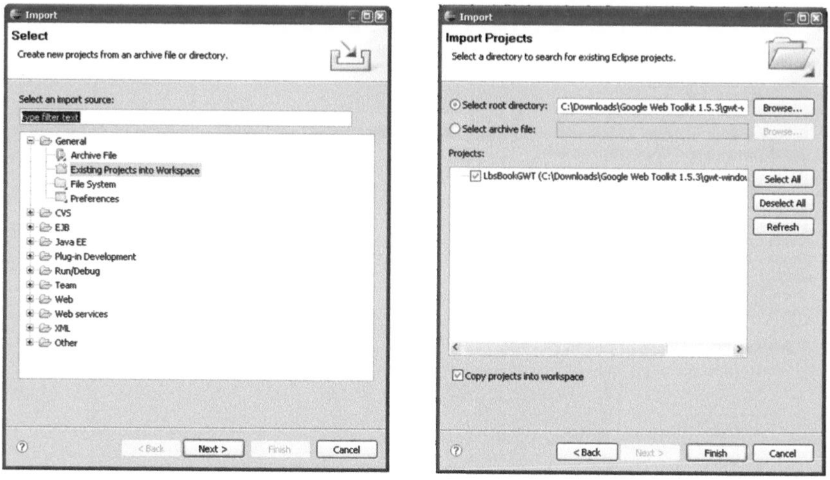

(a) Import window.

(b) Selecting the project to import.

FIGURE 10.4: Importing a GWT project in Eclipse.

rent workspace. All the changes to the project will be done over this copy. Figure 10.4 shows how to import the project. To check that the project was successfully imported, go to the main menu and select *Run→Run*. If everything is configured correctly you should see the screen shown in Figure 10.5. This application provides the skeleton code for you to develop your own application. At this point, the GWT application runs as a Java application that can be modified, debugged, executed, and when ready, compiled into JavaScript code.

Let us explore the source code of the skeleton application. If you look at the Eclipse's IDE, the upper left corner should show the Package Explorer, which shows the project's tree structure. This tree is created automatically by Eclipse and should look similar to the one shown in Figure 10.6.

There are two packages shown under the `src` subtree. These are

- `cse.usf.edu.book`: This package contains, under its public folder, all the Web pages and images (static content) that will be utilized by the project. These are local resources. The package also contains the `GwtBook.gwt.xml` file, which has information that the GWT shell and compiler utilize to link libraries and define the main entry point (the class that executes first) of the application. This file will be explored later.

- `cse.usf.edu.book.client`: This package contains the Java source code of the client-side application. In this package, the file `GwtBook.java`

FIGURE 10.5: Testing the GWT application.

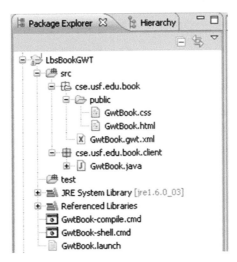

FIGURE 10.6: Eclipse's Package Explorer tree for the GWT project.

serves as the entry point of the application and it is the file that the toolkit executes when the GWT shell runs.

Let us explore the content of the `GwtBook.gwt.xml` file first, which is shown in Listing 10.1. This file is like the application descriptor, as it contains information that the GWT shell and compiler utilize to link libraries and start the application. Line 4 tells the GWT to import all the defaults classes of the GWT framework. Line 9 selects the stylesheet that the application will utilize for the look and feel of the GUI components. Line 17 tells the GWT shell what is the main class of the application, which is the file that executes when the browser loads the Web page. `GwtBook.gwt.xml` contains references to extra modules for the application. We will come back to this file when we add Google Maps in the next chapter.

```
1  <module>
2
3      <!-- Inherit the core Web Toolkit stuff.
          -->
4      <inherits name='com.google.gwt.user.User'/>
5
6      <!-- Inherit the default GWT style sheet.  You can change
          -->
7      <!-- the theme of your GWT application by uncommenting
          -->
8      <!-- any one of the following lines.
          -->
9      <inherits name='com.google.gwt.user.theme.standard.Standard'/>
10     <!-- <inherits name='com.google.gwt.user.theme.chrome.Chrome'/>
          -->
11     <!-- <inherits name='com.google.gwt.user.theme.dark.Dark'/>
          -->
12
13     <!-- Other module inherits
          -->
14
15
16     <!-- Specify the app entry point class.
          -->
17     <entry-point class='cse.usf.edu.book.client.GwtBook'/>
18
19     <!-- Specify the application specific style sheet.
          -->
20     <stylesheet src='GwtBook.css' />
21
22 </module>
```

Listing 10.1: The `GwtBook.gwt.xml` page.

Listing 10.2 shows the content of the `GwtBook.html` file, which can be accessed by double-clicking on the `cse.usf.edu.book\public` folder. This file contains the code that loads the GWT module in the browser and invokes the application (i.e., our `GwtBook` application), which is included in line 22 of the listing. All the final JavaScript code for the GWT client application is contained in several of these `.js` files. The `cse.usf.edu.book.GwtBook. nocache.js` file shown in the listing is the one that is loaded first and depending on the browser, it will invoke other `.js` files. GWT keeps browser compatibility by automatically compiling JavaScript code for the most popular Web browsers (See Figure 10.1). The good thing is that this is done automatically and the developer does not have to worry about browser compatibility issues.

```
1  <!DOCTYPE HTML PUBLIC "-//W3C//DTD HTML 4.01 Transitional//EN">
2  <!-- The HTML 4.01 Transitional DOCTYPE declaration-->
3  <!-- above set at the top of the file will set      -->
4  <!-- the browser's rendering engine into            -->
5  <!-- "Quirks Mode". Replacing this declaration       -->
6  <!-- with a "Standards Mode" doctype is supported,  -->
7  <!-- but may lead to some differences in layout.     -->
8
9  <html>
10   <head>
11     <meta http-equiv="content-type" content="text/html; charset=UTF
           -8">
12     <!--                                            -->
13     <!-- Any title is fine                          -->
14     <!--                                            -->
15     <title>GwtBook</title>
16
17     <!--                                            -->
18     <!-- This script loads your compiled module.    -->
19     <!-- If you add any GWT meta tags, they must     -->
20     <!-- be added before this line.                 -->
21     <!--                                            -->
22     <script type="text/javascript" language="javascript" src="cse.usf.
           edu.book.GwtBook.nocache.js"></script>
23   </head>
24
25   <!--                                              -->
26   <!-- The body can have arbitrary html, or         -->
27   <!-- you can leave the body empty if you want      -->
28   <!-- to create a completely dynamic UI.           -->
29   <!--                                              -->
30   <body>
31
32     <!-- OPTIONAL: include this if you want history support -->
33     <iframe src="javascript:" id="__gwt_historyFrame" tabIndex='-1'
             style="position:absolute;width:0;height:0;border:0"></iframe>
34
35   </body>
36 </html>
```

Listing 10.2: The `GwtBook.html` file.

Listing 10.3 shows the content of the `GwtBook.css` file, which defines the style to be utilized.

```
1  /** Add css rules here for your application. */
2
3  /** Example rules used by the template application (remove for your
       app) */
4  .pc-template-btn {
5    display: block;
6    font-size: 16pt
7  }
8
9  #pc-template-img {
10   margin-top: 20px;
11 }
```

Listing 10.3: The `GwtBook.css` file.

The final file to be explored is the GwtBook.java file located under the cse.usf.edu.book.client package, which implements the client-side application in the Java programming language. This code, which is shown in Listing 10.4, implements the application shown in Figure 10.5.

It is important to mention again that the files containing Listings 10.1, 10.2, 10.3, and 10.4 are created automatically by Eclipse when the project is created. The importance of these files is that they serve as skeletons to build your own application. In this section, it will be shown how to use (modify) these skeleton files to develop a system administration application to create or add devices in the LBIS tracking system. This application requires a window that will ask the system administrator for the new device information, a button to submit the information, and the code to actually submit the information to the server. This will be accomplished by modifying or replacing the onModuleLoad() method included in Listing 10.4 with the code that will show the new window requesting the new device information. As it will be shown later, this new code is the one included in Listing 10.10, which implements the window shown in Figure 10.7.

```
1  package cse.usf.edu.book.client;
2
3  import com.google.gwt.core.client.EntryPoint;
4  import com.google.gwt.user.client.ui.Button;
5  import com.google.gwt.user.client.ui.ClickListener;
6  import com.google.gwt.user.client.ui.DialogBox;
7  import com.google.gwt.user.client.ui.Image;
8  import com.google.gwt.user.client.ui.RootPanel;
9  import com.google.gwt.user.client.ui.VerticalPanel;
10 import com.google.gwt.user.client.ui.Widget;
11
12 public class GwtBook implements EntryPoint {
13   public void onModuleLoad() {
14     Image img = new Image("http://code.google.com/webtoolkit/logo-185
          x175.png");
15     Button button = new Button("Click me");
16     // We can add style names
17     button.addStyleName("pc-template-btn");
18     // or we can set an id on a specific element for styling
19     img.getElement().setId("pc-template-img");
20     VerticalPanel vPanel = new VerticalPanel();
21     vPanel.setWidth("100%");
22     vPanel.setHorizontalAlignment(VerticalPanel.ALIGN_CENTER);
23     vPanel.add(img);
24     vPanel.add(button);
25     // Add image and button to the RootPanel
26     RootPanel.get().add(vPanel);
27     // Create the dialog box
28     final DialogBox dialogBox = new DialogBox();
29     dialogBox.setText("Welcome to GWT!");
30     dialogBox.setAnimationEnabled(true);
31     Button closeButton = new Button("close");
32     VerticalPanel dialogVPanel = new VerticalPanel();
33     dialogVPanel.setWidth("100%");
34     dialogVPanel.setHorizontalAlignment(VerticalPanel.ALIGN_CENTER);
35     dialogVPanel.add(closeButton);
36
37     closeButton.addClickListener(new ClickListener(){
38       public void onClick(Widget sender)
39       {
```

```
40      dialogBox.hide();
41    }});
42    // Set the contents of the Widget
43    dialogBox.setWidget(dialogVPanel);
44    button.addClickListener(new ClickListener(){
45      public void onClick(Widget sender)
46      {
47        dialogBox.center();
48        dialogBox.show();
49      }});
50  }
51 }
```

Listing 10.4: The `GwtBook.java` file.

Listing 10.4 also shows how the event-based GWT code works and executes as a response to an event. In the listing, there are two examples of events added to buttons. For example, line 15 shows how to instantiate a button. The code associated with a click event on this button is added between lines 44 and 48. The `button.addClickListener` in line 44 adds a listener for click events on the button. The manager of the event here is added as an anonymous class that implements the `ClickListener` interface (`new ClickListener()...`). When the user clicks the *Click me* button, the `ClickListener.onClick()` method executes. The code here centers a dialog box and shows it on the screen.

Although most events are triggered by the user when he or she clicks on a button or moves the mouse over some object, there are events that do not rely on GUI events, such as when some data is received from the server, or when a timer expires. GWT provides a complete set of widgets and GUI elements to reutilize for these purposes. The complete set of widgets in GWT 1.5.3 can be found in Google's Website `http://code.google.com/docreader/` searching for GWT 1.5.3 and `DeviceWidgetGallery`.

10.3.1.1 Creating System Administration Functions

This section shows how to implement a "create device" system administration function using the automatically generated skeleton files described before. The process to implement other administrative functions is the same.

In order to create or add a new device in the system, it is imperative to create a window to request the new information from the system administrator and submit it. The code that creates this window and the window itself are shown in Listing 10.5 and Figure 10.7, respectively. To create the code that implements the window, right click on the `cse.usf.edu.book.client` package and click *New→Class*. In the dialog box, write in the name text field `CreateDevice` and click *Finish*. Now copy the content of Listing 10.5 in this file. In the code, line 7 states that the class extends the `Composite` class, which groups several user interface components. In other words, unless the elements of the `Composite` class are exposed with public methods, the whole composite behaves as a whole. This creates a user interface object for adding devices. A class that extends `Composite` can be added to any panel or dialog box.

Let us explore the code further. The method `initializeComponents()` in line 21 instantiates all the GUI components (panel, button, labels, and text fields). While the method `setLayout()` in line 29 adds the components to the `AbsolutePanel`, the `setProperties()` method in line 37 sets their properties such as the height and width of each of the objects. This method also adds a `ClickListener` to the button. When the user clicks on this button, the code executes the `createDevice()` method, which is the one that makes the remote procedure call to the server. For now, this part of the code is left blank. First, it is important to understand how to make RPC calls in GWT.

```
1  package cse.usf.edu.book.client;
2
3  import com.google.gwt.core.client.GWT;
4  import com.google.gwt.user.client.*;
5  import com.google.gwt.user.client.ui.*;
6
7  public class CreateDevice extends Composite{
8    private AbsolutePanel backgroundPanel = null;
9    private Button createDevice = null;
10   private Label deviceNameLabel = null;
11   private Label serialNumberLabel = null;
12   private TextBox deviceNameField = null;
13   private TextBox serialNumberField = null;
14
15   public CreateDevice() {
16     super();
17     initializeComponents();
18     setLayout();
19     setProperties();
20   }
21   protected void initializeComponents(){
22     backgroundPanel = new AbsolutePanel();
23     createDevice = new Button();
24     deviceNameLabel = new Label();
25     serialNumberLabel = new Label();
26     deviceNameField = new TextBox();
27     serialNumberField = new TextBox();
28   }
29   protected void setLayout(){
30     initWidget(backgroundPanel);
31     backgroundPanel.add(createDevice, 150,101);
32     backgroundPanel.add(deviceNameLabel, 30,28);
33     backgroundPanel.add(serialNumberLabel, 29,56);
34     backgroundPanel.add(deviceNameField, 180,28);
35     backgroundPanel.add(serialNumberField, 180,56);
36   }
37   protected void setProperties(){
38     setHeight("170");
39     setWidth("400");
40     backgroundPanel.setWidth("400");
41     createDevice.setText("Create Device");
42     createDevice.addClickListener(new ClickListener(){
43              public void onClick(Widget sender)
44              {
45                  createDevice();
46              }});
47     createDevice.setHeight("25");
48     createDevice.setWidth("120");
49     deviceNameLabel.setText("Device Name");
50     deviceNameLabel.setWidth("146");
51     serialNumberLabel.setText("Serial Number");
52     serialNumberLabel.setWidth("100");
```

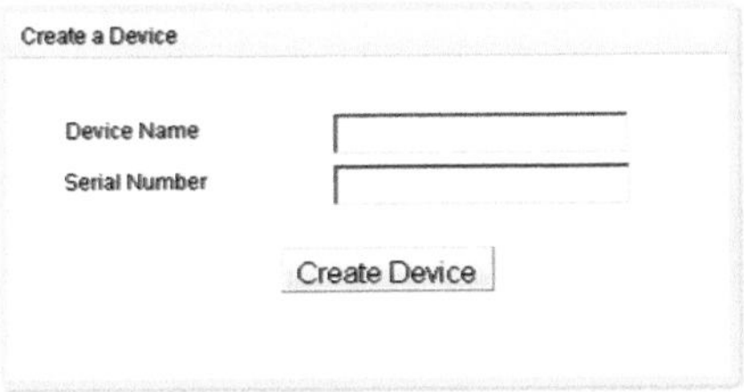

FIGURE 10.7: Window for creating a device.

```
53    deviceNameField.setHeight("23");
54    deviceNameField.setWidth("167");
55    serialNumberField.setHeight("23");
56    serialNumberField.setWidth("168");
57  }
58  public void createDevice(){
59
60  }
61 }
```

Listing 10.5: Code for creating a device.

10.3.1.2 Remote Procedure Calls in GWT

GWT provides an easy approach to make RPC calls to the server. The approach is based on AJAX or Asynchronous JavaScript and XML, which allows the client to send and retrieve data to and from the sever without interfering with the display and the behavior of the existing Web page. In other words, the asynchronous part of the approach does not block the client until the response from the RPC method arrives, but it continues to execute whichever statement comes after the RPC method invocation.

The AJAX-based RPC invocation approach provided by GWT is shown in Figure 10.8. The framework consists of the following elements:

- **Service interface:** This interface abstracts the methods that can be invoked by a client when calling a Web object. Each service interface defines the functions that the system implements. Here, a service interface to implement system administration functions related to devices will be developed. The interface will be used by the client-side application to invoke the function and by the server-side of the application to listen to those invocations and actually implement the function.

- **Asynchronous interface:** This interface abstracts the methods that are actually invoked by the client. This asynchronous interface is needed to manage the responses from the server without blocking the Web browser. This interface is related to the service interface defined before.

- **Client-side service implementation:** This component is the class

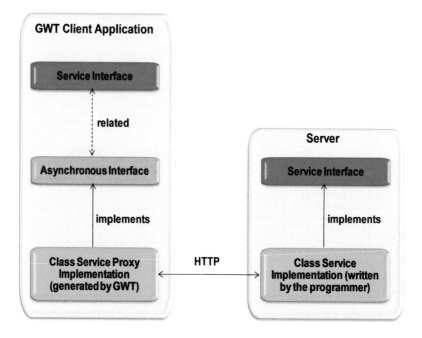

FIGURE 10.8: The AJAX RPC approach.

that actually invokes the RPC procedure by the framework. This class is automatically generated by the GWT and implements the data serialization over HTTP.

- **Server-side service implementation:** This class implements the service interface and it is the class that executes in the server when a client invokes a method of the RPC service interface.

- **Java GWT serializable objects (optional):** A service interface can have as invocation parameters objects that are GWT serializable. These objects can be created by the programmer. A service interface method can also return one of these serializable objects.

A serializable object is an object that can be transmitted and received by the client-side and server-side applications in the same form without the programmer's intervention in coding and decoding it from its state to a byte stream and vice versa. In GWT, a type is serializable if

- The type is a primitive variable, such as char, byte, short, int, long, boolean, float, or double.

- The type is an instance of the String, Date, or a primitive wrapper such as Character, Byte, Short, Integer, Long, Boolean, Float, or Double.

- The type is an enumeration. Enumeration constants are serialized as a name only; none of the field values are serialized.

- The type is an array of serializable types (including other serializable arrays).

- The type is a serializable user-defined class.

- The type has at least one serializable subclass.

For a user-defined class to be GWT serializable, it must comply with at least one of the following rules:

- It can be assigned to `IsSerializable` or `Serializable`, either because it directly implements one of these interfaces or because it derives from a superclass that does.

- All non-final, non-transient instance fields are themselves serializable.

- As of GWT 1.5, it must have a default (zero argument) constructor (with any access modifier) or no constructor at all.

Following the model shown in Figure 10.8, a serializable `Device` class will be created first that will contain the necessary information to create a device in the system. Then, the service interface and its serializable version will be created. Finally, the code that will implement the `createDevice()` method will be shown.

The code that implements the serializable `Device` class is shown in Listing 10.6. To create this class, create a package for the class by first going to the Package Explorer, right-clicking on the `cse.usf.edu.book.client` package and clicking on *New→Package*. Write down the new package's name as `cse.usf.edu.book.client.entities`. Now create the `Device` class in this package as explained before and copy the content of Listing 10.6. As it can be seen from the listing, the class includes the set and get methods to set and get the identifier, name, and serial number of the devices.

```
1  package cse.usf.edu.book.client.entities;
2
3  import com.google.gwt.user.client.rpc.IsSerializable;
4
5  public class Device implements IsSerializable
6  {
7      private int deviceId;
8      private String deviceName;
9      private String serialNumber;
10
11     public Device(){
12     }
13     public void setDeviceId(int val){
14         this.deviceId = val;
15     }
16     public void setDeviceName(String name){
17         this.deviceName = name;
```

```
18        }
19        public void   setSerialNumber(String number){
20            this.serialNumber = number;
21        }
22        public int getDeviceId(){
23            return deviceId;
24        }
25        public String getDeviceName(){
26            return deviceName;
27        }
28        public String getSerialNumber(){
29            return serialNumber;
30        }
31 }
```

Listing 10.6: The `Device.java` GWT serializable class.

The next step is to create the GWT service interface. In order to do this, create a new package called `cse.usf.edu.book.client.services` and then create a new interface under the created package and call it `DeviceServiceManager`. Then, copy the contents of Listing 10.7 to this interface. For an interface to be a GWT service interface, it has to extend the `RemoteService` interface provided by the GWT framework. Also, the type of the interface must be serializable.

Notice that the code included in Listing 10.7 defines several system administration functions related to the devices only, i.e., create, delete, and edit a device. Here, as an example, it will be shown how to implement the `createDevice()` method only, as the process to implement the other functions is the same. Also, notice that many other system administration functions can be included in the system. For example, you might want to implement similar functions to manage users and sessions. For these, separate service interfaces can be defined and implemented in the same manner. Defining these interfaces separately is recommended to keep the functionality of the system modular. In addition to system administration functions, you may also want to define and implement operational interfaces. For example, the LBIS tracking system example is meant to track users in real time; therefore, an interface to handle tracking-related functions such as update, add, and delete GPS fixes, can also be defined and implemented in the same manner. This is the approach used in the next chapter to obtain the fixes from the server and display them in Google Maps.

```
1  package cse.usf.edu.book.client.services;
2
3  import com.google.gwt.user.client.rpc.RemoteService;
4  import cse.usf.edu.book.client.entities.Device;
5
6  public interface DeviceServiceManager extends RemoteService{
7        public Boolean createDevice(Device dev);
8        public Boolean deleteDevice(Device dev);
9        public Boolean editDevice(Device dev);
10       public Device[] getAllDevices();
11 }
```

Listing 10.7: The `DeviceServiceManager.java` GWT service interface.

Now, you must create the asynchronous interface. To do this, create a new interface with the same name as the original service interface but add to the end of the name the suffix `Async`. Listing 10.8 shows the resulting asynchronous interface. The methods of the asynchronous interface are called the same as the service interface; however, they do not return any value; the `AsynCallback` object that is added as a parameter of the method will manage the response.

```
1  package cse.usf.edu.book.client.services;
2
3  import com.google.gwt.user.client.rpc.AsyncCallback;
4  import cse.usf.edu.book.client.entities.Device;
5
6  public interface DeviceServiceManagerAsync {
7      public void createDevice(Device dev, AsyncCallback callback);
8      public void deleteDevice(Device dev, AsyncCallback callback);
9      public void editDevice(Device dev, AsyncCallback callback);
10     public void getAllDevices(AsyncCallback callback);
11 }
```

Listing 10.8: The `DeviceServiceManagerAsync.java` asynchronous GWT service interface.

Now that the code for the required interfaces has been written, it is time to write the code that actually performs the RPC and manages the response back from the server. Please notice that in Listing 10.5, line 58, there was no code in the method `createDevice()`. This is the code that will perform the call to the server using the interfaces created above. The code is shown in Listing 10.9. The code to create other objects (update, delete, and retrieve devices) is left to the readers as a coding exercise.

This code has the following parts:

- **Proxy creation:** The proxy is created in line 3 by the factory method `GWT.create()` using the service interface and returning an object that implements the asynchronous service interface. The proxy transmits the objects using HTTP, hiding the details from the programmer.

- **Remote service location set up:** A remote service location is set up in lines 5–7 where the URL of the Web object that implements the RPC service is located. The `ServiceDefTarget` is an interface defined in the `com.google.gwt.user.client.rpc` package, which was imported at the beginning of Listing 10.5. The `endpoint.setServiceEntryPoint()` method is one of the methods provided by the `ServiceDefTarget` interface.

- **Response manager:** A response manager is set up between lines 9 and 29 where the callback object is created. `AsyncCallback` is an interface that implements two methods. The first, which is `onSuccess()`, is executed when the RPC is completed with success. The other, `onFailure()`, is executed if there is a communication failure with the server.

- **Object preparation and RPC service invocation:** This is done between lines 31 and 34. Line 34 is the line that actually performs the RPC call.

```
1  public void createDevice ()
2  {
3          DeviceServiceManagerAsync theDeviceManager = (
              DeviceServiceManagerAsync) GWT.create(DeviceServiceManager.
              class);
4
5          ServiceDefTarget endpoint = (ServiceDefTarget) theDeviceManager;
6          String remoteServiceURL = "http://192.168.0.2:8080/Lbsbook/
              services/DeviceManager";
7          endpoint.setServiceEntryPoint(remoteServiceURL);
8
9          AsyncCallback callback = new AsyncCallback()
10         {
11           public void onSuccess(Object result)
12           {
13             Boolean res = (Boolean) result;
14
15             if(res.booleanValue())
16             {
17                 Window.alert("Device Added with Success");
18             }
19             else
20             {
21                 Window.alert("The device could not be added. There has
                      been an error in the database");
22             }
23           }
24
25           public void onFailure(Throwable caught)
26           {
27                 Window.alert("An Internal Error has ocurred: " + caught.
                      getMessage());
28           }
29         };
30
31         Device dev = new Device();
32         dev.setDeviceName(this.deviceNameField.getText());
33         dev.setSerialNumber(this.serialNumberField.getText());
34         theDeviceManager.createDevice(dev, callback);
35 }
```

Listing 10.9: The `createDevice()` method of the `CreateDevice.java` class.

The last step calls for the modification of the `onModuleLoad()` method of the `GwtBook.java` file included in Listing 10.4. This method must be entirely replaced by the code in Listing 10.10 to implement our application. This code loads when it starts the `CreateDevice` composite. Now, if you run the application from Eclipse and click the *Create Device* button, the result should be like the one shown in Figure 10.9.

```
1
2  public void onModuleLoad() {
3      VerticalPanel vPanel = new VerticalPanel();
4      vPanel.setWidth("100%");
5      vPanel.setHorizontalAlignment(VerticalPanel.ALIGN_CENTER);
6      // Add image and button to the RootPanel
7      RootPanel.get().add(vPanel);
```

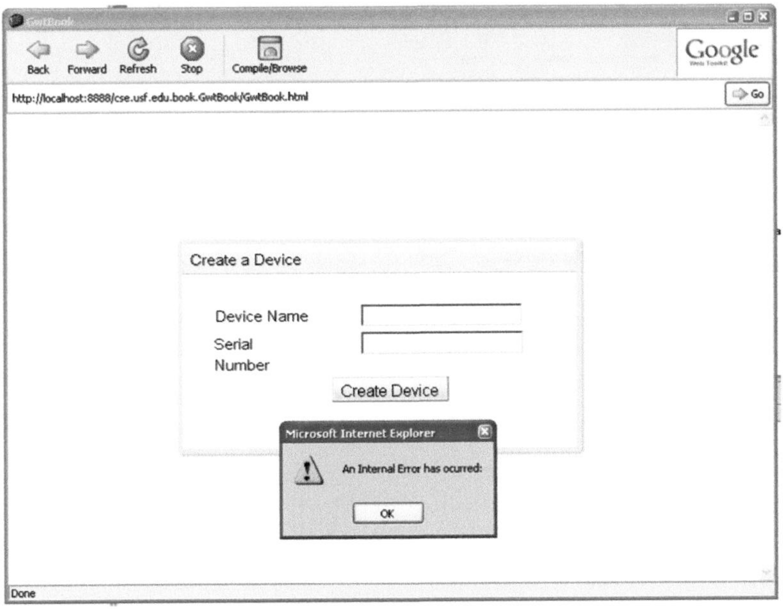

FIGURE 10.9: Executing the `DeviceServiceManager`'s RPC call without service implementation.

```
8
9      // Create the CreateDevice Widget
10
11     CreateDevice theNewDevice = new CreateDevice();
12
13     // Create the dialog box
14     final DialogBox dialogBox = new DialogBox();
15     dialogBox.setText("Create a Device");
16     dialogBox.setAnimationEnabled(true);
17     dialogBox.add(theNewDevice);
18     dialogBox.center();
19     dialogBox.show();
20   }
```

Listing 10.10: Modifying the `onModuleLoad()` method for showing the `CreateDevice.java` composite.

This finalizes the client-side code and the code needed to invoke the remote service. The next section shows how to create the server-side code.

10.3.2 Server-Side Code

The server-side code consists of the same serializable class and the implementation of the same service interface defined in the client code. The service implementation includes the methods that, upon the invocation from the client, implement the requested functions in the server, in this case, create

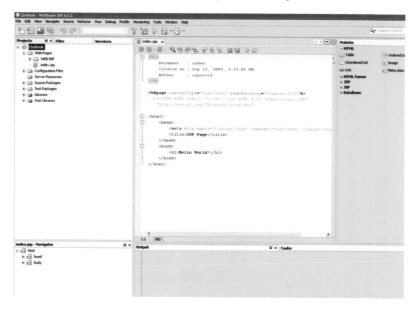

FIGURE 10.10: NetBeans' window after the Web project is created.

a new device in the system. As explained before, this code is developed in NetBeans.

The first step is to create a new project. In NetBeans, click on menu *File→New*, select *Java Web* from the *Categories* list, and *Web Application* from the *Projects* list. Then, click *Next*. In the next dialog box, write in the project name (LbsBook in our case), and click *Next*. In the next screen, select *Glassfish V2* from the server combo box and click *Finish*.

The second step is to add the GWT library to your project. Once the project is created, you should see a screen like the one shown in Figure 10.10. Now, in the *Projects* tab (upper left), right-click on *LbsBook* and select *Properties*. Then, select the option *Libraries* from the *Categories*. You should see a screen like the one shown in Figure 10.11. In this screen, click on *Add JAR/Folder*. Now go to your GWT installation directory and select the file called gwt-servlet.jar. Click *Open* and *OK*.

The next step is to create the same Device serializable class that was created for the client. In order to do so, a new package needs to be created with the same name, i.e., cse.usf.edu.book.client.entities, and include the same code utilized in the client-side code, which is included in Listing 10.6. To create the package, right-click on *Source Package* in the *Project* panel, and click on *New→Java Package*. After the package is created, go to the *Project* panel, right-click on the package, and click on *New→Java Class* to create the new class.

The next step is to create the corresponding service interface, the

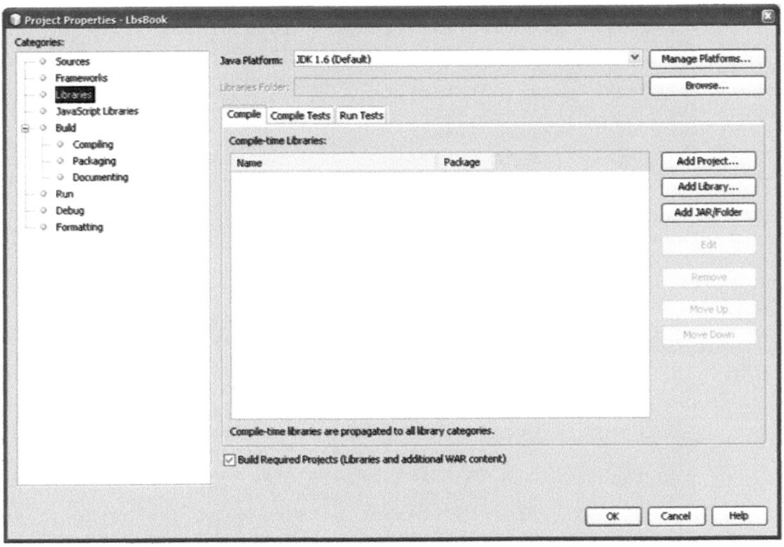

FIGURE 10.11: Adding libraries to the project.

one that upon the request from the client will create a new device in the database. In order to do this, create a package with the same name as the package that contains the service interface in the client (`cse.usf.edu.book.client.services`) and also create the implementation class. This time, name it exactly as you named the service interface of the client but with the `Impl` at the end, i.e., `DeviceServiceManagerImpl`.

The final step is to write the code that will implement the method specified in the service, i.e., the `createDevice()` method of the `DeviceServiceManager` interface. This code is shown in Listing 10.11 and explained next. See that in line 12 of the code, the `DeviceServiceManagerImp` is extending the `RemoteServiceServlet` class. Further, the class implements the methods of our GWT interface.

Another important part of the code is related to the database. For example, the code within lines 16 and 18 use a JDBC resource of the server to obtain a connection to the database. To insert the device's information into the database, the `PreparedStatement` object is created in line 19 in which the device's identifier is generated using a SQL sequence generator. Lines 20–21 insert the device's name and serial number into the `PreparedStatement` object and line 22 executes the update to the database. If there are no errors, the code should return true. Else, an exemption is thrown in the server and the code returns false. This code assumes that you have created a JDBC resource to connect to the database, which is explained in Section A.2.6.2.

```
1  package cse.usf.edu.book.client.services;
2
```

```
 3  import com.google.gwt.user.server.rpc.RemoteServiceServlet;
 4  import cse.usf.edu.book.client.entities.Device;
 5  import java.sql.Connection;
 6  import java.sql.PreparedStatement;
 7  import java.sql.SQLException;
 8  import java.util.logging.Level;
 9  import java.util.logging.Logger;
10  import javax.naming.NamingException;
11
12  public class DevicerServiceManagerImpl extends RemoteServiceServlet
        implements DeviceServiceManager{
13
14      public Boolean createDevice(Device dev){
15              try{
16                      javax.naming.InitialContext ic = new javax.naming
                            .InitialContext();
17                      javax.sql.DataSource dataSource = (javax.sql.
                            DataSource)ic.lookup("jdbc/lbsbook");
18                      Connection conn = dataSource.getConnection();
19                      PreparedStatement insertStatement = conn.
                            prepareStatement("insert into tracking(
                            deviceid,devicename,serialnumber) values(
                            nextval('dev_seq'),?,?)");
20                      insertStatement.setString(1, dev.getDeviceName());
21                      insertStatement.setString(2, dev.getSerialNumber()
                            );
22                      insertStatement.executeUpdate();
23                      conn.close();
24                      return true;
25              }
26              catch (NamingException ex){
27                      Logger.getLogger(DevicerServiceManagerImpl.class.
                            getName()).log(Level.SEVERE, null, ex);
28              }
29              catch (SQLException ex){
30                      Logger.getLogger(DevicerServiceManagerImpl.class.
                            getName()).log(Level.SEVERE, null, ex);
31              }
32              return false;
33      }
34
35      public Boolean deleteDevice(Device dev) {
36          throw new UnsupportedOperationException("Not supported yet.");
37      }
38
39      public Boolean editDevice(Device dev) {
40          throw new UnsupportedOperationException("Not supported yet.");
41      }
42
43      public Device[] getAllDevices() {
44          throw new UnsupportedOperationException("Not supported yet.");
45      }
46  }
```

Listing 10.11: Server-side GWT service implementation.

The next step is to register the implementation class with the server. GWT services are an extension of the Java Servlets technology. Therefore, they work above the servlet layer. In order to register the server, go to the *Project* panel, click on the + sign of the label *Configuration* and double click over the web.xml file. After that, a page that contains the configuration of the application appears on the right side. Click on the *Servlets* button and click the *Add Servlet Element* button. In the window, write GwtDeviceManager in the

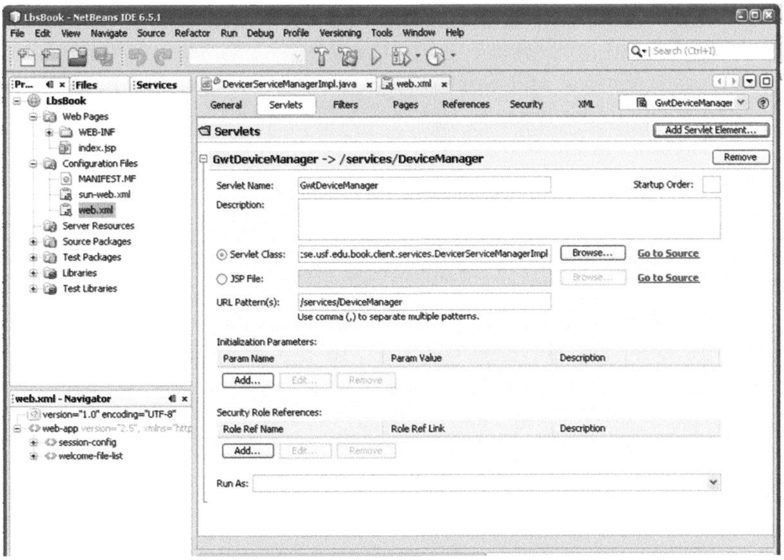

FIGURE 10.12: Configuring the GWT servlet.

Name textfield. In the Servlet class, click on the *Browse* button and look for the DeviceServiceManagerImpl.java class. In URL Pattern(s), write /services/DeviceManager. This name makes part of the endpoint address for the service invocation in the GWT application (line 6 in Listing 10.9). Click *OK* and now you should see a screen like the one shown in Figure 10.12. At this point, the application is ready to be deployed and tested.

To deploy the application, go to the *Projects* panel, right click on the project, and choose the *Clean and Build* option. After the building process is completed, go again to the *Projects* panel, right click on the project, and choose the *Deploy* option.

In order to test the application, go to Eclipse and run the GWT application. Fill in the text fields and click on the *Create Device* button. If everything is working correctly, you should see a dialog box stating that the information was successfully saved.

10.3.3 Compiling and Deploying the Application with GWT

Now that the client and server codes have been developed and tested, it is time to compile the application with GWT and deploy it along with the Web Project. The following steps indicate how to accomplish this:

1. **Compile the Eclipse project with GWT:** Run the Eclipse project as explained in the previous section (Figure 10.9) and click on the *Compile/Browse* button.

2. **Copy the compiled files to the Web project application:** Using the Windows Explorer, go to the Eclipse's GWT project location (e.g., `C:\Documents and Settings\ajperez4\workspace\LbsBookGWT`) and copy the folder www to the Web folder of the NetBeans project (e.g., `C:\DocumentsandSettings\ajperez4\MyDocuments\NetBeansProjects\LbsBook`).

3. **Build and Deploy:** Using NetBeans, build the Web project and deploy it as it was shown in the previous section.

After the Web application has been deployed, it can be executed from a Web browser. In our case the URL to use would be `http://192.168.0.2:8080/LbsBook/www/GwtBook.html`, which consists of the path where the application resides in the server with IP address 192.168.0.2.

10.4   System Administration and the LBIS Tracking System Example

This chapter teaches how to implement system administration functions using the Google Web Toolkit framework. The LBIS tracking system example described in Chapter 1 needs to implement some system administration functions in order to maintain the system. Functions like creating new users, devices, sessions; modifying the current information; retrieving such information, etc., can be implemented using this framework. Under this framework, the system administrator can use the Web browser of his/her preference from a computer connected to the Internet, in our case the "main control station," to send and receive data from the database of the system, which is located in one of the servers. This chapter shows how to implement a function to add devices to the system. More important than the function itself is the fact that the process to implement it can be followed to create any other one.

Chapter 11

Data Visualization

11.1   Introduction

The LBIS tracking system example described in Chapter 1 includes a "main control station" connected to the Internet to visualize the positions of the users in real time. Instead of showing plain coordinate numbers, it is definitively more practical and useful to display the users in a graphical interface, such as a map. This chapter explains how to use the Google Web Toolkit framework described in Chapter 10 along with Google Maps and Google Earth to visualize (track) users in real time. As in the case of system administration functions, this process also implies software development for the client (i.e., the control station) and the server.

11.2   Visualizing the Users' Positions in Google Maps

This section show how to use the GWT framework to create a Web application that will allow the continuous monitoring of the positions of the active users of the system in a Google Maps interface. In our specific LBIS tracking system example, this application is meant to run in the main control station; however, as a Web application, it can be run in any computer connected to the Internet.

The development of this Web application follows the same procedure described in Chapter 10 to develop the "create device" system administration function using the GWT framework (see Section 10.2 and Figure 10.1). In general, there must be a client-side software to query the server for the GPS fixes in a periodic manner and a server-side software with a service interface to listen and respond to these queries. Once the GPS fixes are received in the control station, the client-side software uses the Google Maps interface to display the fixes on the map.

11.2.1   Configuring the GWT Project

One of the main differences between the Web application developed in Chapter 10 to create a device in the system and this Web application to visualize the users in Google Maps is the use of the latter. Therefore, after the GWT project is created in Eclipse, as shown in Section 10.3.1, the GWT needs to be configured to utilize the Google Maps API. This configuration is accomplished with the following steps:

1. **Sign up for a Google Maps key:** Google Maps require you to sign up for a Google Maps key, which can be obtained from `http://code.google.com/apis/maps/`. You should sign up for two keys, one for developing the application and the other one for deploying it. First, sign up for a key for the developing domain `http://localhost:8888/`, which will be utilized to develop and test the application within the GWT browser. Then, obtain another key for the production domain, which is the URL where the application will be deployed, in our case `http://192.168.0.2:8080/`.

2. **Download the Google Maps API library for GWT:** The Google Maps API is a JavaScript API, but there is a project that encapsulates the JavaScript API for using it in GWT. This library (`gwt-maps-1.0.4.zip`) can be downloaded from Google's Website at `http://code.google.com/p/gwt-google-apis/` or from the book's Website at `http://www.csee.usf.edu/~labrador/LBIS`.

3. **Import the library into the GWT Eclipse Project:** Once the `.zip` file has been downloaded and extracted, the `gwt-maps.jar` file has to be added to the GWT project.

4. **Configure the GWT project `.xml` file and develop your code:** Add the map module in the GWT `.xml` file and configure it using the development API key that was obtained in step 1.

The first two steps are self-explanatory following the directions in their respective Websites. The last two steps are explained next.

11.2.1.1   Import the Library into the GWT Eclipse Project

To import the Google Maps API library into the GWT Eclipse project, open Eclipse, go to the *Package Explorer*, right click on the project's name and click on *Properties*. Once the window appears, on the left panel select the *Java Build Path*, and then click on the *Libraries* tab panel. You should see a window like the one shown in Figure 11.1. Now click on *Add external JAR*, and find the `gwt-maps.jar` file that you downloaded. Click *Open* and then *OK*.

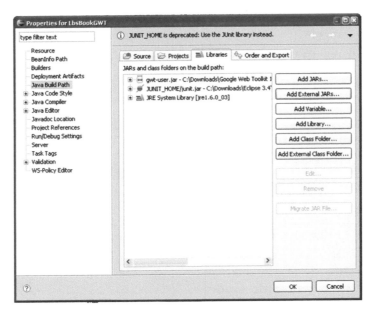

FIGURE 11.1: Adding the Google Maps API into GWT.

11.2.1.2 Configure the GWT Project .xml File

In order to configure the GWT project .xml file, open the GwtBook.gwt.xml file and modify the file so it looks like the file shown in Listing 11.1. This is the same file utilized in Chapter 10 shown in Figure 10.6 and Listing 10.1. Two new lines have been added to the configuration file. The first one, which is line 12, links the GWT maps library to the project. The second line, line 20, inserts the Google Maps key. The key obtained in the previous step for the development and testing domain http://localhost:8080 should replace the characters that come after key= in line 20. After this, the software development process can be initiated following the process sketched in Figure 10.1, the same process used in Chapter 10 to develop the system administration "create device" function.

```
1  <module>
2          <!-- Inherit the core Web Toolkit stuff.
               -->
3          <inherits name='com.google.gwt.user.User'/>
4
5          <!-- Inherit the default GWT style sheet.  You can change
               -->
6          <!-- the theme of your GWT application by uncommenting
               -->
7          <!-- any one of the following lines.
               -->
8          <inherits name='com.google.gwt.user.theme.standard.Standard'/>
9          <!-- <inherits name='com.google.gwt.user.theme.chrome.Chrome'/>
               -->
```

```
10     <!-- <inherits name='com.google.gwt.user.theme.dark.Dark'/>
          -->
11
12     <inherits name='com.google.gwt.maps.GoogleMaps'/>
13
14     <!-- Other module inherits
          -->
15     <!-- Specify the app entry point class.
          -->
16     <entry-point class='cse.usf.edu.book.client.GwtBook'/>
17
18     <!-- Specify the application specific style sheet.
          -->
19     <stylesheet src='GwtBook.css' />
20   <script src="http://maps.google.com/maps?gwt=1&amp;file=api&amp;v
          =2&amp;key=
          ABQIAAAAMjJ4YSAY1XGY632iJMQNUhQUHfw7juUOIptNf38LMYliOu-5
          YBTsUf_Ylw-SdAb_GUxMQM_j7owt1g"/>
21 </module>
```

Listing 11.1: Configuring GWT project to utilize Google Maps.

11.2.2   Client-Side Code

This section develops the software to display the positions of the active sessions in a Google Maps interface in the main control station. Every 10 seconds, this application will invoke a GWT service to obtain the last positions of the active users in the system and display them in the Google Maps GUI.

Let us start by creating the initial tracking component without getting the data from the server. For this, create a new class in the package name cse.usf.edu.book.client and call it TrackingWindow. The content of the class is shown in Listing 11.2. This is similar to the CreateDevice class of the previous chapter (see Listing 10.5), and as such, the TrackingWindow class also extends the Composite class. Line 14 declares the MapWidget object that will be used as the base map. The MapWidget component is the basic class for the maps in the Google Maps GWT library. All the objects that will be shown in the map utilize this component in some fashion. The API allows to add markers, points, polylines, and polygons. Since the interest here is to show the active sessions in the system, the example code shows how to add a marker.

In the code, lines 22–23 create a marker to be added to the map. The marker is added in line 25, the map is centered in the coordinates of the marker (line 27), and line 26 sets the zoom level to 14. Line 32 instantiates a MapWidget object and the next line adds it to the background panel of the class. Lines 48 and 49 set the dimensions of the map and lines 50–51 add the controls to the map, which are the map type (map, satellite) and the large map control (zoom level and map movement). Finally, line 54 is the updateActiveSessions() method that should make the RPC call to the server and obtain the latest positions of the active sessions in the system. The code implementing this method is included later.

```
1  package cse.usf.edu.book.client;
2
3  import com.google.gwt.maps.client.MapWidget;
4  import com.google.gwt.maps.client.control.LargeMapControl;
5  import com.google.gwt.maps.client.control.MapTypeControl;
6  import com.google.gwt.maps.client.geom.LatLng;
7  import com.google.gwt.maps.client.overlay.Marker;
8  import com.google.gwt.user.client.*;
9  import com.google.gwt.user.client.ui.*;
10
11 public class TrackingWindow extends Composite {
12
13   private AbsolutePanel backgroundPanel = null;
14   private MapWidget theMapWidget = null;
15
16   public TrackingWindow() {
17     super();
18     initializeComponents();
19     setLayout();
20     setProperties();
21
22     LatLng coordinates = LatLng.newInstance(28.055166, -82.413511);
23     Marker theNewMarker = new Marker(coordinates);
24
25     theMapWidget.addOverlay(theNewMarker);
26     theMapWidget.setZoomLevel(14);
27     theMapWidget.setCenter(coordinates);
28   }
29
30   protected void initializeComponents(){
31     backgroundPanel = new AbsolutePanel();
32     theMapWidget = new MapWidget();
33     backgroundPanel.add(theMapWidget,1,1);
34   }
35
36   protected void setLayout(){
37     initWidget(backgroundPanel);
38
39   }
40
41   protected void setProperties(){
42     setHeight("600");
43     setWidth("800");
44
45     backgroundPanel.setHeight("600");
46     backgroundPanel.setWidth("800");
47
48     theMapWidget.setHeight("600");
49     theMapWidget.setWidth("800");
50     theMapWidget.addControl(new LargeMapControl());
51     theMapWidget.addControl(new MapTypeControl());
52   }
53
54   public void updateActiveSessions()
55   {
56
57   }
58 }
```

Listing 11.2: The client-side tracking component.

The next step is to create the classes and interfaces needed to obtain the GPS fixes from the server using GWT's remote procedure calls. As in the example included in the last chapter, a serializable class (TrackingUpdate class) and two interfaces (the service interface and the asynchronous in-

terface) have to be created. As shown at the end of Listing 11.2, the
`updateActiveSessions()` method will be used to invoke the server and manage the response; this method is invoked periodically to obtain the current
position of the users and show updated information on the Google map. GWT
provides the class `Timer` to perform actions periodically.

Let us start with the `TrackingUpdate` serializable class, which is shown in
Listing 11.3. Just as with the `Device` class example included in Listing 10.6,
the class `TrackingUpdate` implements the `IsSerializable` interface, which is
placed in the `cse.usf.edu.book.client.entities` package. This time, the
class contains methods to set and get the session id, username, and coordinates.

```
1  package cse.usf.edu.book.client.entities;
2
3  import com.google.gwt.user.client.rpc.IsSerializable;
4
5  public class TrackingUpdate implements IsSerializable{
6     private double latitude;
7     private double longitude;
8     private int sessionid;
9     private String username;
10
11    public TrackingUpdate(){
12
13    }
14    public int getsessionId(){
15       return sessionid;
16    }
17    public String getUsername(){
18       return username;
19    }
20    public double getLatitude(){
21       return latitude;
22    }
23    public double getLongitude(){
24       return longitude;
25    }
26    public void setSessionid(int sessionid){
27       this.sessionid = sessionid;
28    }
29    public void setUsername(String usr){
30       this.username = usr;
31    }
32    public void setLatitude(double lat){
33       this.latitude = lat;
34    }
35    public void setLongitude(double lng){
36       this.longitude = lng;
37    }
38 }
```

Listing 11.3: The `TrackingUpdate` serializable class.

The next step is to define and write the service and asynchronous
interfaces, this time not to perform system administration functions
but to get GPS fixes. These interfaces, which are now named as
`TrackingServiceManager` and `TrackingServiceManagerAsync`, are included
in the `cse.usf.edu.book.client.services` package. The new interfaces consist of one method, the `getTrackingUpdates()` method, which returns an

array of `TrackingUpdate` objects. The interfaces are shown in Listings 11.4 and 11.5, respectively.

```
1  package cse.usf.edu.book.client.services;
2
3  import com.google.gwt.user.client.rpc.RemoteService;
4  import cse.usf.edu.book.client.entities.TrackingUpdate;
5
6  public interface TrackingServiceManager extends RemoteService{
7    public TrackingUpdate[] getTrackingUpdates();
8  }
```

Listing 11.4: The `TrackingServiceManager` service interface.

```
1  package cse.usf.edu.book.client.services;
2
3  import com.google.gwt.user.client.rpc.AsyncCallback;
4
5  import cse.usf.edu.book.client.entities.TrackingUpdate;
6
7  public interface TrackingServiceManagerAsync {
8    public void getTrackingUpdates(AsyncCallback callback);
9  }
```

Listing 11.5: The `TrackingServiceManager` asynchronous interface.

Once the classes and interfaces have been written, the next step is to write the `updateActiveSessions()` method included at the end of Listing 11.2. The code of this function obtains the locations of the active users in the system and places those locations in Google Maps. The function is shown in Listing 11.6.

```
1  public void updateActiveSessions()
2  {
3        TrackingServiceManagerAsync theTrackingManager = (
            TrackingServiceManagerAsync) GWT.create(
            TrackingServiceManager.class);
4
5        ServiceDefTarget endpoint = (ServiceDefTarget)
            theTrackingManager;
6        String remoteServiceURL = "http://192.168.0.2:8080/Lbsbook/
            services/TrackingManager";
7        endpoint.setServiceEntryPoint(remoteServiceURL);
8
9        AsyncCallback callback = new AsyncCallback(){
10         public void onSuccess(Object result){
11           TrackingUpdate theUpdates[] = (TrackingUpdate[]) result;
12           if(theUpdates != null)
13           {
14               theMapWidget.clearOverlays();
15
16               for(int i = 0; i < theUpdates.length; i++)
17               {
18                   final LatLng coordinates = LatLng.newInstance(theUpdates
                       [i].getLatitude(), theUpdates[i].getLongitude());
19                   final String theString = "Username: "+theUpdates[i].
                       getUsername()+"<br>Session id:"+theUpdates[i].
                       getsessionId();
20                   Marker theNewMarker = new Marker(coordinates);
21
```

```
22              MarkerClickHandler theHandler = new MarkerClickHandler ()
                {
23                public void onClick ( MarkerClickEvent event ) {
24                  theMapWidget . getInfoWindow () . open ( coordinates , new
                        InfoWindowContent ( theString )) ;
25                }
26              };

27
28              theNewMarker . addMarkerClickHandler ( theHandler );
29              theMapWidget . addOverlay ( theNewMarker );
30            }
31          }
32        }
33
34        public void onFailure ( Throwable caught ){
35          Window . alert ("An Internal Error has ocurred : " + caught .
                getMessage ()) ;
36        }
37      };
38
39      theTrackingManager . getTrackingUpdates ( callback );
40    }
```

Listing 11.6: The `updateActiveSessions()` method.

As shown in the previous chapter, the `updateActiveSessions()` method creates the proxy (line 3), sets up the remote service location (lines 5–7), sets up the manager of the response (lines 9–37), and invokes the service (line 39). The code between lines 11 and 29 updates the map.

Line 11 obtains the `TrackingUpdate` vector that the RPC call returns. Line 14 deletes all the previous overlays of the map, and the code between lines 18 and 29 creates a new marker. This example creates a marker per active session in the system; also a click event per marker is added between lines 22 - 26. The event will open a window above the marker that displays the username and the session identifier.

The only part missing from the GWT client is the `Timer` that will fire the `updateActiveSessions()` method periodically. This code is shown in Listing 11.7. The timer is a way to schedule repetitive events in GWT. In the code, the `trackingTimer` object is set up to fire and invoke the `updateActiveSessions()` method every 10000 milliseconds (10 seconds). This code should be included in the `initializeComponents()` method of the client-side tracking component code presented in Listing 11.2. This finalizes the client-side code.

```
1  // this code assumes that there is a field in the class called
       trackingTimer .
2  // to do this , add the following field Timer trackingTimer to the
       class .
3
4  protected void initializeComponents (){
5      backgroundPanel = new AbsolutePanel ();
6      theMapWidget = new MapWidget ();
7      backgroundPanel . add ( theMapWidget , 1 ,1);
8
9      trackingTimer = new Timer ()
10     {
11       public void run ()
```

```
12        {
13            updateActiveSessions ();
14        }
15      };
16      trackingTimer . scheduleRepeating (10000);
17    }
```

Listing 11.7: Modifying the `initializeComponents()` method to initialize the timer.

11.2.3   Server-Side Code

The next step is to create the service implementation in the server. In order to create the service in the server, we need to almost replicate the packages, classes, and interfaces built for the client (see Figure 10.8). The main difference is that the service interface implementation will contain the code to execute the service, in this case, query the database and return the list of GPS fixes.

The first step is to create the serializabe class `TrackingUpdate` with the methods to set and get the GPS fixes. In order to do this, open your Net-Beans project and create the `cse.usf.edu.book.client.entities` package and include the code presented in Listing 11.3. The second step is to create the `cse.usf.edu.book.client.services` package and the service interface `TrackingServiceManager` exactly as shown in Listing 11.4. The final step is to implement the service interface, which is given by the class `TrackingServiceManagerImpl`, also named exactly as its client counterpart but with the suffix "Impl." This class includes the code that implements the methods defined in the service, as shown in Listing 11.8. In this case, the service interface implementation only includes one method, the `getTrackingUpdates()` method.

The job of the implementation is to invoke the database and retrieve the last location and session information of all the active sessions in the system. Once it obtains the information from the database, it returns a vector of `TrackingUpdate` that the GWT application utilizes to update the locations in the map. The code for the service implementation is shown in Listing 11.8. Also the `postgis-1.3.3.jar` library needs to be added to the project. This file is found in the JDBC folder of your PostgreSQL installation.

```
1  package  cse . usf . edu . book . client . services ;
2
3  import  com . google . gwt . user . server . rpc . RemoteServiceServlet ;
4  import  cse . usf . edu . book . client . entities . TrackingUpdate ;
5  import  java . sql . Connection ;
6  import  java . sql . PreparedStatement ;
7  import  java . sql . ResultSet ;
8  import  java . sql . SQLException ;
9  import  java . util . Iterator ;
10 import  java . util . LinkedList ;
11 import  java . util . List ;
12 import  java . util . logging . Level ;
13 import  java . util . logging . Logger ;
14 import  javax . naming . NamingException ;
```

```
15  import org.postgis.Point;
16
17  public class TrackingServiceManagerImpl extends RemoteServiceServlet
        implements TrackingServiceManager{
18
19    public TrackingUpdate[] getTrackingUpdates()
20    {
21      try{
22          javax.naming.InitialContext ic  = new javax.naming.
                InitialContext();
23          javax.sql.DataSource dataSource = (javax.sql.DataSource)ic.
                lookup("jdbc/lbsbook");
24          Connection theConnection = dataSource.getConnection();
25
26          PreparedStatement queryStatement = theConnection.prepareStatement
                ("select fieldsession.sessionid as sesid, fielduser.username
                as uname, ST_AsText(tracking.position) as pos from
                fieldsession, tracking,fielduser, (select max(idtracking) as
                idtrack from fieldsession, tracking where fieldsession.
                datestop is NULL and fieldsession.sessionid=tracking.
                sessionid group by fieldsession.sessionid) as s2 "+
27        "where fieldsession.datestop is NULL and fieldsession.sessionid =
                tracking.sessionid and "+
28            "tracking.idtracking = s2.idtrack and fieldsession.iduser =
                fielduser.iduser");
29          ResultSet rs = queryStatement.executeQuery();
30          List returnList = new LinkedList();
31          while(rs.next()){
32            TrackingUpdate newUpdate = new TrackingUpdate();
33            newUpdate.setSessionid(rs.getInt("sesid"));
34            newUpdate.setUsername(rs.getString("uname"));
35
36            Point theNewPoint = new Point(rs.getString("pos"));
37
38            newUpdate.setLongitude(theNewPoint.getX());
39            newUpdate.setLatitude(theNewPoint.getY());
40            returnList.add(newUpdate);
41          }
42          theConnection.close();
43          if(!returnList.isEmpty())
44          {
45              TrackingUpdate theReturnVector[] = new TrackingUpdate[
                    returnList.size()];
46              int i = 0;
47              for (Iterator it = returnList.iterator(); it.hasNext();)
48              {
49                  TrackingUpdate theUpdate = (TrackingUpdate) it.next();
50                  theReturnVector[i] = theUpdate;
51                  i++;
52              }
53              return theReturnVector;
54          }
55          return null;
56        }
57      catch (NamingException ex){
58          Logger.getLogger(DevicerServiceManagerImpl.class.getName()).
                log(Level.SEVERE, null, ex);
59      }
60      catch (SQLException ex){
61          Logger.getLogger(DevicerServiceManagerImpl.class.getName()).
                log(Level.SEVERE, null, ex);
62      }
63      return null;
64    }
65  }
```

Listing 11.8: Server-side tracking service implementation.

This code connects to the database in lines 22–24. After the connection has been established, it prepares a query in lines 26–28 to obtain the last location from all active sessions. In the database model, a session is active if the value of the `datestop` field is NULL. Since the location of all the sessions is kept in the tracking list, the query performs a subquery in the from statement of the query to retrieve the maximum `idtracking` for all active sessions, which would be the identification of the last GPS fix received from every active session. This result is then joined with the session, tracking, and fielduser tables to obtain the following fields:

- `sessionid`: Obtained from the fieldsession table.

- `username`: Obtained from the fielduser table after joined with the fieldsession table on the iduser.

- `location`: Obtained after joining the s2 subquery (see query statement in Listing 11.8) table (on idtracking) with the tracking table and fieldsession (on sessionid).

Lines 31–41 obtain the information for each of the sessions and place that information in a `TrackingUpdate` object. In the query, the location is obtained as a `String` and the coordinates have to be converted into a `double` value. This is performed in line 36 where the `Point` object (from the PostGIS library) obtains the location as `String` from the `ResultSet` and converts it into `double` value (line 38 for longitude and line 39 for latitude). Since the size of the `ResultSet` is unknown (the number of active sessions), the information is placed in a `LinkedList`. After this, the information is placed in a vector that is returned to the GWT application (lines 47–53).

Once the client and server side codes have been developed and tested, they can be compiled, tested, and deployed with GWT. For this, follow the same process explained in Section 10.3.3.

11.3   Google Earth

The GPS fixes of active users can also be displayed in a Google Earth GUI. Google Earth is a 3D mapping application designed as a geographical browser to show maps, satellite images, and location data in an interactive fashion. Just as with Google Maps, Google Earth allows to place overlays on the maps with the advantage of being able to show those overlays in 3D. An example of the Google Earth GUI is shown in Figure 11.2.

Google Earth can show customized information over the globe's surface using an XML schema originally called Keyhole Markup Language (KML). Designed by Keyhole, Inc., KML became an Open Geospatial Consortium

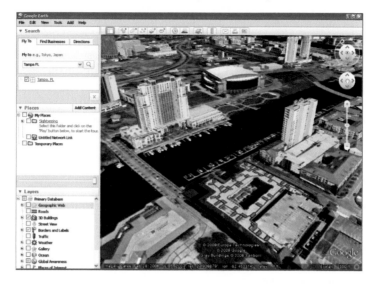

FIGURE 11.2: Google Earth graphical user interface.

(OGC) standard in April 2008. This section briefly explains KML and the process to show the location information of the active sessions of our LBIS tracking system example in Google Earth.

11.3.1 KML Language

KML is a markup language designed to encode information to be shown in an Earth browser [6]. Similar to HTML, KML is an XML language formed by a hierarchy of tags with nested elements and attributes. With KML, placemarks describing geographical places (e.g., restaurants, hospitals, houses) can be created. Also, it can be utilized to show tracking journeys (e.g., hurricanes, cars) and to share information among several geographical data providers (e.g., NOAA, NASA, UNESCO, Smithsonian, Google). As with HTML, KML documents are written in plain text, following a specification. The following list includes the most important tags available in KML:

- <kml>...< /kml>: Declares the root element of a KML file. It is used to define the namespace of the file. The content of the KML file must be placed within these tags. Before the <kml> tag, the <?xml version="1.0" encoding="UTF-8"? > must be placed, as these tags define the XML version and the encoding of the document.

- <Document>...< /Document>: The Document tag defines a container for features and styles. A style is an attribute that assigns the look of a feature. As styles can be shared among features, this tag defines the shared styles for the features. In Google Earth, a feature is an object that can be shown in the globe. Such features form the KML document.

- <**Folder**>...< /**Folder**>: Allow to arrange features in a hierarchical fashion. Folders can be contained in other folders and also within a Document tag. Folders are optional and a document can be made up of several folders.

- <**Placemark**>...< /**Placemark**>: A Placemark is a feature that is associated with a Geometry. The Placemark is the basic object that can be shown and georeferenced in Google Earth. The basic Placemark is a placemark with a Point geometry and an icon that marks a coordinate in the globe. Placemarks may have other geometries such as a Line or a Polygon, and even be associated with collections of basic geometries, forming a even more complex geometry, such as a building.

Listing 11.9 shows a simple example of a KML document that puts a placemark in the coordinates of the University of South Florida. To see this in Google Earth, save the code using Notepad with a .kml extension, open Google Earth, go to the menu *File→Open*, and open the file. This KML file will be the basis for creating a dynamic script that will generate a KML document on demand, as explained in the next section.

```
 1 <?xml version="1.0" encoding="UTF-8"?>
 2 <kml xmlns="http://www.opengis.net/kml/2.2">
 3    <Document>
 4      <Placemark>
 5        <name>University of South Florida, Tampa Campus</name>
 6        <description>A Placemark showing USF Campus</description>
 7        <Point>
 8          <coordinates>-82.413511,28.055166,0</coordinates>
 9        </Point>
10      </Placemark>
11    </Document>
12 </kml>
```

Listing 11.9: A simple KML file example.

11.3.2 Generating KML Documents Dynamically

Using the example in Listing 11.9, this section explains how to generate this KML document in a dynamic fashion. The first step is to create a servlet to generate the KML document. In order to do this, open your NetBeans project, right-click in the project's name in the *Projects* panel, and select *New→Servlet*. In the dialog box that appears, write KMLTrackingServlet in the *Class Name* text field. In the package select the cse.usf.book.client. services. In the next dialog box write in KMLTrackingServlet as the servlet name and /services/KMLTrackingServlet in URL pattern(s). Click *Finish* to create the servlet. NetBeans automatically creates and open a new Java file, which is shown in Listing 11.10.

```
 1  package cse.usf.book.client.services;
 2
 3  import java.io.IOException;
 4  import java.io.PrintWriter;
 5  import javax.servlet.ServletException;
 6  import javax.servlet.http.HttpServlet;
 7  import javax.servlet.http.HttpServletRequest;
 8  import javax.servlet.http.HttpServletResponse;
 9
10
11  public class KMLTrackingServlet extends HttpServlet {
12
13      protected void processRequest(HttpServletRequest request,
            HttpServletResponse response)
14      throws ServletException, IOException {
15          response.setContentType("text/html;charset=UTF-8");
16          PrintWriter out = response.getWriter();
17          try {
18              /* TODO output your page here
19              out.println("<html>");
20              out.println("<head>");
21              out.println("<title>Servlet NewServlet</title>");
22              out.println("</head>");
23              out.println("<body>");
24              out.println("<h1>Servlet NewServlet at " + request.
                  getContextPath() + "</h1>");
25              out.println("</body>");
26              out.println("</html>");
27              */
28          } finally {
29              out.close();
30          }
31      }
32
33      @Override
34      protected void doGet(HttpServletRequest request,
            HttpServletResponse response)
35      throws ServletException, IOException {
36          processRequest(request, response);
37      }
38
39
40      @Override
41      protected void doPost(HttpServletRequest request,
            HttpServletResponse response)
42      throws ServletException, IOException {
43          processRequest(request, response);
44      }
45
46      @Override
47      public String getServletInfo() {
48          return "Short description";
49      }
50  }
```

Listing 11.10: Creating the `KMLTrackingServlet` servlet to generate KML documents dynamically.

Once the servlet is created, the next step is to write its `processRequest()` method. The code is similar to the code for the `getTrackingUpdates()` method in Listing 11.8. The main difference is that this method generates a KML feed instead of returning a GWT serializable vector. Listing 11.11 shows the code that produces the KML output.

```
1  protected void processRequest(HttpServletRequest request,
       HttpServletResponse response)
2      throws ServletException, IOException {
3          response.setContentType("text/html;charset=UTF-8");
4          PrintWriter out = response.getWriter();
5          try{
6              response.setContentType("application/vnd.google-earth.kml+
                   xml");
7
8              out.write("<?xml version=\"1.0\" encoding=\"UTF-8\"?>");
9              out.write("<kml xmlns=\"http://www.opengis.net/kml/2.2\">"
                   );
10
11             List returnList = getDBTrackingUpdates();
12
13             if((returnList!=null) && (!returnList.isEmpty()))
14             {
15                 out.write("<Document>");
16                 out.write("<Folder>");
17                 out.write("<name>Active Tracking Sessions</name>");
18                 out.write("<open>1</open>");
19                 out.write("<description>Contains the active sessions in
                       the Tracking system</description>");
20
21                 String thePlacemarkString = "";
22                 for (Iterator it = returnList.iterator(); it.hasNext();)
23                 {
24                     TrackingUpdate theUpdate = (TrackingUpdate) it.next
                           ();
25
26                     thePlacemarkString = "<Placemark>";
27                     thePlacemarkString = thePlacemarkString + "<name>"+
                           theUpdate.getUsername()+"</name>";
28                     thePlacemarkString = thePlacemarkString + "<
                           description>"+theUpdate.getUsername()+" with
                           sessionid: "+theUpdate.getsessionId()+"</
                           description>";
29                     thePlacemarkString = thePlacemarkString+"<Point><
                           coordinates>"+theUpdate.getLongitude()+","+
                           theUpdate.getLatitude()+","+0+"</coordinates></
                           Point>";
30                     thePlacemarkString = thePlacemarkString + "</
                           Placemark>";
31
32                     out.write(thePlacemarkString);
33                 }
34                 out.write("</Folder>");
35                 out.write("</Document>");
36                 out.write("</kml>");
37             }
38             else
39             {
40                 out.write("</kml>");
41             }
42             out.close();
43         }
44         finally
45         {
46             out.close();
47         }
48     }
```

Listing 11.11: The processRequest() method of the KML servlet.

The code begins by setting the content type for the servlet's response, which is "application/vnd.google-earth.kml+xml" for Google Earth (line

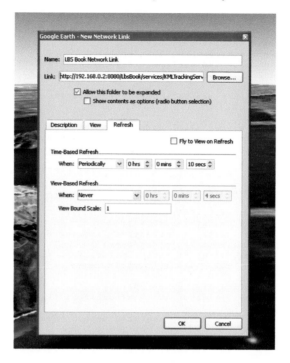

FIGURE 11.3: Creating a network link in Google Earth.

6). Lines 8 and 9 write to the output stream the header of the KML file. Since the code that obtains the information from the database is similar to that of Listing 11.8 (getTrackingUpdates()), this method has been named getDBTrackingUpdates(), which returns a list of TrackingUpdates objects. The function returns NULL if there is a database connection error and an empty list if there are no active sessions in the system. On the other hand, if there is at least one active session, then the for loop iterates over the list (lines 22–33) and writes a placemark per active session in the system. Within that loop, line 28 adds the username plus the session identifier as the placemark's description and line 29 sets the location's coordinates for the placemark. Finally, line 32 writes the placemark to the output stream.

Now that the KML is generated, the next step is to replace the processRequest() method that was created automatically by NetBeans in Listing 11.10 with this one (Listing 11.11). Then, *Clean and Build* the application, and *Deploy* it.

The last step is to create a Network Link so the Google Earth client in the main control station can obtain a feed of GPS fixes from the server and display them. Open Google Earth and go to the menu *Add→Network Link*. In the dialog box that appears (Figure 11.3), write in the name text field LBS Book Network Link and the URL of your KML tracking service in the

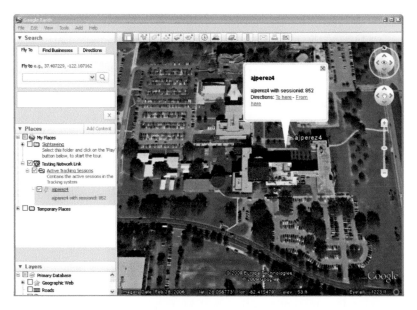

FIGURE 11.4: An active tracking session as shown in Google Earth.

Link text field (for us it is `http://192.168.0.2:8080/LbsBook/services/` `KMLTrackingServlet`). Then, click on the *Refresh* panel. There are two major options that instruct Google Earth when to update the network link. One is by time and the other is by a change in the view. For a time-based option, select in the *When* combo box of the *Time-Based Refresh*, then the *Periodically* option and set the time to update. In this example, the time was set to 10 seconds. Now click *Ok*. If there are active sessions in your tracking system, they should be shown like in Figure 11.4 and refreshed every 10 seconds. The *View-Based Refresh* option allows you to refresh the view every time there is a change in it.

11.3.3 Embedding Google Earth in a Web Application

Last section shows how to display the GPS fixes of the active sessions in the system in a Google Earth GUI. However, the placemarks, once displayed, are static and can't be manipulated to provide additional information. For example, you may want to click on one of those placemarks and see the buildings and landmarks around it, as if you were standing there, walking in the street. The Google Earth API (`http://code.google.com/apis/earth/`) and the Google Earth Plugin were developed for this purpose.

The Google Earth API is a JavaScript programming interface utilized to program Google Earth as if it was a complement of your application. The programming interface is a complement to the KML language that allows to control events in Google Earth, which cannot be done by KML only. This last section of the chapter explains how to embed Google Earth into a Web application with the GWT. In order to do this, one of the advanced concepts of the GWT needs to be explained: the GWT JavaScript Native Interface.

11.3.3.1   The GWT JavaScript Native Interface

The GWT JavaScript Native Interface is one of the most advanced concepts of the GWT. It allows you to write methods in JavaScript and invoke these methods from Java GWT code and vice versa, i.e., call Java GWT methods from JavaScript code. Listing 11.12 shows an example of JavaScript code embedded into Java GWT. The code has the following characteristics:

- The name of the method is `addNumbers()`.

- The JavaScript code is written within the characters /*-{ and }-*/.

- The scope of the method is private, meaning that this native code can be invoked within the class and instances of this class only. As with regular Java methods, native methods can have any of the three modifying scopes: public, private, or protected.

```
1  private int addNumbers (int op1 , op2)
2  /*-{
3      return op1 + op2;
4  }-*/;
```

Listing 11.12: A native JavaScript GWT method.

In order to invoke Java methods from JavaScript, the following method signature has to be used [31]:

`[instance-expr.]@class-name::method-name(param)(arguments)`

where:

- `[instance-expr.]`: Instance of the class that has the method the code is invoking. The instance is always mandatory unless the code is invoking a static method.

- `class-name::method-name`: Class and method signature for the method that is going to be invoked.

- `param`: Types of each of the parameters that are passed to the method. Each of the parameters is separated by a semicolon (;). Depending on the type, its signature can be as:

  - boolean: Z.
  - int: I.
  - double: D.

- [type]: Where type is a primitive type signature.
- any object: Lpackage/object. Here package is separated by back-slash (e.g., `java.lang.String` becomes `Ljava/lang/String`).

- `arguments`: The argument list, comma-separated.

Two remaining aspects that need to be mentioned from the JavaScript native interface are the variables that refer to the browser and the document. These are

- `$wnd`: Refers to the Window JavaScript element properties and methods. It is utilized to call the browser's methods and external JavaScript libraries associated with the project.

- `$doc`: Refers to the HTML elements in the page.

11.3.3.2 Loading Google Earth in a GWT Web Application

This section explains how to load Google Earth from a GWT Web application. The main idea is to modify the visualization application to utilize Google Earth as a mapping platform instead of Google Maps. The application will invoke the server every 10 seconds to update the location information and use the code developed in this section to add the updated locations to the Google Earth globe. The code included in this section is based on the code developed by Samuel Charron, which is available at `http://earth-api-samples.googlecode.com/svn/trunk/demos/gwt-earth/`. It assumes that the Google Earth Plugin is installed and a Google Maps API key is available (see Section 11.2.1).

Let us start by modifying the project's HTML and css (cascade style sheet[1]) files to include the following:

- In your project's HTML file (created in Section 10.3.1 and shown in Listing 10.2) include the following lines to import the Google Earth API to your document:

```
1    <head>
2        ....
3        ....
4        <script src="http://www.google.com/jsapi?hl=en&key=
             YOUR_GWT_KEY"></script>
5        <script>google.load("earth", "1");</script>
6    </head>
```

- In your project's css file (created in Section 10.3.1 and shown in Listing 10.3) include the following lines to setup the starting size of the `div` element for the Google Earth Globe:

---

[1]CSS files contain the styles of all HTML objects.

```
1  . map3dcontainer {
2     border : 1px solid silver ;
3     height : 500px ;
4  }
5
6  . map3d {
7     height : 100%;
8  }
```

Using the GWT JavaScript native interface, the code that initializes Google Earth is invoked. The idea is to wrap it up in a Widget that can be utilized as a GUI component for any screen that you need. Therefore, this Widget can be part of other GUI components and be shown in the browser. Listing 11.13 shows the Widget code that loads the GWT globe.

```
1  package cse.usf.edu.book.client;
2
3  import java.util.ArrayList;
4
5  import com.google.gwt.core.client.GWT;
6  import com.google.gwt.core.client.JavaScriptObject;
7  import com.google.gwt.user.client.*;
8  import com.google.gwt.user.client.ui.*;
9
10 public class GoogleEarthTrackingWidget extends Widget
11 {
12    private JavaScriptObject ge;
13    public static int globeId = 0;
14    private ArrayList pluginReadyListeners = new ArrayList();
15
16    public GoogleEarthTrackingWidget()
17    {
18       HTML html = new HTML(
19          "<div class='map3dcontainer' id='map3dcontainer" + globeId + "
             '>" +
20          "<div class='map3d' id='map3d" + globeId + "'></div></div>");
21       setElement(html.getElement());
22    }
23
24    public void init() {
25       initializeGoogleEarth(globeId);
26       globeId++;
27    }
28
29    public void addGELoadedListener(GELoadedListener listener)
30    {
31       this.pluginReadyListeners.add(listener);
32    }
33
34    public void ready(JavaScriptObject ge) {
35       for (int i = 0; i < pluginReadyListeners.size(); ++i) {
36          ((GELoadedListener)pluginReadyListeners.get(i)).geReady(ge);
37       }
38    }
39
40    private native void initializeGoogleEarth(int id) /*-{
41    var instance = this;
42
43    function initCB(obj)
44    {
45        ge = obj;
46        ge.getWindow().setVisibility(true);
```

```
47
48          instance.@cse.usf.edu.book.client.GoogleEarthTrackingWidget::
                 ready(Lcom/google/gwt/core/client/JavaScriptObject;)(ge);
49
50          var navControl = ge.getNavigationControl();
51          navControl.setVisibility(ge.VISIBILITY_SHOW);
52      }
53
54      function failureCB(object)
55      {
56          alert('load failed:'+object);
57      }
58      $wnd.google.earth.createInstance($doc.getElementById("map3d" + id),
                 initCB, failureCB);
59  }-*/;
60
61  }
```

Listing 11.13: Google Earth GWT Widget.

Let us explore the code. The code extends the Widget class, creating a custom-designed user interface object. The constructor of this method (lines 16–22) creates an HTML component. The HTML component creates two new div elements called map3dcontainer+globeId and map3d+globeId on the fly. Notice that these two lines in the class property invoke the map3dcontainer and the map3d css element classes in the project's css file (see Listing 10.3). After this, line 21 sets the element of the Widget to be the element defined by the HTML code.

Lines 29–39 show how to implement a listener to make sure Google Earth has been loaded correctly. To create this listener, you need to create an interface called GELoadedListener (shown in Listing 11.14). With this in mind, the method addGELoadedListener() (lines 29–32) adds a GELoadedListener object to the array of listeners and the ready() method (lines 34–38) fires the geReady() method of all the listeners once Google Earth has been loaded.

```
1  package cse.usf.edu.book.client;
2
3  import com.google.gwt.core.client.JavaScriptObject;
4
5  public interface GELoadedListener {
6
7      public void geReady(JavaScriptObject ge);
8  }
```

Listing 11.14: The GELoadedListener interface.

The next part of the code is the native method that performs the Google Earth's invocation. This method is the initializeGoogleEarth() method (lines 40–59). This code declares the functions (initCB) and (failureCB) that Google Earth will fire upon loading. The initCB JavaScript function sets the Globe to be visible, and invokes the ready() function (calling the Java GWT ready function from the JavaScript native code), which then fires the geReady() method of the listeners. The failureCB function shows an alert on the screen if Google Earth fails to load. Finally, line 58 invokes the Google Earth API function that loads Google Earth. This JavaScript function has three parameters, which are the elements where the globe will be added, and the two JavaScript functions (`initCB` and `failureCB`).

Now it is time to write a class that extends the `Composite` class and utilizes the already developed Google Earth widget. When completed, this class will perform the same functionality as Listing 11.2, invoking the server to update the locations and showing them in the Google Earth Globe.

Initially, create a class named `GoogleEarthTrackingWindow` under the package `cse.usf.edu.book.client` and copy the code included in Listing 11.15. Line 18 states that the `GoogleEarthTrackingWindow` class extends the `Composite` GWT object and implements the `GELoadedListener` class. This class has four fields, which are a vertical panel (line 20), a `GoogleEarthTracking` widget (line 21), a timer (line 22), and a vector of GWT features (line 24). This vector is utilized to store the placemarks for the locations created by Google Earth through the native methods shown in Listing 11.17.

Lines 26–32 contain the constructor of the `GoogleEarthTrackingWindow` class and create a new instance of the `GoogleEarthTracking` class. The most important part of this method is in line 30 where the code adds the current class as a listener of the `gew` object. When loaded successfully, the `gew` object fires the `geReady()` method (lines 34–45), which activates a timer (lines 37–44) to invoke the `updateActiveSessions()` method every ten seconds (as stated in line 44). Finally, the `updateActiveSessions()` method (lines 47–50) invokes the server to obtain the updated locations of those active sessions in the system.

After this, the next step is to modify the `onLoadMethod()`, as shown in Listing 11.16, to create an instance of `GoogleEarthTrackingWindow` and load it in the browser. Remember that the `onLoadMethod()` is the entry point, i.e., the main method, of the Web application. This listing modifies the entry point of the application so it loads the `GoogleEarthTrackingWindow` when the client Web application starts. Line 7 creates an instance of the `GoogleEarthTrackingWindow` and the next two lines set the size of such `Composite`. Finally, save the files and run the project in the GWT browser. You should see an image like the one shown in Figure 11.5. In this code, the timer that invokes the `updateActiveSessions()` method is triggered after the Google Earth is successfully loaded in the browser. If you try to add something else to the globe before it is loaded, an unexpected behavior may occur.

Please notice that we are using the same service interface defined in the last section for the client-side code with Google Maps. That is why in the code the class `GoogleEarthTrackingWindow` imports the `TrackingUpdate`, `TrackingServiceManager`, and the `TrackingServiceManagerAsync` classes.

```
1 package cse.usf.edu.book.client;
2
3 import java.util.Vector;
4
```

```
 5 import com.google.gwt.core.client.GWT;
 6 import com.google.gwt.core.client.JavaScriptObject;
 7 import com.google.gwt.user.client.Timer;
 8 import com.google.gwt.user.client.Window;
 9 import com.google.gwt.user.client.rpc.AsyncCallback;
10 import com.google.gwt.user.client.rpc.ServiceDefTarget;
11 import com.google.gwt.user.client.ui.Composite;
12 import com.google.gwt.user.client.ui.VerticalPanel;
13
14 import cse.usf.edu.book.client.entities.TrackingUpdate;
15 import cse.usf.edu.book.client.services.TrackingServiceManager;
16 import cse.usf.edu.book.client.services.TrackingServiceManagerAsync;
17
18 public class GoogleEarthTrackingWindow extends Composite implements
      GELoadedListener
19 {
20   private VerticalPanel vp = new VerticalPanel();
21   public GoogleEarthTrackingWidget gew = new GoogleEarthTrackingWidget
        ();
22   private Timer trackingTimer = null;
23
24   public Vector gwtFeatures = new Vector();
25
26   public GoogleEarthTrackingWindow()
27   {
28     vp.add(gew);
29     vp.setCellHeight(gew, "500px");
30     gew.addGELoadedListener(this);
31     initWidget(vp);
32   }
33
34   public void geReady(JavaScriptObject ge)
35   {
36     updateActiveSessions();
37     trackingTimer = new Timer()
38     {
39       public void run()
40       {
41         updateActiveSessions();
42       }
43     };
44     trackingTimer.scheduleRepeating(10000);
45   }
46
47   public void updateActiveSessions();
48   {
49
50   }
51 }
```

Listing 11.15: The `GoogleEarthTrackingWindow` `Composite` class.

```
 1 public void onModuleLoad() {
 2     AbsolutePanel theTest = new AbsolutePanel();
 3     theTest.setSize("95%", "95%");
 4
 5     RootPanel.get().add(theTest);
 6
 7     GoogleEarthTrackingWindow gew = new GoogleEarthTrackingWindow();
 8     gew.setHeight("500px");
 9     gew.setWidth("700px");
10
11     theTest.add(gew,0,0);
12     gew.gew.init();
13
```

FIGURE 11.5: Google Earth loaded in a Web application.

```
14        theTest . setVisible ( true );
15  }
```

Listing 11.16: Modifying the onModuleLoad() method.

At this point, the GoogleEarthTrackingWindow class can be further developed to show the users in real time. The first step to do this is to modify the GoogleEarthTrackingWidget class by adding the code shown in Listing 11.17. This code has two new native methods, the addPlacemark() method for adding a feature to the globe and the removePlacemark() method to remove a feature from the globe.

The addPlacemark() method of the GoogleEarthTrackingWidget creates and shows placemarks in the Google Earth globe. This method is a native JavaScript method that returns (as shown in line 1) a JavasScriptObject. This object is just an abstraction of an object that is created within a native method. In this particular method, the returned JavaScriptObject represents a newly created placemark in the Google Earth globe. The reference is needed, so it can be used later to remove it from the map. The addPlacemark() method receives three parameters, which are the latitude, longitude, and the caption for the placemark. Line 4 creates a new instance of a placemark, line 5 sets its caption, and line 6 adds the placemark as a feature of the Google Earth globe. At this point, the placemark has neither its location nor its style. The style for the placemark is created between lines 9 and 13, where a red circle as the icon for the placemark is selected. The location for the placemark is created between lines 17 and 19 and added to the placemark in line 21. Finally, line 22 returns a newly created instance of a placemark. The second method in this listing is the `removePlacemark()` method, which receives a `JavaScriptObject` as a parameter instance that represents a previously created placemark. The removal of such placemark is finally performed by the code in line 28.

```
1  public native JavaScriptObject addPlacemark (double latitude, double
        longitude, String caption)
2  /*-{
3
4          var placemark = ge.createPlacemark('');
5          placemark.setName(caption);
6          ge.getFeatures().appendChild(placemark);
7
8          // Create style map for placemark
9          var icon = ge.createIcon('');
10         icon.setHref('http://maps.google.com/mapfiles/kml/paddle/red-
                circle.png');
11         var style = ge.createStyle('');
12         style.getIconStyle().setIcon(icon);
13         placemark.setStyleSelector(style);
14
15         // Create point
16
17         var point = ge.createPoint('');
18         point.setLatitude(latitude);
19         point.setLongitude(longitude);
20
21         placemark.setGeometry(point);
22         return placemark;
23
24     }-*/;
25
26     public native void removePlacemark(JavaScriptObject obj)
27     /*-{
28          ge.getFeatures().removeChild(obj);
29     }-*/;
```

Listing 11.17: Adding and removing features using the native interface.

The next step is to write the code to invoke the server, get location updates, and show the updated locations in the globe. This is similar to the code that was developed in Listing 11.6, but instead of adding such locations to the map, this code will add them to the globe. The code is shown in Listing 11.18. Notice that since the changes have been done in the GWT client application, there is no need to change the service's implementation code in the server. At this point, you should be able to run the GWT client application and get location updates to be added to the Globe every 10 seconds.

Listing 11.18 shows the `updateActiveSessions()` method of the `GoogleEarthTrackingWindow`. This code updates the locations invoking a service at the server. There are three major parts: Lines 3–7 create the endpoint (destination address) of the service to be invoked; lines 9–34 show the code that executes when there is a successful invocation of the remote service (`onSuccess()` method) or there is a failure in the invocation (`onFailure()`); line 37 performs the service invocation to the server.

Let's take a look at the onSuccess() method (lines 10–28). The first line in the method (line 11) casts the returned result of the remote procedure as an array of TrackingUpdate objects. If the array is not null, then all previous placemarks shown in the Google Earth globe are removed. This is performed between lines 14–18 of the listing, where the gwFeatures vector is traversed and each of the JavaScriptObject instances stored in the vector are obtained and removed from the globle (line 17). Remember that the JavaScriptObject instances represent placemarks created using the native methods of the GoogleEarthTrackingWidget class. After each of the placemarks is removed from the globe, all the objects of the gwtFeatures vector (line 20) are also removed. Finally, between lines 22 and 27, each of the tracking updates is added to the Google Earth globe, where the placemarks' locations are given by the coordinates obtained from the server and the placemarks' captions are the usernames (line 24). The newly created placemarks are also stored in the gwtFeatures vector (line 25).

```
1  public void updateActiveSessions()
2  {
3      TrackingServiceManagerAsync theTrackingManager = (
           TrackingServiceManagerAsync) GWT.create(TrackingServiceManager
           .class);
4
5      ServiceDefTarget endpoint = (ServiceDefTarget) theTrackingManager;
6      String remoteServiceURL = "http://192.168.0.2:8080/Lbsbook/
           services/TrackingManager";
7      endpoint.setServiceEntryPoint(remoteServiceURL);
8
9      AsyncCallback callback = new AsyncCallback(){
10         public void onSuccess(Object result){
11             TrackingUpdate theUpdates[] = (TrackingUpdate[]) result;
12             if(theUpdates != null)
13             {
14               for(int i = 0; i < gwtFeatures.size(); i++)
15               {
16                 JavaScriptObject thePrevLoc = (JavaScriptObject)
                       gwtFeatures.get(i);
17                 gew.removePlacemark(thePrevLoc);
18               }
19
20               gwtFeatures.removeAllElements();
21
22               for(int i = 0; i < theUpdates.length; i++)
23               {
24                 JavaScriptObject theNewPlacemark = gew.addPlacemark(
                       theUpdates[i].getLatitude(), theUpdates[i].
                       getLongitude(), theUpdates[i].getUsername());
25                 gwtFeatures.add(theNewPlacemark);
26               }
27             }
28         }
29
30         public void onFailure(Throwable caught)
31         {
32             Window.alert("An Internal Error has ocurred: " + caught.
                   getMessage());
33             trackingTimer.cancel();
34         }
35     };
36
```

```
37    theTrackingManager . getTrackingUpdates ( callback );
38  }
```

Listing 11.18: The **updateActiveSessions**() method for updating locations in Google Earth.

11.4 Data Visualization and the LBIS Tracking System Example

This chapter describes how to show the active sessions in the LBIS system in a Google Map or Google Earth graphical user interface. The main control station queries the database in the server to obtain and display the active sessions in the interface in real time. This query-response method is executed, at a pre-established frequency, using the Google Web Toolkit, which facilitates the transfer of information between client and server hiding from the programmer all the low-level details of such transfers. Implementing the visualization capabilities described in this chapter allow emergency officers, caregivers, parents, guardians, etc., to visualize the users of the system in real time in a very compelling graphical interface from any computer connected to the Internet.

Chapter 12

Processing the Data

12.1 Introduction

Location-based applications provide services based on the geographical location of the device. In order to provide enhanced LBS services or to provide the services in a more efficient manner, LBIS perform some data processing to transform that data into information and run algorithms to improve its performance. According to the software architecture described in Section 1.4, this data processing can be done in a local fashion (mobile device-side processing), as shown in Figure 1.5, in a remote machine (server-side processing), as shown in Figure 1.6, or in a combined or collaborative fashion between the mobile device and the server.

The decision on where to do the processing depends on the application, the service, and the resources needed. Some applications require local processing to provide immediate feedback to the user. Some other applications require this processing to be performed in a more powerful machine because of the mobile device's limitations on computing power, memory, communication, and energy. Further, data availability is also an aspect to consider since the data might not be available locally.

This chapter provides examples of data processing in the mobile device and the server. The first example performs local data processing to reduce the communication and energy costs of sending unnecessary GPS fixes to the server. Then, two examples of data processing in the server are included to show how to enhance the LBS service beyond real-time tracking.

12.2 Mobile Device-Side Processing

Consider our LBS tracking system example and assume that to track a device in real time the application in the mobile device sends position data to the server every second, i.e., $24*3600 = 86400$ position updates to the server every day. This has strong implications in terms of 1) energy consumption in the mobile device, 2) bandwidth consumption, which is costly and scarce in cellular networks, and 3) data storage in the server. And this is for one device only!

Assume that the device does not move 50% of the day. Does the application really need to send all the GPS fixes to track the device? Definitively, not. In this case, approximately 43200 unnecesary position updates would be sent on a daily basis! Now, assume that the device moves, but it remains in a 800 square meters area the entire day. Is it necessary to send all the position updates to keep track of this device if all you need to know is whether the device goes beyond this particular area? Is it necessary to send all the fixes if you know that the device is not changing its direction and you know how fast it is moving? The answers to these questions seem to be no. The challenge is to design and implement position update algorithms that would reduce the number of updates, and therefore, reduce network traffic (save scarce bandwidth and reduce communication costs), save energy, and reduce the server overhead while being able to accurately track the device. These algorithms, which are implemented in the mobile device tracking application to filter out unnecessary position updates, are named here as Critical Point Algorithms (CPA) [16].

CPA can be implemented in many different ways. In this chapter, one of those possible implementations is shown, which uses the distance and time traveled by the device and the accuracy of the fixes to make the decision as to whether to send or not a GPS fix to the server. The algorithm, which is shown in Listing 12.1, works as follows. Initially, when the tracking application is started in the mobile device, the first valid position that the mobile device calculates is marked as a critical point and sent to the server. After this, the distance from every valid position to the last critical point is calculated. If the distance is greater than some distance threshold, then the last valid coordinate is marked as critical and sent to the server. If the distance is less than the threshold, then the algorithm compares the horizontal diluted of precision (HDOP) values of the last critical position and the last valid position. A lower HDOP value means less error, and therefore better accuracy. If the last valid position is more accurate than the last critical point, then the position is marked as critical and sent to the server. If the GPS receiver does not provide the HDOP data directly, the location API provides the `getHorizontalAccuracyy()` method, which is a good substitute, as shown in Listing 12.1.

If neither of the two conditions described above marks the last valid position as critical point, then the elapsed time from the last critical position to this last valid position is calculated. If the elapsed time is greater than a time threshold, then the last valid coordinate is marked as critical and sent to the server.

```
1  // This code assumes that there is a valid position called
       lastCriticalLocation
2  // which represents the last position sent to the server.
3  // distThresshold is a double value in meters > 0.
```

```
4  // timeThresshold is a time in milliseconds thresshold > 0.
5
6  public boolean distanceBasedCP(Location lastValidLocation)
7  {
8      QualifiedCoordinates theLastCriticalPoint = lastCriticalLocation.
           getQualifiedCoordinates();
9      QualifiedCoordinates theValidLastCoordinates =  lastValidLocation.
           getQualifiedCoordinates();
10
11     if(theLastCriticalPoint.distance(theValidLastCoordinates) >
           distThresshold)
12     {
13         lastCriticalLocation = lastValidLocation;
14         return true;
15     }
16     else if(theValidLastCoordinates.getHorizontalAccuracy() <
           theLastCriticalPoint.getHorizontalAccuracy())
17     {
18         lastCriticalLocation = lastValidLocation;
19         return true;
20     }
21     else if(lastValidLocation.getTimestamp() - lastCriticalLocation.
           getTimestamp() > timeThresshold)
22     {
23         lastCriticalLocation = lastValidLocation;
24         return true;
25     }
26     return false;
27 }
```

Listing 12.1: The distance-time-based critical point algorithm.

The distance threshold plays an important role in the algorithm: if the distance threshold is set too high, then the mobile device will send very few fixes to the LBIS server, and therefore, it will be very difficult to track the device accurately. Further, it may imply a long time between critical points, which might be critical for some real-time applications. For example, by the time the system gets a critical point, it might be too late to provide the intended service. On the other hand, if the distance threshold is set too low, then many unnecessary position updates will be sent, wasting precious resources.

Figure 12.1 shows the effect of applying the critical point algorithm in an application used to track an individual while walking through the Tampa campus of the University of South Florida. In this example, the distance threshold was set to 20 meters and the time threshold to 30 seconds. This means that the device will send a position update every second only if it is moving at a rate faster than 20 m/s (72 Km/h) or every 30 seconds in the worst case. Figure 12.1(a) shows all the GPS fixes calculated by the device and sent to the server without the CPA; a total of 386 GPS fixes recorded in a seven-minute walk. Figure 12.1(b) shows the same walk but using the CPA algorithm. In this case, only 20 fixes (roughly 5%) from all recorded ones were marked as critical points and sent to the server. This algorithm was also tested while moving in cars. In that scenario, it marked between 20%–30% of all the fixes as critical and still allowed to track the vehicle during the entire trip.

Of course, different policies and threshold values could be implemented. The beauty of the critical point algorithm presented above is that it is totally customizable, as these values can be easily changed according to the specific needs of the application.

12.3   Server-Side Processing

Server-side processing is usually performed to enhance the service beyond simple tracking. In this section, two examples of server-side processing are described, one to find the closest friend to the user's location, and one to provide situational awareness.

12.3.1   Finding the Closest Friend

In addition to tracking a user in real time, a location-based information system could provide a service that, upon the user's request, will return the position and name of the closest friend to the user's location. The user may want to know whether there is a friend close enough to have lunch with, or maybe to ask for help during an emergency. This is a very general application, as "friend" can be replaced by restaurant, attraction, movie theater, hospital, etc.

This enhancement to the service can be implemented by a servlet that would query the database in search of the active sessions in the system. The query would take as parameters the location of the device that is invoking the service and return all active sessions with the distances in meters to that location. Once the result of the query is obtained, the algorithm would iterate over the result and find the nearest session. Then it would return a string with the session information to the device that invoked the service. The following paragraphs describe how to implement this enhanced service.

The first step is to create a servlet. To do this, right-click on the project name in the *Project* panel. In the menu that appears, click on *New→Servlet*. In the dialog box that appears, write `NearestSessionServlet` in the *Class Name* text field. In the package, select the `cse.usf.book.client.services`, which is the package that was created as part of the server-side code in Chapter 10, Section 10.3.2. In the next dialog box, write in servlet name `NearestSession`, and in URL pattern(s) write `/services/Nearest`. Click *Finish* to create the servlet. NetBeans should open a new Java file as shown in Listing 12.2.

```
1  package cse.usf.book.client.services;
2
3  import java.io.IOException;
4  import java.io.PrintWriter;
5  import javax.servlet.ServletException;
6  import javax.servlet.http.HttpServlet;
7  import javax.servlet.http.HttpServletRequest;
```

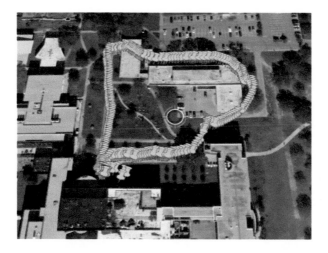

(a) Trip without the CPA algorithm. Position updates are sent to the server every second.

(b) Trip with the CPA algorithm. Only critical points are sent to the server.

FIGURE 12.1: The distance-time-based critical point algorithm.

```
 8| import javax.servlet.http.HttpServletResponse;
 9|
10|
11| public class NeaerestSessionServlet extends HttpServlet {
12|
13|     protected void processRequest(HttpServletRequest request,
   |         HttpServletResponse response)
14|     throws ServletException, IOException {
15|         response.setContentType("text/html;charset=UTF-8");
16|         PrintWriter out = response.getWriter();
17|         try {
18|             /* TODO output your page here
19|             out.println("<html>");
20|             out.println("<head>");
21|             out.println("<title>Servlet NewServlet</title>");
22|             out.println("</head>");
23|             out.println("<body>");
24|             out.println("<h1>Servlet NewServlet at " + request.
   |                 getContextPath() + "</h1>");
25|             out.println("</body>");
26|             out.println("</html>");
27|             */
28|         } finally {
29|             out.close();
30|         }
31|     }
32|
33|     @Override
34|     protected void doGet(HttpServletRequest request,
   |         HttpServletResponse response)
35|     throws ServletException, IOException {
36|         processRequest(request, response);
37|     }
38|
39|
40|     @Override
41|     protected void doPost(HttpServletRequest request,
   |         HttpServletResponse response)
42|     throws ServletException, IOException {
43|         processRequest(request, response);
44|     }
45|
46|     @Override
47|     public String getServletInfo() {
48|         return "Short description";
49|     }
50|
51| }
```

Listing 12.2: Server-side servlet example.

Now, modify the `processRequest()` method as shown in Listing 12.3. Using the database model described in Chapter 7, the query finds the last received locations from all the active sessions in the system and for each one it calculates the distance to the location passed by the request. The query is shown between lines 22 and 29, which utilizes the PostGIS function `ST_distance_sphere()`. This PostGIS function returns the distance in meters between two locations that are in the same spherical model. The query contains a subquery in the "from" statement to obtain the identifier of the last received location per session. The result of the subquery is utilized as a table to join with the others and obtain the username, location, and session information. Lines 31 and 32 set the values of the parameters in the query.

Once it is executed (line 34), the code iterates over the result of the query to obtain the nearest session (lines 47–49). Finally, line 53 writes the information to the output stream.

To invoke this code, you will have to use an HTTP client. To test this example, clean, build, and deploy the project and open your browser. Write the URL http://your_server:your_port/LbsBook/services/services/Nearest?lat=-82.6&lng=28, where your_server:your_port is the IP address of the server where the application is deployed.

```
1  //this code asumes that it is executed inside a servlet.
2  //it takes as parameters the latitude and longitude from the request
3  //and returns the information of the nearest session to the request.
4
5  protected void processRequest(HttpServletRequest request,
       HttpServletResponse response)
6       throws ServletException, IOException {
7     response.setContentType("text/html;charset=UTF-8");
8   PrintWriter out = response.getWriter();
9
10  double distance = Double.MAX_VALUE;
11  TrackingUpdate theClosestOne = new TrackingUpdate();
12  try
13  {
14    try{
15        javax.naming.InitialContext ic  = new javax.naming.
               InitialContext();
16        javax.sql.DataSource dataSource = (javax.sql.DataSource)ic.
               lookup("jdbc/lbsbook");
17        Connection theConnection = dataSource.getConnection();
18
19        double latitude = Double.parseDouble(request.getParameter("lat
               "));
20        double longitude = Double.parseDouble(request.getParameter("lng
               "));
21
22        PreparedStatement queryStatement = theConnection.
               prepareStatement("select fieldsession.sessionid as sesid,
               fielduser.username as uname, ST_AsText(tracking.position)
               as pos , ST_distance_sphere(tracking.position,
               ST_GeomFromText('POINT(? ?)', 32661)) as distance "+
23        "from fieldsession, tracking,fielduser, (select max(idtracking)
               as idtrack "+
24                                  "from fieldsession,
                                       tracking "+
25                                  "where fieldsession.
                                       datestop is NULL
                                       and fieldsession.
                                       sessionid =
                                       tracking.sessionid
                                       "+

                                  "group by
                                       fieldsession.
                                       sessionid) as s2 "+
26        "where fieldsession.datestop is NULL and "+
27        "fieldsession.sessionid = tracking.sessionid and "+
28        "tracking.idtracking = s2.idtrack and "+
29        "fieldsession.iduser = fielduser.iduser ");
30
31        queryStatement.setDouble(1, longitude);
32        queryStatement.setDouble(2, latitude);
33
34        ResultSet rs = queryStatement.executeQuery();
```

```
35
36        double d_temp = 0.0;
37        while(rs.next())
38        {
39            d_temp = rs.getDouble("distance");
40            if(d_temp < distance)
41            {
42                theClosestOne.setSessionid(rs.getInt("sesid"));
43                theClosestOne.setUsername(rs.getString("uname"));
44                Point theNewPoint = new Point(rs.getString("pos"));
45
46                theClosestOne.setLongitude(theNewPoint.getX());
47                theClosestOne.setLatitude(theNewPoint.getY());
48                distance = d_temp;
49            }
50        }
51
52        String theReturnString = "<";
53        theReturnString = theReturnString + ";"+theClosestOne.
              getUsername()+";"+theClosestOne.getsessionId()+";"+
              theClosestOne.getLongitude()+";"+theClosestOne.getLatitude()
              +">";
54        out.write(theReturnString);
55    }
56    catch (NamingException ex){
57        Logger.getLogger(DevicerServiceManagerImpl.class.getName()).log(
              Level.SEVERE, null, ex);
58    }
59    catch (SQLException ex){
60                    Logger.getLogger(DevicerServiceManagerImpl.class.
                          getName()).log(Level.SEVERE, null, ex);
61    }
62  }
63  finally
64  {
65      out.close();
66  }
67 }
```

Listing 12.3: Server-side processing example.

As the reader can easily realize, there are many types of enhanced services that can be provided doing some processing in the server. The "find the closest friend" service is just one example. Other examples include traffic alert notifications with or without alternate routes, situational awareness alerts, geofencing services for people with Alzheimer's disease, geofencing service to watch your children, location-based advertisement, finding restaurants, hospitals, services, etc., emergency services, fleet and asset management, pet tracking, roadside assistance, navigation, city sightseeing, and many others. The next section provides details of an enhanced service for situational awareness.

12.3.2   Integration of LBIS and Wireless Sensor Networks for Situational Awareness

Wireless sensor networks (WSNs) are self-configured, infrastructureless wireless networks made of small and cheap devices equipped with specialized sensors used to collect data from the environment and send it to a reporting

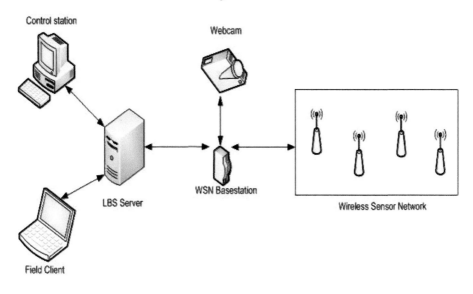

FIGURE 12.2: Integration of WSNs and LBIS.

site where the data can be observed and analyzed [35, 40]. Usually, WSNs are utilized to monitor a variable of interest in a remote environment or in dangerous places for human beings. The idea is to deploy (maybe throwing) many WSN nodes in the area of interest and use the network in a disposable manner until it dies. Given the cheap nature of the devices, WSN nodes are very constrained in terms of computational, memory, energy, and communication capabilities, similar to cellular phones.

Normally, WSNs are static, meaning that once the WSN devices are deployed in the area of interest, they do not move. Although some mobile wireless sensor networks exist, they are complex and usually restricted to a rather small number of nodes and applications. The concept of participatory sensing described in Chapter 1 can be seen as a mobile version of a possibly very large wireless sensor network.

There are many applications in which WSNs can be used. WSNs have been used in transportation to measure traffic conditions; in environmental applications to monitor for gases, air pollution, water levels, etc.; in disaster prevention to monitor the possibility of mudslides; in military and security applications to detect intruders; in engineering applications to monitor bridge structures; in home automation applications; in health care to monitor patients; in industry to monitor manufacturing processes, etc.

This section shows how WSNs can be integrated into a LBIS in a military setting to provide situational awareness to mobile users (soldiers). Figure 12.2 shows the basic architecture of a WSN and its integration into a LBIS system. The WSN nodes are equipped with infrared sensors for intrusion detection. The nodes are deployed in such a linear manner that the infrared sensors build a "virtual" fence in a specific area. Upon an intrusion, the sensors notify the base station, which at the same time takes a picture with a Web camera. The base station then assembles a message with the notification and the picture and sends it to the LBIS server. At the same time, the LBIS system has been tracking the soldiers in real time, so it knows the whereabouts of each soldier in the system. Upon receiving the intrusion notification from the wireless sensor network, the LBIS server takes two actions. First, it immediately sends the notification to the "main control station," so 24/7 monitoring personnel knows about the situation instantly. Second, the LBIS server finds all the soldiers within a radius of 200 meters from the virtual fence (WSN) and sends the same notification to all of them, so they also know at the same time that an intrusion has occurred. Further, since they also receive the picture, they also know the type of intrusion.

12.4   Processing the Data and the LBIS Tracking System Example

The relationship of this chapter with our LBIS tracking system example is straightforward and direct. Without any data processing at the mobile device and the server, we could not be able to improve the performance of the system nor provide a reasonable service to the end users. One example of processing at the mobile device was given as well as two examples of server-side processing to enhance the service beyond plain tracking.

Many other processing possibilities exist, in particular at the server-side, given that the back-end of the LBIS system, 1) can store user data for a long time and therefore has access to historical data about the users, and 2) may have access to different databases located anywhere in the world where to obtain additional information pertaining the service. For example, imagine that the service is meant to provide users with real-time traffic congestion notifications. Once a particular user has been tracked for a long time, historical travel data of that particular user can be utilized to predict where the user is heading once he or she begins a new trip. With that prediction, the system can query real-time traffic databases and obtain congestion information about the roads the user is about to use. With all that information the system can send notifications to the user way before he or she hits a congested road. Further, the system could also calculate and provide the user with alternate routes.

Appendix A

Installing the Software Development Environments (SDE)

A.1 Introduction

This appendix lists the software and hardware components required to implement the LBIS tracking system example described in this book. It guides the reader through the software installation process in order to have the application development environment ready.

In the following sections, this appendix describes the installation procedure of the software components needed in the server as well as the development environments needed to develop applications for different mobile devices, in the following order:

- **Server:** The server is the component in the architecture where the data from all clients is stored and where additional intensive computations can be performed; therefore, it needs a database and an application server.

- **Server-side application development environment:** This corresponds to the Java development environment for servers. Server-side applications perform data analysis and run computationally intensive algorithms to enhance the system's performance and provide additional services to the user.

- **Client-side application development environment:** It consists of the Java development environment for regular computers, such as desktops, laptops, etc., i.e., computers without memory, energy, and computing power limitations.

- **Mobile-side application development environment:** This consist of the Java development environment for resource-constraint devices, such as cellular phones, PDAs, and the like.

The installation assumes that the server has Windows XP Service Pack 3 installed, with at least 1 GB of RAM, and the user has administration permissions.

A.2 Server-Side Software Development Environment

The server is the core of the system, as it provides two fundamental resources for all applications: storage space and computational power. The server will be used as the main repository for all the information generated by the different LBS clients. In addition, server-side applications will be run in this machine for further data processing and analysis, visualization, and decision making, such as providing real-time feedback to the users. In order to perform these tasks, the server needs to be equipped with a database for storage and an application server to develop and run applications for data analysis. The following list contains the software that needs to be installed in the server:

- Sun Java Development Kit Standard Edition, or Java SE, version 6, update 13 or better.

- Sun Glassfish Enterprise Server V 2.1 or better.

- Postgres 8.3.7-1 or better.

- Postgis 1.3.6-1 or better (check compatibility with current Postgres version).

- JDBC version 3 drivers for Postgres.

In the following, the installation process of each of these items is explained. Given that most of these software packages have their own application installer, this appendix will focus only on those steps where the user is asked to define parameters that are critical for the correct installation of the environment.

A.2.1 Sun Java Development Kit (JDK) Standard Edition

The first component to be installed is the Sun JDK SE. The installer can be downloaded from Sun's Website at `http://java.sun.com/javase/downloads/` or from the book's Website at `http://www.csee.usf.edu/~labrador/LBIS`.

The installation process of this software is self-explanatory; it only requires to double-click on the icon of the executable file.

A.2.2 GlassFish Application Server

The next component to be installed is GlassFish, the application server. The installer can be downloaded from `https://glassfish.dev.java.net/public/downloadsindex.html` or from the book's Website.

The installation process of this component is mostly self-explanatory, with the exception of the following steps:

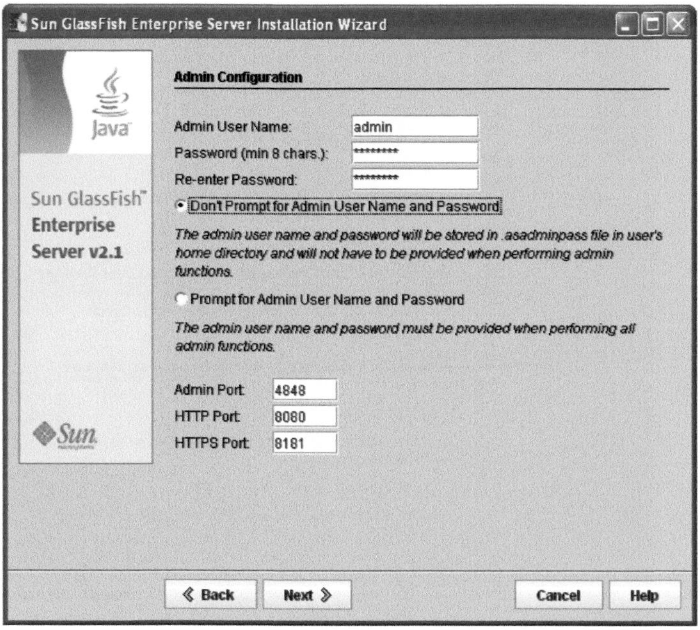

FIGURE A.1: Administrator information and communication ports for GlassFish.

A.2.2.1 Administrator Information and Communication Ports

In this step, as shown in Figure A.1, the user is required to define the user name and password of the administrator of the server. In addition, the server requires the definition of three communication ports:

- **Admin port:** This port is used for the administrator to configure the server: registering applications, installing available resources like databases, etc. The default value for this port is *4848*.

- **HTTP port:** This port is used by the clients to access their applications. The default value for this port is *8080*.

- **HTTPS port:** This port is used by the clients to access their applications in a secure manner, implementing an encryption scheme. The default value for this port is *8181*.

A.2.2.2 Recommended Options

The server requires the administrator to define a series of options for general performance. These options, as shown in Figure A.2, are the following:

- **Upgrade from Previous Version:** If this option is chosen, the server

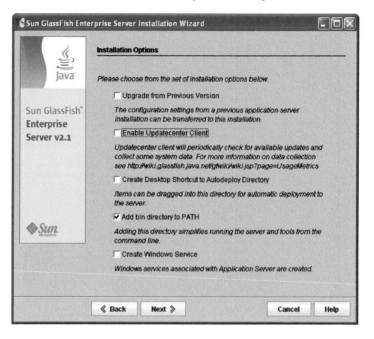

FIGURE A.2: Recommended options for the server.

will import the settings from an existing installation. Here, it is assumed that the server has never had GlassFish installed before; therefore, this option is left unchanged.

- ***Enable Updatecenter Client:*** If checked, this option allows the server to install updates automatically. This option is left unchecked to have more control and avoid conflicts with existing applications.

- ***Create Desktop Shortcut to Autodeploy Folder:*** This option allows the administrator to deploy applications directly to the server. In the proposed platform, the application deployment will be performed using NetBeans, so the shortcut is not selected.

- ***Add bin directory to PATH:*** This option allows the administrator to execute the configuration tools of the server from the command line without having to find the application server's folder in the machine.

- ***Create Windows Service:*** This option allows the administrator to control the server from the Windows services options. This option was not selected to keep manual control of the server activity.

FIGURE A.3: Location of the files to be replaced in GlassFish.

A.2.2.3 Special File Replacement

During the GlassFish installation process, it was detected that the current version had problems working with the Java Persistence API in Postgres. Given that this problem was not present in previous versions, it was solved replacing the two files related with these operations. The correct files, which are included in the Website of the book, are the following:

- toplink-essentials.jar

- toplink-essentials-agent.jar

These files are located in the `lib` folder of the server installation, e.g., C:\Program Files\glassfish-v2ur2\lib or C:\Sun\AppServer\lib, as shown in Figure A.3. If you are not completely sure about replacing these files, you can always change the names of the current files as a backup measure.

A.2.2.4 Starting and Stopping the Application Server

Once the application server has been installed, it is time to get it started. Based on the recommended options previously mentioned, it is assumed that the user will be using the command line. The command that allows the user to control the activity of the server is `asadmin`. It can be used as a command with a list of parameters, or when called alone, it opens a shell environment where more than one command can be executed in the server.

```
C:\WINDOWS\system32\cmd.exe - asadmin                                    _ □ x
Microsoft Windows XP [Version 5.1.2600]
(C) Copyright 1985-2001 Microsoft Corp.

C:\Documents and Settings\Research>cd \

C:\>cd sun\AppServer\bin

C:\Sun\AppServer\bin>asadmin
Use "exit" to exit and "help" for online help.
asadmin> start-domain domain1
Starting Domain domain1, please wait.
Default Log location is C:\Sun\AppServer\domains\domain1\logs\server.log.
Redirecting output to C:/Sun/AppServer/domains/domain1/logs/server.log
Domain domain1 is ready to receive client requests. Additional services are bein
g started in background.
Domain [domain1] is running [Sun GlassFish Enterprise Server v2.1 (9.1.1) (build
 b60e-fcs)] with its configuration and logs at: [C:\Sun\AppServer\domains].
Admin Console is available at [http://localhost:4848].
Use the same port [4848] for "asadmin" commands.
User web applications are available at these URLs:
[http://localhost:8080 https://localhost:8181 ].
Following web-contexts are available:
[/web1  /__wstx-services ].
Standard JMX Clients (like JConsole) can connect to JMXServiceURL:
[service:jmx:rmi:///jndi/rmi://enb213d:8686/jmxrmi] for domain management purpos
es.
Domain listens on at least following ports for connections:
[8080 8181 4848 3700 3820 3920 8686 ].
Domain does not support application server clusters and other standalone instanc
es.

asadmin> _
```

FIGURE A.4: Starting the application server.

In the example shown in Figure A.4, the second option was used. Even though the `asadmin` program was added on the PATH, it was decided to go directly to the folder that contains the application just to show its location in the server's folders. Once `asadmin` is run and the shell environment is active, the application server is started by typing the following command:

    start-domain <name of the domain>

By default, the application server creates an initial domain called `domain1`, which is the one used in the example. During the process, the shell shows a list of available services with their respective ports, such as the administration console, regular and secure Web applications, available Web content, and others.

In order to test whether the server was started correctly and is up and running, you can open the server's initial Web page from your favorite browser, as shown in Figure A.5, by typing the following URL `http://<server'sIPaddress>:8080`.

Similarly, the command to stop the application server is the following:

    stop-domain <name of the domain>

A.2.3 Postgres

Postgres is one of the most popular databases in the market today, not only because is a free open source program but also because is one the most

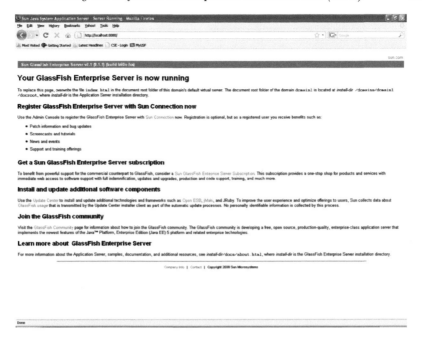

FIGURE A.5: Test Web page to check if the server is running correctly.

robust and reliable databases available. The installer's executable file can be downloaded from `http://www.postgresql.org/download/`.

The installation process of this database is very simple and self-explanatory for the most part. Just two steps require some extra attention: the administrator information and the communication ports. This information is critical to connect the database with the application server.

A.2.3.1 Administrator Information

In this step, Postgres creates a superuser for the database named `postgres`. In Windows, this user has total control over the operation of the database and is responsible for all activities executed in the database.

If there is no previous version of Postgres installed in the server, the program just asks for a new password, as shown in Figure A.6. In other cases, it requires the password of the existing `postgres` superuser.

A.2.3.2 Communication Port

In this step, the installer asks you to define the communication port that Postgres will use to listen for connections. By default, Postgres uses port *5432*, as shown in Figure A.7. This port is necessary to register the database as a resource in the application server.

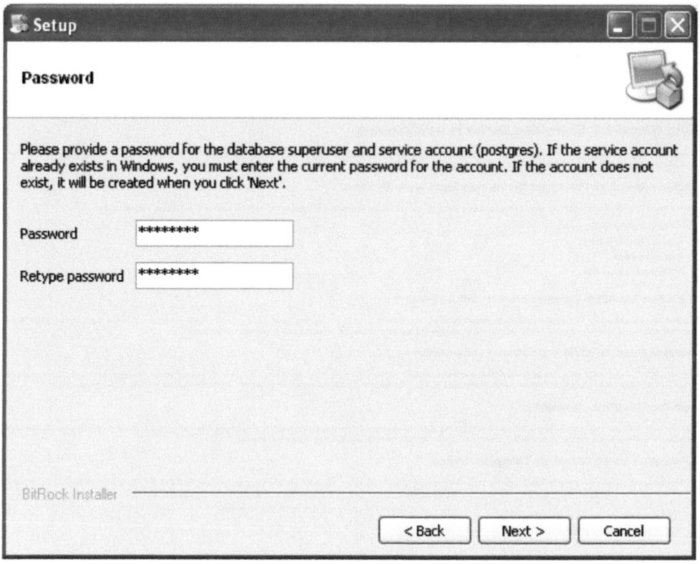

FIGURE A.6: Administrator information.

A.2.4 PostGIS

PostGIS is an extension that adds support for geographic objects to the Postgres object-relational database necessary to store and manage the location of the mobile clients. The installer's executable file can be downloaded from http://postgis.refractions.net/download/.

The installation process of PostGIS creates a template table in Postgres that contains the appropriate definition of the data types and large set of functions for processing geographic information. Based on this template, the user can create the tables of its own geographic information system.

In order to create the template table, the installer requires the user to include the information of the database administrator and the communication port, as shown in Figure A.8.

A.2.4.1 Database Information

PostGIS also offers the option to create a geographic (spatial) database during the installation process. Figures A.9 and A.10 show how to select this option and name the new database, respectively.

A.2.5 JDBC Drivers

In order for the application server to connect with the databases, the appropriate JDBC drivers need to be installed. It is important to make sure that the version of the drivers is compatible with the version of Postgres installed

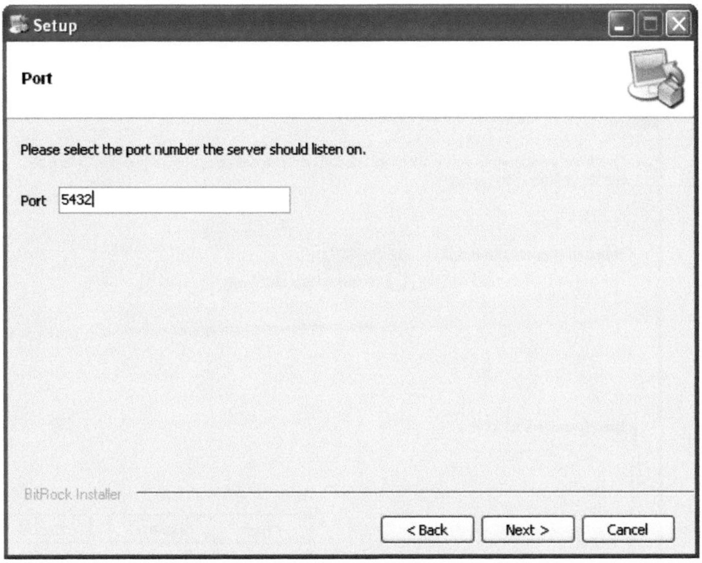

FIGURE A.7: Communication port.

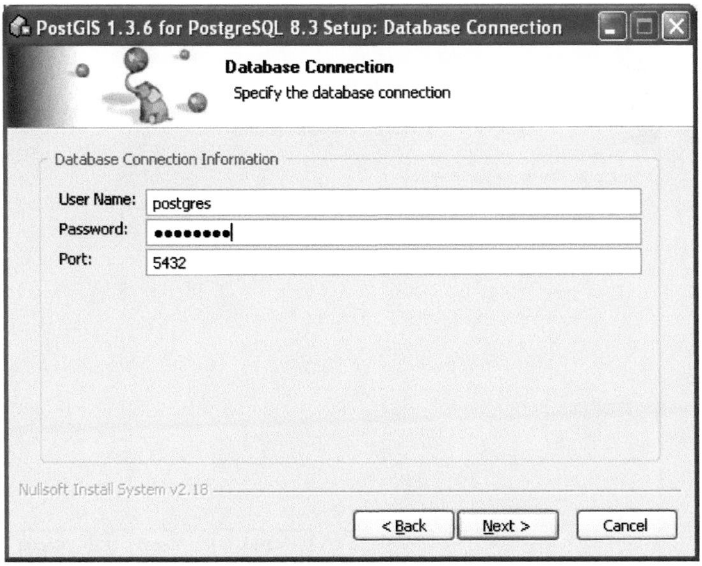

FIGURE A.8: Postgres's administrator information and communication port for PostGIS.

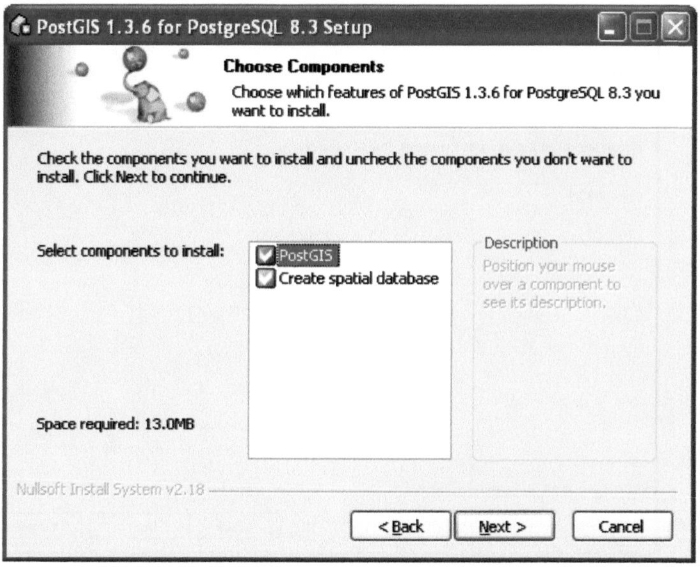

FIGURE A.9: Option to create a new geographic database.

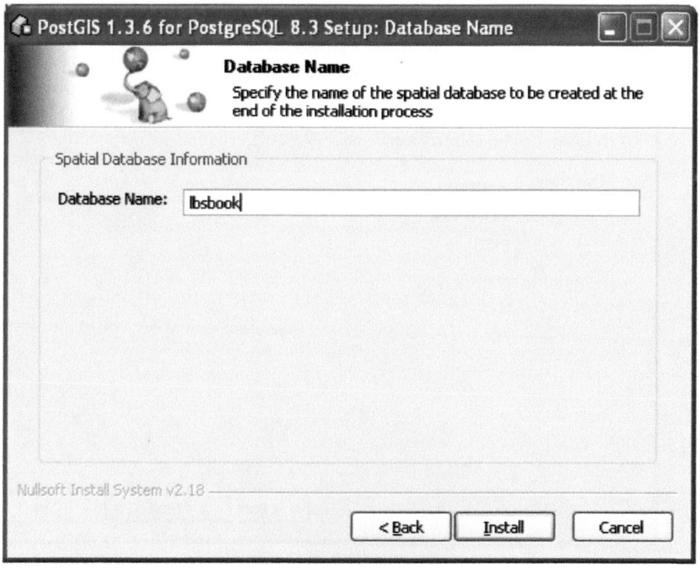

FIGURE A.10: Name of the new geographic database.

in your machine. The JDBC drivers for Postgres are a single *jar* file that can be downloaded from `http://jdbc.postgresql.org/download.html`.

The drivers of PostGIS are automatically installed in the JDBC folder of Postgres, as shown in Figure A.11.

Both Postgres and PostGIS *jar* files must be copied into the server's folders to make them available. The path where these files must be copied is, as shown in Figure A.12, on the external libraries of the domain where the applications will be running, in this case domain1 `C:\Sun\AppServer\domains\domain1\lib\ext`.

A.2.6   Registering the Database in the Server

At this point, the application server, the database, and the drivers have been installed. However, they still do not know about the existence of each other. Thus, the next step is to register the database in the list of resources of the application server.

Assuming that the application server has been already started, the first step is to log-in in GlassFish's administration console. The login screen, shown in Figure A.13, is accessed by typing the URL `http://`<`IPaddressoftheserver`>`:4848` in the browser of your preference.

The installation of the database in the server requires two steps:

- **Creating a connection pool:** This element is in charge of defining the access to the database by setting variables like the maximum number of concurrent connections, timeout for disconnection, location of the database, administrator information, communication port, etc.

- **Creating a JDBC resource:** This element is in charge of defining the database as a resource for the applications that will be running in the server. The idea of having these two elements separately is to procure independence between the application and the actual database, so changes can be done to the second one without virtually changing anything in the applications.

These two elements can be found in the tree of options in the *Common Tasks* panel, located on the left side of the administration console. From the initial tree of options, go to *Resources*. From the options that appear under *Resources*, click on *JDBC*. After this click, the options that refer to connection pools and JDBC resources will appear, as shown in Figure A.14.

A.2.6.1   Creating a Connection Pool

The first step is to create a connection pool that will serve as the access door for the database. From the *Common Tasks* panel, select the *Connection Pools* option, as shown in Figure A.14.

The panel on the right shows the existing connection pools. To create a

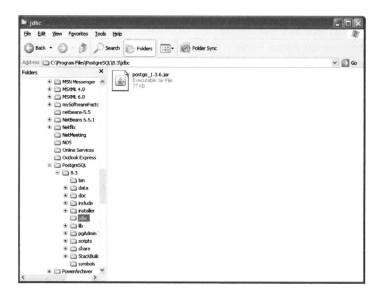

FIGURE A.11: Location of the JDBC drivers.

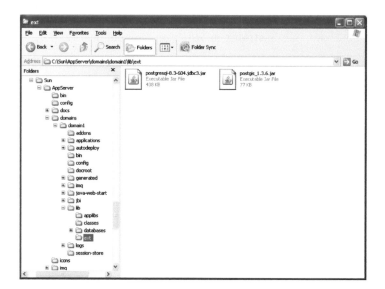

FIGURE A.12: Location of the PostGIS and Postgres JDBC drivers in the application server.

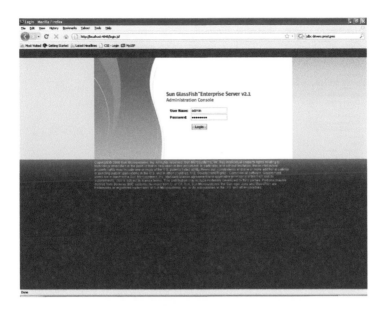

FIGURE A.13: Administration console of the application server.

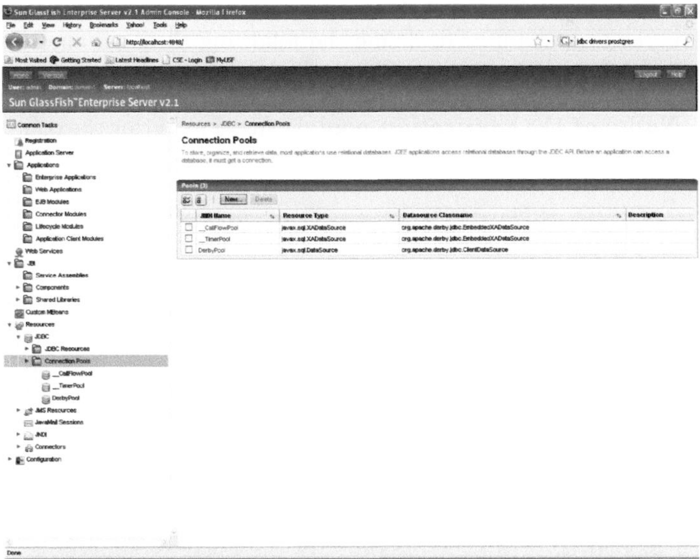

FIGURE A.14: Location of the option for creating a connection pool in the application server.

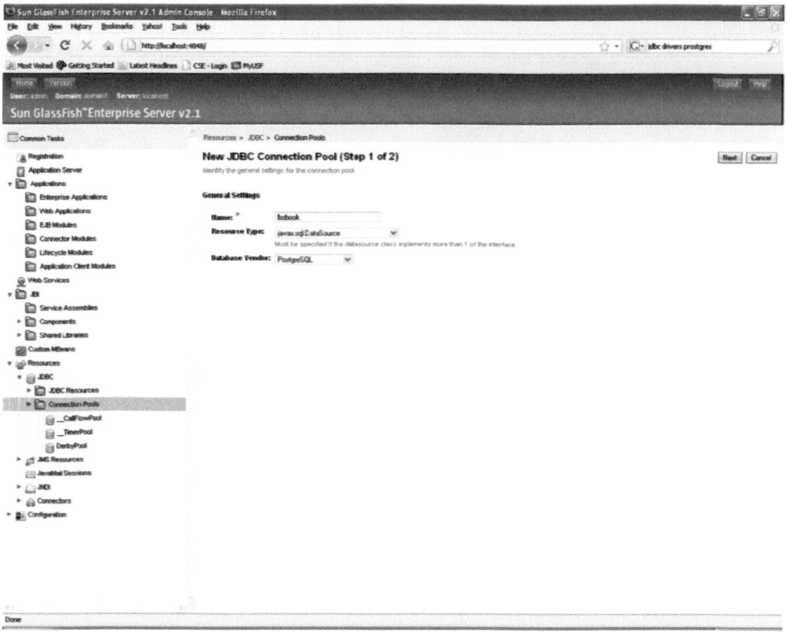

FIGURE A.15: General information about the nature of the connection pool.

new one, click on the *New...* button on the top row of the table. The next window requires the user to define the following three parameters, as shown in Figure A.15:

- *Name of the connection pool:* Define a name for the connection pool, e.g., lbsbook.

- *Resource type:* Select javax.sqlDataSource.

- *Database vendor:* Select PostgreSQL.

The next step offers the user many options, as shown in Figures A.16 and A.17. For this installation, most of the variables will be set to their default values, except the following parameters from the lower section of the configuration parameters, as it can be seen in Figure A.17:

- *DatabaseName:* Write the name of the database created when installing PostGIS.

- *Password:* Write the password of the Postgres superuser.

- *PortNumber:* Write *5432* or the port number you defined when installing Postgres.

- *User:* Write *Postgres*.

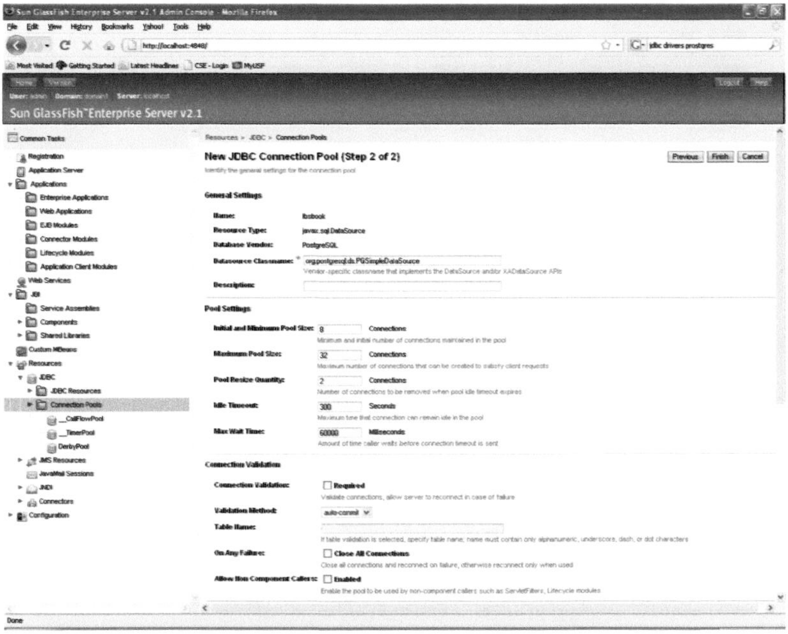

FIGURE A.16: Upper section of the configuration parameters.

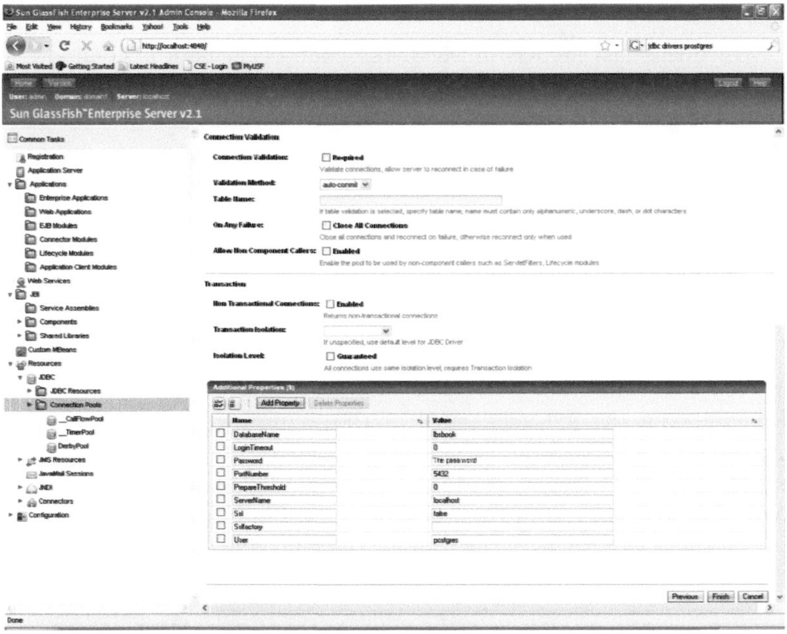

FIGURE A.17: Lower section of the configuration parameters.

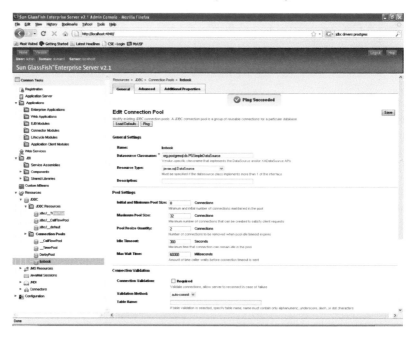

FIGURE A.18: Testing the connection to the database from the connection pool.

Once this last step is finished, the connection pool is created. Now it is time to check whether the connection can effectively connect to the database. From the table of connection pools, click on the one that you just created. It will show a panel similar to the one with all the configuration options, except for a pair of buttons on top of the right panel: *Load Defaults* and *Ping*. To test the connection to the database, click on the *Ping* button. The panel should change and look like the one showed in Figure A.18.

A.2.6.2 Creating a JDBC Resource

The process to create a JDBC resource is much simpler than the one used to create a connection pool. The first step is to click on the option *JDBC Resources* on the left-side panel of the administration console, just above the *Connection Pools* option. Once you click on the option, a table with the existing JDBC resources appears in the right-side panel. Click on the button *New...*, in the top row of this table, as shown in Figure A.19.

The next window asks the user for the following general information about the JDBC resource, as shown in Figure A.20:

- *Java Naming and Directory Interface (JNDI) Name:* Define a name for the JDBC Resource name. Even though in theory it could be any name, experience working with the platform suggests to start the

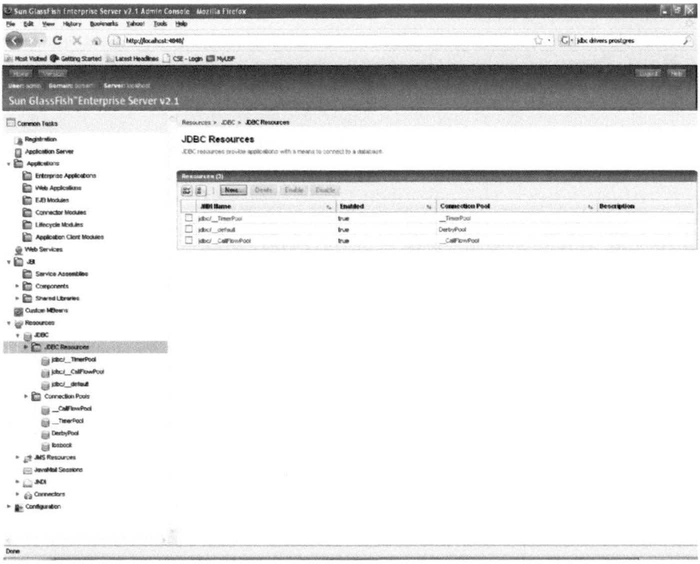

FIGURE A.19: Location of the option for creating a connection pool on the application server.

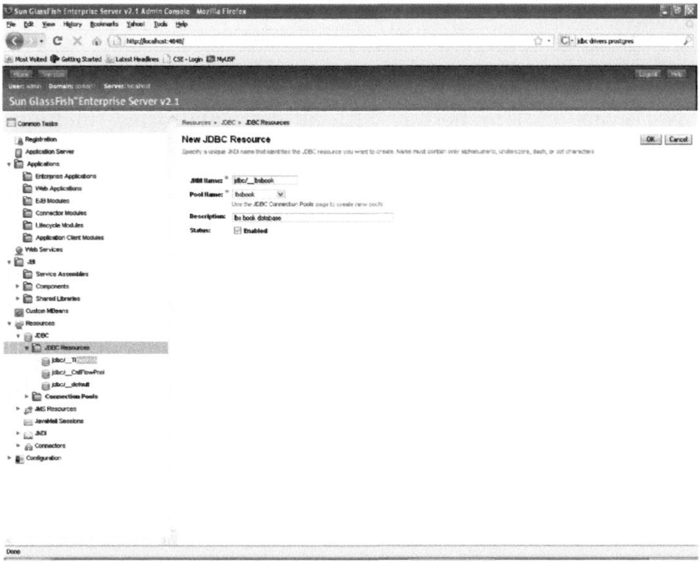

FIGURE A.20: General information about the nature of the connection pool.

name with the prefix `jdbs_`. In this installation, the name of the resource will be `jdbs_lbsbook`.

- **Pool Name:** Select the connection pool that you just created. In this example: `lbsbook`.

- **Description:** Write a short description of the resource.

- **Enable:** Check the resource to be enabled.

Once the JDBC resource is created, the server installation is complete, as all common resources needed by all applications housed in the server are now available. The next section describes the installation procedure of the software components needed to develop server-side applications.

A.3   Server-Side Application Development Environment

Applications running in the server are part of the proposed architecture because they utilize the data stored in the server's database and the server's computational power to process and analyze that data and take some actions, such as providing real-time feedback to the users. Therefore, in addition to the database, drivers, etc., the server needs to have the application development environment to develop these applications, which includes the following components:

- Sun Java Development Kit, version 6, update 13 or better.

- NetBeans 6.5.1 or better, with all Java platforms (including Java Enterprise Edition, or Java EE and the different GlassFish application servers).

Both installers are self-explanatory. The installation of the Sun JDK is the same described in Section A.2.1. One aspect to consider is that the installation of NetBeans gives you the option to also install the application server GlassFish and the Apache server. In order to have more control over the location of the folders, versions, etc., without having to depend on NetBeans, it is recommended to make these installations separately, i.e., install NetBeans only. To make this decision, you must select the customized installation option. This version of the installation shows the list of components to be installed with NetBeans. From that list, uncheck GlassFish and the Apache server.

A.3.1   Registering NetBeans

The machine utilized to develop the server-side applications needs a way to deploy the application files into the server. NetBeans offers this functionality

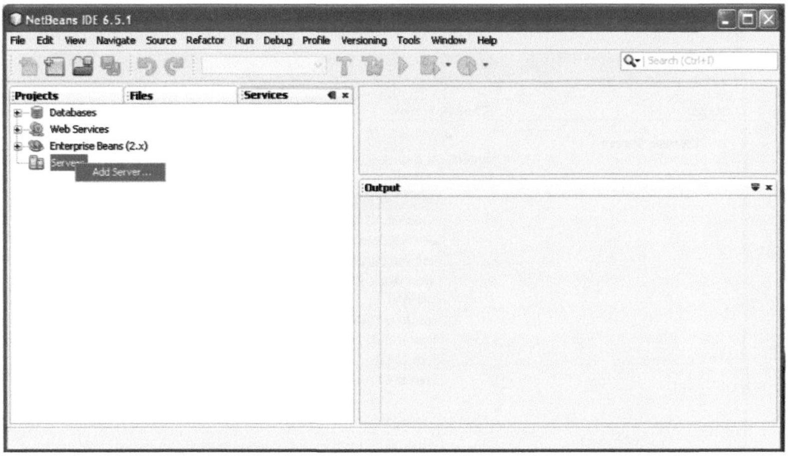

FIGURE A.21: Addition of a server in NetBeans.

when the server is registered as a service. This subsection describes this registration process in those cases where NetBeans is installed in the same server machine and in a different machine. This process consists of the following five steps:

1. The first step of the registration process is to get to the *Service* tab on the left-sided panel of NetBeans' main window. From that list of services, right-click on *Servers* and select the option *Add Server*, as shown in Figure A.21.

2. In the Add Server Instance window, NetBeans shows a lists of possible application servers that it supports. Select *GlassFish V.2*, as shown in Figure A.22.

3. The next window shows the different options to install a server. In the case of a locally installed application server, there are two possible options: *Register Local Default Domain* and *Register Local Domain*. The first option will register the default domain. In this case, the system automatically knows the directory (path) of the default domain. If you have more than one domain in the server, then select the second option and provide the location of the folder and the administration communication port of the specific domain to register. In this installation, the default option was selected, as shown in Figure A.23.

4. If the server is installed in another computer, select the option *Register Remote Domain*, as shown in Figure A.24. The next step requires the user to define the location of the server and the administration communication port, as shown in Figure A.25.

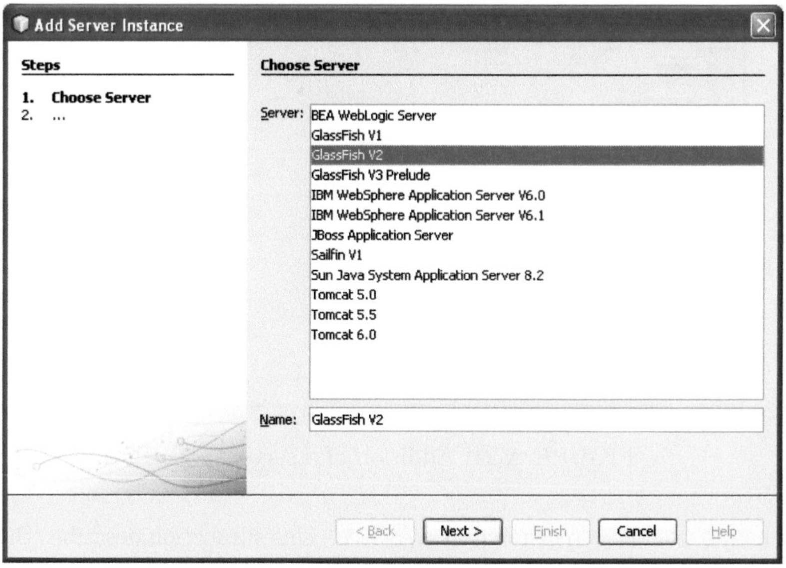

FIGURE A.22: Selecting the type of server.

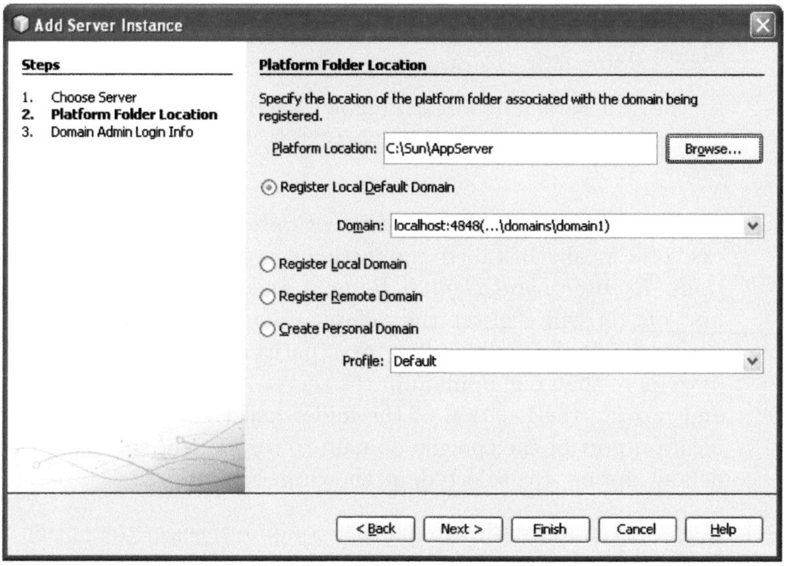

FIGURE A.23: Registering a local server with the default domain.

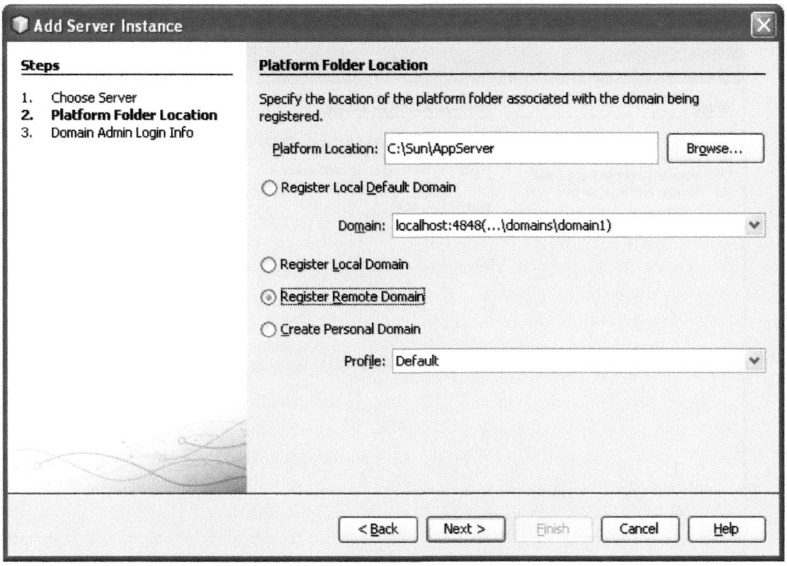

FIGURE A.24: Registering a remote server.

5. Once the location of the server has been defined (in both cases of local and remote servers), NetBeans requires the information of the server's user administrator, as shown in Figure A.26. After this step, click on the *Finish* button to finalize the installation process.

If the installation is successful, the new server should be included in the server's list. In addition, it must show a small green arrow under the GlassFish icon to show that the connection with the sever was successful, as shown in Figure A.27.

A.4 Client-Side Application Development Environment

This section describes the installation procedure of those components needed to develop applications that will run on powerful devices, such as PCs, laptops, and the like. These components are the following:

- Sun Java Development Kit, version 6, update 13 or better.

- Google Web Toolkit 1.5.3 (recommended version).

- Google Web Toolkit Maps API.

- Eclipse Ganynemede, Europe or current (check compatibility).

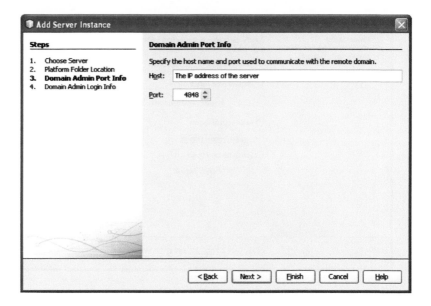

FIGURE A.25: Location information of the remote server.

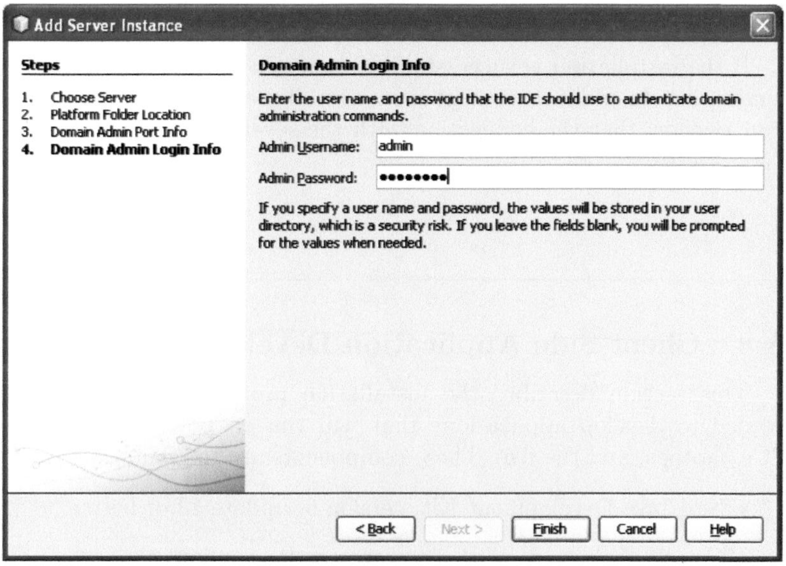

FIGURE A.26: Adding the information of the server's user administrator.

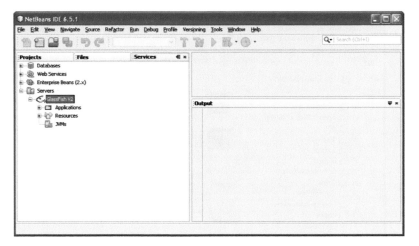

FIGURE A.27: Final view of the registration of the new server.

A.4.1   Sun Java Development Kit

The installation of the Sun JDK is the same described for the server in Section A.2.1; therefore, it will not be repeated here.

A.4.2   Google Web Toolkit (GWT) and the GWT Maps API

The Google Web Toolkit is a module that compiles applications written in Java into JavaScript, so they can be embedded in Web pages. The GWT Maps API, on the other hand, provides GWT with interfaces to include functionalities from Google Maps. This is very convenient and useful for location-based services because this API makes it possible to display the geographical information obtained from the mobile clients in a Google Map.

The GWT version 1.5.3 used in this book is not the most updated version, but it is recommended because it creates a folder with the compiled files that will be included in the server applications. This functionality is no longer available in the current versions of GWT. The GWT version 1.5.3 is available for download from the book's Website at `http://www.csee.usf.edu/ ~labrador/LBIS` or from `http://code.google.com/webtoolkit/versions. html`. The GWT Maps API can be downloaded from the book's Website as well as from `http://code.google.com/p/gwt-google-apis/`.

The installation process of the GWT and GWT Maps API consists of extracting the files in the developer's computer. It is recommended that a known and accessible folder is selected for the location of these files. Figure A.28 shows a possible path to save the extracted files of these two applications.

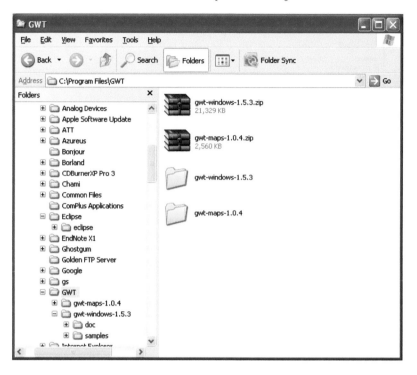

FIGURE A.28: Installation of the GWT and the GWT Maps API.

A.4.3   The Eclipse Integrated Development Environment

Eclipse is an integrated development environment (IDE) tool very similar to NetBeans. It is recommended to use Eclipse in the developer's computer because the GWT was originally designed by Google to work with this IDE. Therefore, there are no integration or compatibility issues and it runs very smoothly. This program can be downloaded from the books's Website or from `http://www.eclipse.org/downloads/`.

The installer file of Eclipse consists of a compressed file that contains a folder with the application. Thus, the installation process consists of extracting the files and running the Eclipse executable file. Figure A.29 shows the recommended path for the extraction of the folder with the IDE.

A.4.4   Installing the GWT in Eclipse

Chapter 10 describes in more detail how the Google Web Toolkit and Eclipse work together to create the client application. All is needed is to create a folder where to copy and decompress the `gwt-windows-1.5.3.zip` file. The procedure to create a GWT project for Eclipse is described in Chapter 10, Section 10.3.1.

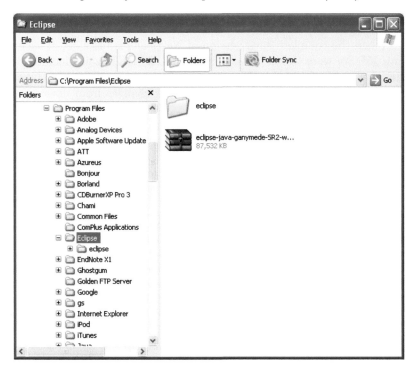

FIGURE A.29: Installation of the Eclipse IDE.

A.5 Mobile-Side Software Development Environment

This section describes the installation procedure of those components needed to develop applications that will run on resource-constrained devices, such as cellular telephones, PDAs, and the like. These components are the following:

- Sun Java Development Kit, version 6, update 13 or better.

- NetBeans 6.5.1 or better, with all Java platforms (including Java Platform Micro Edition, or Java ME).

- Cellular phones emulators.

  - Generic cellular phone emulator included in NetBeans.
  - Sprint Wireless Web Toolkit (or Sprint SDK).

- Apple Quicktime standalone, version 7.6 or better.

The procedures to install the Sun JDK and NetBeans will not be repeated here. Please refer to the instructions given in Sections A.2.1 and A.3.

A.5.1   Cellular Phone Emulators

When the complete Java version of NetBeans is installed, it includes the Java ME Software Development Kit (Java ME SDK), which includes the Java ME platform to develop applications for resource-constrained mobile devices. However, the configuration of this platform changes from device to device, depending on the manufacturer.

When a new application is being developed, it is a good idea to check the level of compliance of the application in different target devices. Cellular phone emulators provide an easy way to test the application in different platforms without having to install it in several different physical devices.

Java ME provides generic cellular phone platforms with all the implementations of the Java ME CLDC and MIDP defined up to date (CLDC 1.0, CLDC 1.1, and MIDP 1.0, MIDP 2.0, MIDP 2.1) and also four different cellular phone layouts: gray-scale phone, color phone, cellular phone with media hotkeys in the keyboard, and a full QWERTY keyboard model.

In addition to these generic options, some cellular phone manufacturers and operators provide model-specific emulators for commercial devices, so applications can be tested using the real capabilities of the specific models.

The following section shows how to install and use the set of platforms provided by the cellular phone operator Sprint. The selection of this specific set of platforms is completely optional. The purpose of this section is to show how to register these new modules in NetBeans to be used later in the development of the mobile device application.

A.5.1.1   Sprint Wireless Web Toolkit (SWWT)

The Sprint Wireless Web Toolkit is the set of Java ME libraries needed to develop applications for most of Sprint's mobile phones. This tool is very useful for developers because they have exact images of the libraries that exist in the phones, so the applications can be tested for compatibility among different models. The book's Website (`http://www.csee.usf.edu/~labrador/LBIS`) contains a compressed executable file, which is the installer application.

Even though the process is very straightforward, it is very important to know that the Java Development Kit must be installed in the machine. In addition, if the developer is going to create multimedia applications, the installation of Apple's Quicktime is recommended. The installer for Quicktime is also included in the book's Website, and the installation process is self-explanatory.

The process to install the Java ME module included in the Sprint WWT in NetBeans consists of the following six steps:

1. The first step is to open NetBeans and click on *Tools* and *Java Platforms*, as shown in Figure A.30.

2. Once the *Java Platforms* window is open, click on the button *Add Platform*, as shown in Figure A.31.

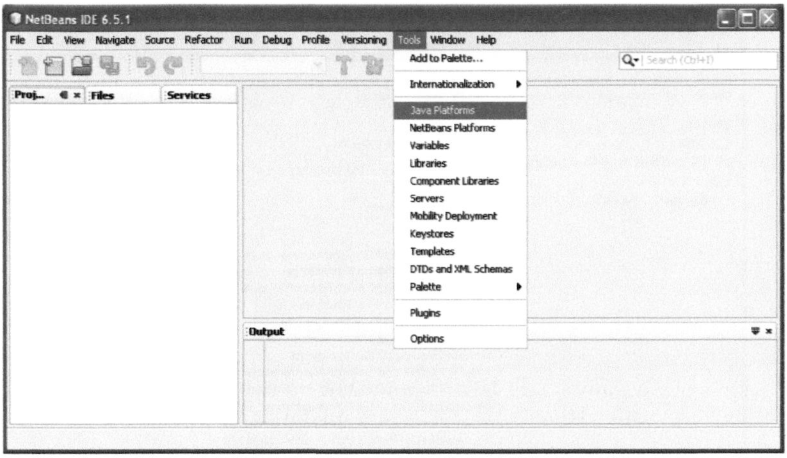

FIGURE A.30: Select Java Platforms from the Tools menu.

3. The *Add Platform* window offers a series of options for different kinds of platforms. Select the option *Java ME MIDP Platform Emulator*, as shown in Figure A.32.

4. Once the option is selected, NetBeans will try to find the new platform. If the program cannot find it, NetBeans will show you a file selection window. Find the folder where the Sprint WWT was installed and select the folder, as shown in Figure A.33.

5. Once the folder is selected, click *Open*. Now the Add Platform window will show the Sprint WWT platform folder as pendent for detection, as shown in Figure A.34. NetBeans will inspect for Java ME platforms in the folder. Click *Next* to continue with the installation process.

6. The detection process will recognize all the available emulators that the Sprint WWT offers, as shown in Figure A.35. Once the detection process is finished, click on the *Finish* button to finalize the installation process.

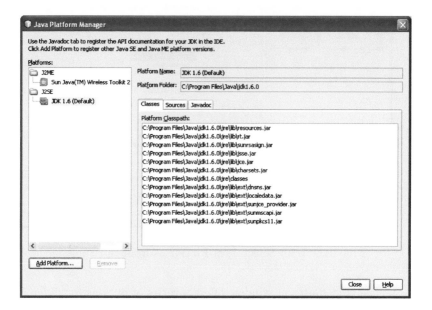

FIGURE A.31: The Add Platform window.

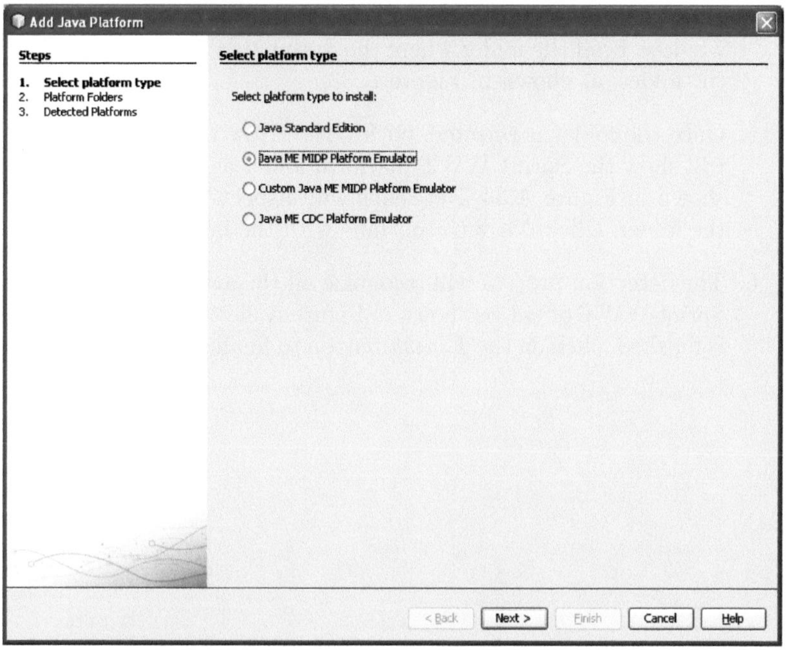

FIGURE A.32: Selection of the proper type of platform.

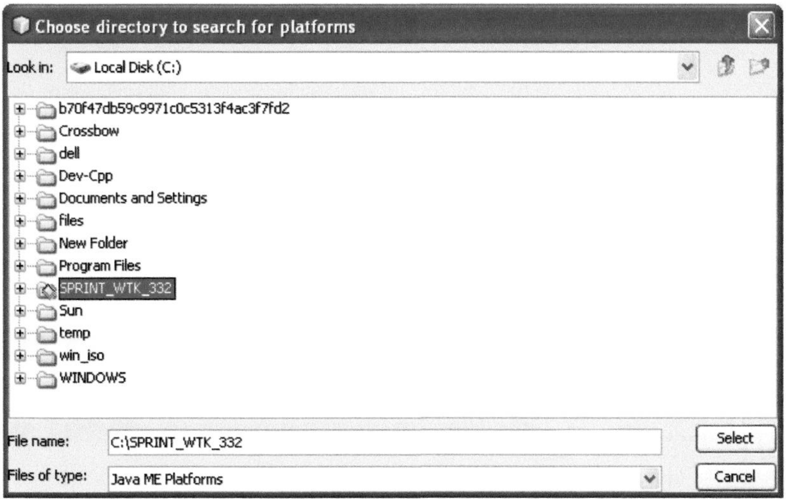

FIGURE A.33: Location of the Sprint WWT platform.

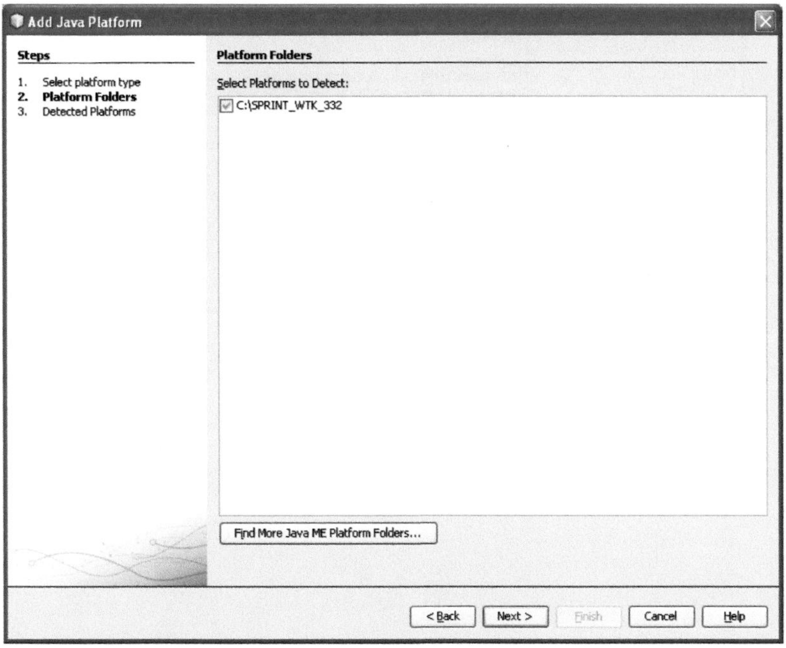

FIGURE A.34: Selection of the Sprint WWT platform for inspection.

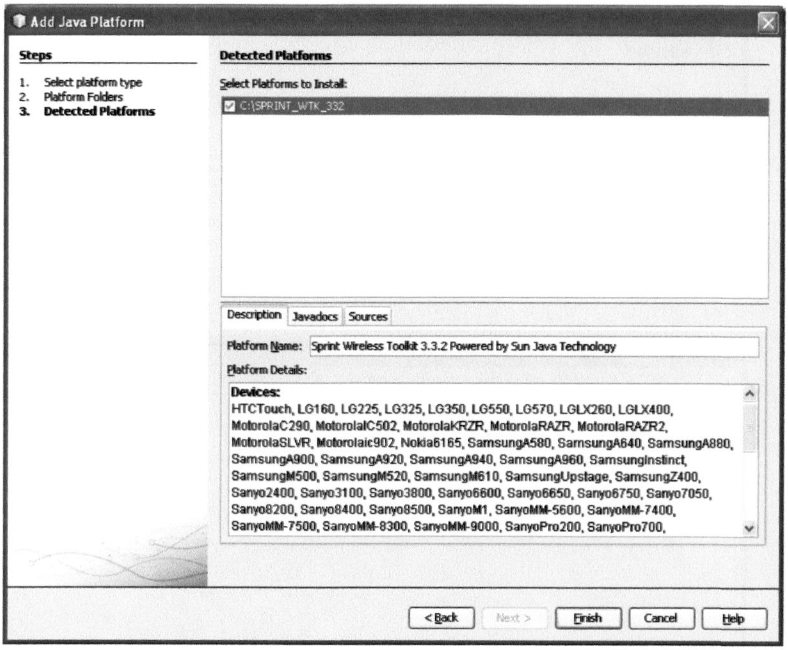

FIGURE A.35: Final window of the installation process of the Sprint WWT.

Bibliography

[1] AeroScout. http://www.aeroscout.com/.

[2] ARM Limited. http://www.arm.com/.

[3] Ekahau. http://www.ekahau.com/.

[4] Intel Place Lab. http://www.placelab.org/.

[5] Loc-Aid Technologies, Inc. http://www.loc-aid.net/portal/.

[6] *Open Geospatial Consortium KML 2.2*. Open Geospatial Consortium Inc. 2008.

[7] *PostGIS 1.5.0 Manual*. Available for download online at http://postgis.refractions.net/docs/.

[8] TechnoCom. http://www.technocom-wireless.com/.

[9] Useful Networks. http://www.useful-networks.com/.

[10] Veriplace. http://www.veriplace.com/.

[11] Where. http://www.where.com/.

[12] JSR 179 Location API for J2ME. Technical report, Java Community Process/JSR 179 Expert Group, 2006.

[13] JSR 293 Location API 2.0. Technical report, Java Community Process/JSR 293 Expert Group, 2008.

[14] ABI. GPS-Enabled Location-Based Services (LBS) Subscribers Will Total 315 Million in Five Years. *ABI Research, available online at: http://www.abiresearch.com/abiprdisplay.jsp?pressid=731*, September 2006.

[15] ABI. Personal Locator Services to Reach More Than 20 Million North American Consumers by 2011. *ABI Research, available online at: http://www.abiresearch.com/abiprdisplay.jsp?pressid=766*, November 2006.

[16] S. Barbeau, M. A. Labrador, A. Perez, P. Winters, N. Georggi, D. Aguilar, and R. Perez. Dynamic Management of Real-Time Location Data on GPS-Enabled Mobile Phones. In *Proceedings of Ubicomm*, 2008.

[17] S. Barbeau, M. A. Labrador, P. Winters, R. Perez, and N. Georggi. Location API 2.0 for J2ME — A New Standard in Location for Java-enabled Mobile Phones. *Computer Communications*, Vol. 1, No. 6:1091–1103, 2008.

[18] S. Barbeau, M. A. Labrador, P. Winters, R. Perez, and N. L. Georggi. A General Architecture in Support of Interactive, Multimedia, Location-based Mobile Applications. *IEEE Communications Magazine*, pages 156–163, November 2006.

[19] S. Barbeau, R. Perez, M. A. Labrador, A. Perez, P. Winters, and N. Georggi. LAISYC — A Location-Aware Framework to Support Intelligent Real-time Applications for GPS-Enabled Mobile Phones. *IEEE Pervasive Computing (to appear)*, 2009.

[20] P. Bellavista and A. Corradi. *The Handbook of Mobile Middleware*. Auerbach Publications, 2006.

[21] T. Berners-Lee, R. Fielding, and L. Masinter. *Uniform Resource Identifiers (URI): Generic Syntax*. IETF, RFC 2396, August 1998.

[22] C. Bettini, S. Jajodia, P. Samarati, and S. X. Wang (Eds.). *Privacy in Location-Based Applications*. Springer, 2009.

[23] Broadcom. BCM4751 Product Page. http://bit.ly/ceoJcP.

[24] A. T. Campbell, N. D. Lane, E. Miluzzo, R. A. Peterson, H. Lu, X. Zheng, M. Musolesi, K. Fodor, S. B. Eisenman, and G.-S. Ahn. The Rise of People-Centric Sensing. *IEEE Internet Computing*, pages 12–21, July/August 2008.

[25] D. D. Chamberlin and R. F. Boyce. SEQUEL: A Structured English Query language. In *Proceedings of the ACM SIGFIDET (now SIGMOD) Workshop on Data Description, Access and Control*, pages 249–264, 1974.

[26] E. F. Codd. A Relational Model of Data for Large Shared Data Banks. *Communications of the ACM*, 13(6):377–387, 1970.

[27] M. Debbabi, M. Saleh, C. Talhi, and S. Zhioua. *Embedded Java Security*. Springer, 2007.

[28] T. Dierks and E. Rescorla. *The Transport Layer Security (TLS) Protocol Version 1.2*. IETF, RFC 5246, August 2008.

[29] R. Fielding, J. Gettys, J. Mogul, H. Frystyk, L. Masinter, P. Leach, and T. Berness-Lee. *Hypertext Transfer Protocol — HTTP/1.1*. IETF, RFC 2616, June 2009.

[30] E. Giguere. Using Threads in J2ME Applications. In *http://developers.sun.com/mobility/midp/articles/threading2/*.

[31] Google. Google Web Toolkit Developer's Guide Version 1.5. `http://code.google.com/docreader/\#p=google-web-toolkit-doc-1-5\&s=google-web-toolkit-doc-1-5\&t=DevGuideJavaFromJavaScript`.

[32] M. S. Grewal, L. R. Weill, and A. P. Andrews. *Global Positioning Systems, Inertial Navigation, and Integration.* John Wiley & Sons, 2007.

[33] R. Housley, W. Ford, W. Polk, and D. Solo. *Internet X.509 Public Key Infrastructure — Certificate and CRL Profile.* IETF, RFC 2459, January 1999.

[34] B. Kaliski and J. Staddon. *PKCS #1: RSA Cryptography Specifications, Version 2.0.* IETF, RFC 2437, October 1998.

[35] H. Karl and A. Willig. *Protocols and Architectures for Wireless Sensor Networks.* Wiley, 2006.

[36] K. W. Kolodziej and J. Hjelm. *Local Positioning Systems: LBS Applications and Services.* Taylor & Francis, 2006.

[37] A. Kupper. *Location-Based Services: Fundamentals and Operation.* John Wiley & Sons, 2005.

[38] A. Kupper, G. Treu, and C. Linnhoff-Popien. TraX: A Device-Centric Middleware Framework for Location-Based Services. *IEEE Communicatioins Magazine*, Vol. 44, No. 9:114–120, 2006.

[39] J. Kurose and K. Ross. *Computer Networking: A Top Down Approach Featuring the Internet.* Pearson, 2008.

[40] M. A. Labrador and P. M. Wightman. *Topology Control in Wireless Sensor Networks.* Springer, 2009.

[41] H. Lu, W. Pan, N. D. Lane, T. Choudhury, and A. T. Campbell. SoundSense: Scalable Sound Sensing for People-Centric Sensing Applications on Mobile Phones. In *Proceedings of 7th ACM Conference on Mobile Systems, Applications, and Services (MobiSys)*, 2009.

[42] T. Mikkonen. *Programming Mobile Devices — An Introduction for Practitioners.* Wiley, 2007.

[43] E. Miluzzo, N. D. Lane, K. Fodor, R. A. Peterson, H. Lu, M. Musolesi, S. B. Eisenman, X. Zheng, and A. T. Campbell. Sensing Meets Mobile Social Networks: The Design, Implementation and Evaluation of the CenceMe Application. In *Proceedings of International Workshop on Urban, Community, and Social Applications of Networked Sensing Systems (UrbanSense)*, 2008.

[44] M. Mun, S. Reddy, K. Shilton, N. Yau, P. Boda, J. Burke, D. Estrin, M. Hansen, E. Howard, and R. West. PEIR, the Personal Environmental Impact Report, as a Platform for Participatory Sensing Systems Research. In *Proceedings of the 7th Annual International Conference on Mobile Systems, Applications and Services, Mobisys*, 2009.

[45] A. Patil, J. Munson, D. Wood, and A. Colin. Bluebot: Asset Tracking Via Robotic Location Crawling. *Computer Communications*, Vol. 1, No. 6:1067–1077, 2008.

[46] A. J. Perez, M. A. Labrador, and S. Barbeau. G-Sense: A Scalable Architecture for Global Sensing and Monitoring. *IEEE Networks Magazine*, 24, No. 4:57–64, 2010.

[47] N. B. Priyantha, A. Chakraborty, and H. Balakrishnan. The Cricket Location-Support System. In *Proceedings of ACM Mobicom*, 2000.

[48] N. Ramanathan, T. Schoelhammer, E. Kohler, K. Whitehouse, T. Harmon, and D. Estrin. Suelo: Human-assisted Sensing for Exploratory Soil Monitoring Studies. In *Proceedings of the 7th ACM Conference on Embedded Networked Sensor Systems (SenSys)*, 2009.

[49] D. Rebollo-Monedero, J. Forne, A. Solanas, and A. Martinez-Balleste. Private Location-Based Information Retrieval through User Collaboration. *Computer Communications*, 33(6):762–774, April 2010.

[50] S. Reddy, K. Shilton, J. Burke, D. Estrin, M. Hansen, and M. Srivastava. Evaluating Participation and Performance in Participatory Sensing. In *Proceedings of International Workshop on Urban, Community, and Social Applications of Networked Sensing Systems (UrbanSense)*, 2008.

[51] S. Reddy, K. Shilton, J. Burke, D. Estrin, M. Hansen, and M. Srivastava. Using Context Annotated Mobility Profiles to Recruit Data Collectors in Participatory Sensing. In *Proceedings of the 4th International Symposium on Location and Context Awareness (LOCA)*, 2009.

[52] G. Riccardi. *Principles of Database Systems with Internet and Java Applications*. Addison Wesley, 2001.

[53] K. Ridley. Global Mobile Phone Use to Hit Record 3.25 Billion. *Reuters, available online at: http://www.reuters.com/article/email/idUSL2712199720070627*, June 2007.

[54] J. Ryder, B. Longstaff, S. Reddy, and D. Estrin. Ambulation: A Tool for Monitoring Mobility Patterns Over Time Using Mobile Phones. In *Proceedings of IEEE International Conference on Social Computing: Workshop on Social Computing with Mobile Phones and Sensors: Modeling, Sensing and Sharing*, 2009.

[55] J. Schiller and A. Voisard. *Location-Based Services.* Morgan Kaufmann, 2004.

[56] Sun. The Class Thread. `http://java.sun.com/javase/6/docs/api/java/lang/Thread.html`.

[57] Sun. The Java Tutorials: Concurrency. `http://java.sun.com/docs/books/tutorial/essential/concurrency/index.html`.

[58] Sun. J2ME Building Blocks for Mobile Devices — White Paper on KVM and the Connected, Limited Device Configuration (CLDC). *Sun Microsystems*, 2000.

[59] Sun. Connected, Limited Device Configuration Specification Version 1.1. *Sun Microsystems*, 2003.

Index

T - #0198 - 221019 - C288 - 234/156/13 - PB - 9780367383480